PARTNERING
for
CHANGE

Figures and Tables

Figures

Tables

Acknowledgments

I would like to thank all of the contributors. Not only do they tell interesting stories and do valuable work, but they made editing this book an ease and a pleasure. Special thanks also to Manny Ness, editor of *WorkingUSA*. His encouragement in having me put together several special issues of the journal provided the impetus to make this collection happen. All of us who work for a revived labor movement appreciate his dedication in keeping this quality journal going. Thanks to the staff at M.E. Sharpe for their enthusiasm for this project and the ease of final production. Finally, I would like to acknowledge Hal Stack, director of the Labor Studies Center, for his continued support and excitement for my research and activism around labor-community coalitions. He is a model boss.

Introduction

Bringing Together the Seeds of Change

"Over the past few years, once-insular movements have been reaching out to cooperate at the local level. They have created literally hundreds of coalitions and alliances, large and small, formal and informal."[1] So wrote Jeremy Brecher and Tim Costello on the eve of the 1990s in their edited work on labor-community coalitions, *Building Bridges*. Looking back at the 1980s—in many ways a depressing decade for those committed to social and economic justice—they saw promising signs of newfound common cause and energy at America's grass roots.

Our new collection carries that hope forward into a new century. The seeds that Brecher and Costello detected continued to grow. Indeed, within the ranks of labor, building coalitions with community groups is officially part of current national AFL-CIO policy. On the community side, organizations such as the Association of Community Organizations for Reform Now (ACORN) and the National Interfaith Committee for Worker Justice view working with unions as a central part of what they do. However, just as in Brecher and Costello's time, the main drivers of labor-community partnerships come at the grassroots. The plant closing alliances of the 1980s, for example, fed into the corporate accountability and living wage movements of today. Local and regional economic development—so long the terrain of business people and professional administrators—has become a rich source of grassroots organizing by unions and community groups.

Why Are Labor-Community Coalitions Developing Now?

While today's labor-community coalitions seem innovative within the context of recent years, in fact they have a long American tradition. Indeed, the question is not why are such alliances happening now, but rather why they were so relatively rare in the post–World War II era. The history of the U.S.

labor movement offers several clear lessons. Union ranks have not grown incrementally decade after decade, but have surged during distinct periods of worker unrest. Such pivotal times have seen labor organizations and community groups forge strong alliances and common cause. These eras represent mass social awakenings when great grassroots movements have transformed America. During these periods, building workplace organizations and reforming society were one and the same cause.

The last great labor upsurge in the 1930s and early 1940s, for example, saw unemployed workers joining with Autolite strikers to battle the Ohio National Guard while farmers aided the Minneapolis general strike of 1934. Organizing unions and battling to protect and extend the New Deal were spoken of as issues of industrial democracy, fundamental social justice, and fulfilling the democratic promise of the country. The connections between unions and the community ran deep. In 1941, for example, African American community and religious leaders risked dire reprisals from Henry Ford to come to the defense of the United Auto Workers (UAW). Their support helped defeat Ford's attempt to use racial violence to defeat the union. In turn, the newly formed UAW Local 600 fought not only for desegregation within Ford but also the community—including founding the area's first integrated bowling league. Today, many Detroit area residents live in decent affordable housing built with UAW financing.

These strong connections between unions and community groups fell into decline from the 1950s onward. Part of the explanation lies in the Cold War. Corporate leaders actively fostered anticommunist hysteria as a way of driving back and containing union gains. Those persecuted as "radicals" were often the activists who most embodied union-community partnership. At the same time, corporate money flowed into civil groups, business-church alliances, and media campaigns aimed at fostering an ethic of individualism and self-advancement in working class communities.[2]

During the postwar period, the liberal carrot often accompanied the anti-"radical" stick. The New Deal, the civil rights laws, the Great Society, and other liberal reforms marked genuine progress in the nation's social and economic agenda. They would not have happened without mass organizing and unrest. However, liberal reformism also had some damaging messages. Liberalism abandoned comprehensive thinking for fragmented specialization. Social, economic, and environmental problems were not outcomes of a single capitalist system, but separate issues to be addressed with separate policy. The message for reform movements was clear: organize around your specific interests, ignore other groups, don't talk about corporate power as The Issue, and you can win changes from those government institutions in which liberalism holds dominance. Cold War liberalism and its interest group politics broke many of the ties between labor and other currents of social reform. While individual unions and leaders participated in the great upheavals of the civil rights and 1960s eras, organized labor as a whole was notable either for its absence or calls for reforms far milder than those heard in the streets.

Time and corporate restructuring have done much to dismantle the postwar barriers to labor-community cooperation. The fall of the Berlin Wall and the collapse of the Soviet Union rendered red-baiting left-leaning activists a far less effective tool. At the same time, corporate liberalism has given way to corporate conservatism. The era of never-ending growth that "lifts all boats" is over. As has been well documented, the vast majority of Americans have seen their standards of living stagnate or fall over the past two decades. Corporations have sought to increase the bottom line by shredding unions, community standards, and democratic controls. Unions and many community groups face the same situation. The dominant corporate agenda places their base constituency under attack at the same time that the old ways of doing things have become less and less effective. Innovation has become not a luxury, but a means for survival. While the conservative agenda has been painful, ugly, and threatening, it has also helped progressive activism by thoroughly discrediting mainstream liberalism. The establishment no longer has the liberal tools to co-opt and narrow popular unrest the way it did in the postwar period. For the foreseeable future, no New Deal or Great Society is on the horizon. The terrain of significant social and economic reform has been left for union and community allies to bring to the table.

What Is Distinct About the Coalitions Covered in this Book

With literally hundreds of examples of labor-community cooperation around the country, our collection had to be selective. Our examples aim for broad alliances in which the community is not supporting labor's agenda, or the other way around, but in which groups come together around new agendas of mutual concern. Indeed, our cases look toward transcending the traditional agendas of each partner to establish far-reaching projects—efforts that can transform the local or regional political terrain in ways that support more group-to-group cooperation and support. Ultimately, our cases revolve around not simply winning this or that reform, but building power.

We do not focus primarily on labor support efforts in which community and religious groups aid union organizing and contract campaigns. We recognize that this is important work. Especially in the areas of organizing and winning a first contract, the laws protecting workers are so weak and corporations often so aggressive that community involvement has increasingly become a necessity for unions. Many of the chapters in this book touch upon examples of such cooperation since labor support work is often a component of larger projects. Our primary focus, however, is on these larger, longer term coalitions. For the same reason, we do not focus upon cases of paired partnership between specific labor bodies and community organizations such as the ACORN-Central Labor Council Partnership in Little Rock or the United Steelworker's outreach to student activists.

Partnerships that build regional or local power display one or more of the following key elements: coalition building, governance, public debate, leadership development, victories, and organizational growth. Each is worth a brief explanation.

Deep Coalition Building

Even though one side may take the lead, labor and community groups develop mutual agendas that transcend their past activities. Together, partners expand the scope of their actions into broad projects beyond their individual capacities and traditional sense of the possible. Through deep coalitions, labor and community partners position themselves at the center of a broad regional movement for economic change.

Preparing for Governance

Simply electing majorities of union- and community-endorsed candidates does not necessarily mean that labor and its allies have acquired regional power. A governing coalition must have a concrete program for progressive change. This agenda is more than simply a laundry list of coalition partners' specific issues. Rather, it combines a broad vision of local or regional transformation with specific public policy reforms that build toward that vision. In addition, power building requires grassroots political machinery—both a shared mobilization capacity and as a process for developing activist candidates prepared to champion the progressive agenda. In short, labor and community groups must engage in the activities that in theory political parties are supposed to do, but which the loose candidate-centered networks that pass for political parties in the United States fail to do.

Shifting the Public Debate

Specific reforms and other victories cannot take place as isolated events. The corporate Right has been very successful in pushing agendas that over time have moved public debate to terms in which economic prosperity becomes a question of enhancing "the market"; personal freedom means less government; and few public figures dare propose raising taxes on the wealthy or expanding should participate in policy coalitions in order to build power in a general sense—one connected to, but not defined exclusively by, adding immediate new members.

Bob Brownstein works as the policy director of an organization centered around one of the most developed regional power-building projects in the country: Working Partnerships USA. This nonprofit was established in 1995 as the research and policy component of a broader revitalization strategy launched by the Santa Clara County Central Labor Council. Brownstein details the development of the partnership's multipronged strategy to build a progressive movement for economic change in Silicon Valley. California offers a network of related experiments in regional power building. The Los Angeles Alliance for a New Economy (LAANE) (described in the chapter by Reynolds and Kern) has similarly developed a multipronged agenda that includes pioneering work to secure community benefit agreements on large private development projects. The East Bay Alliance for a New Economy has used living wage activism in San Francisco, Oakland, and elsewhere to bring together a regional economic justice coalition. Meanwhile, the Center for Policy Initiatives works to develop the pieces of progressive activism in conservative San Diego.

As examples such as Working Partnerships and LAANE enjoy relatively large foundation-funded staffs, they can seem rather intimidating to activists who do not live in a major metropolitan area. The chapter by Mary Jo Connelly, Peter Knowlton, Pete Capano, and Harneen Chernow offers cases from Massachusetts in which local activists, working mainly on volunteer energy, have begun to piece together modest labor-community coalitions around economic development. Most of the activists involved found themselves delving into an arena of which they knew very little. Thus, the process involved no small amount of self-education: unearthing the misplaced priorities of current public policies, identifying the levers of decision making, and reaching out to the wide range of labor and community groups. As the authors show, even the most initial steps taken by these local coalitions have revealed pieces of what promises to be a sustained and far reaching source of labor-community activism.

This book focuses on labor-community efforts that arise largely in opposition to the dominant business agenda. Yet, as part IV details, progressive activists can ill afford to treat private businesses as a monolith. Ultimately, local and regional policy activism can only go so far. Barring greater structural changes, basic economic decision-making power will remain in the hands of private business owners. Labor and community activists need to understand the complexity of the business community—its many divisions, conflicting agendas, and disparate needs. Corporate politics often attempts to split labor and community groups. Labor and community coalitions can do the same to business.

Annette Bernhardt, Laura Dresser, and Joel Rogers of the Center on Wisconsin Strategy have worked for years to build projects of joint benefit to labor, the community, and business. While corporate restructuring has funneled public resources into private hands and sought to slash public standards, it has also neglected effective workforce development policies and other forms of cooperative economic problem solving. Unlike a good part of the developed world, the United States has no systematic worker training system outside of a college education. The public programs that exist are typically underfunded and woefully disconnected to actual work needs. At the same time, most employers invest only reluctantly in worker training. As a result, the United States has a profound shortage of skilled workers in a wide range of professions. This general absence of extensive lifelong learning opportunities erodes employers' ability to pursue the kinds of high-wage, high-skill business strategies (which the authors call the high road) sought by organized labor and its community allies. As the authors argue, unions and the community must revitalize their historic role as solvers of the basic economic obstacles to the high road that individual businesses are unable to address. This starts by offering leadership in building high-road training, modernization, and employee involvement partnerships between business, labor, the community, and government. The authors use the example of the pioneering Wisconsin Regional Training Partnership (WRTP) to illustrate how unions and the community can develop broad support for a high-road agenda. Unlike business-driven "win-win" projects which often draw labor and community groups into a corporate agenda, the WRTP offers an example of a genuine partnership in which unions and the community become important players in the development of key regional industries. The goal is to imbed business success in a web of grassroots standards and institutions.

Notes

1. Jeremy Brecher and Tim Costello, *Building Bridges: The Emerging Grassroots Coalition of Labor and Community* (New York: Monthly Review Press, 1990), p. 9.

2. See Patricia Cayo Sexton, *The War on Labor and the Left: Understanding America's Unique Conservatism* (Boulder, CO: Westview Press, 1991) and Elizabeth Fones-Wolf, *Selling Free Enterprise: The Business Assault on Labor and Liberalism 1945–1960* (Chicago: University of Illinois Press, 1994).

I

Dynamics of
Labor-Community Coalitions

1

Labor-Environmental Coalitions

Fred Rose

The phrase "Teamsters and Turtles" captured the public's imagination during the heady days of protest that shut down the World Trade Organization (WTO) deliberations in Seattle in 1999. For a moment, a powerful grassroots coalition of unions, environmentalists, and other activists seemed poised to block the plans of global elites to reorganize the international economy. Two years later, in 2001, the International Brotherhood of Teamsters captured national headlines again for leading the campaign *against* environmentalists to allow oil exploration in the Alaska National Wildlife Refuge (ANWR). The Bush administration successfully courted the Teamsters to advocate for its energy plan that would advance the interests of the oil industry. This reversal of allegiances by the largest private-sector union in the country illustrates the rocky history of relations between labor unions and environmentalists.

Whether environmental and labor organizations cooperate has real political and policy implications. The fair trade coalition in Seattle protested for both worker and environmental protections. As Teamsters Union president Jimmy Hoffa said, "This is going throughout the world to oppressed people everywhere, that we care, that we're going to change WTO or we're going to get rid of WTO. We come with a message to stop what you're doing, stop the mindless trade deals, stop the oppression of workers throughout the world, stop the rape of the environment."[1] But during the debate over ANWR, the Teamsters characterized environmentalists as extremists and claimed that the job benefits of drilling far outweighed the minor environmental risks. The union stated in a paid radio ad, "Why are some folks who call themselves environmentalists so intolerant and excessive? Don't they know that if we want to stabilize prices we have to carefully find and develop new energy sources? That includes a remote area of Alaska—ANWR."[2] Whether environmental protections are conceived of as a benefit or a barrier to jobs is directly correlated with whether environmentalists are allied or at odds with workers and unions.

This chapter examines the prospects for a sustained alliance between the labor and environmental movements. To what extent are these coalitions temporary opportunistic alliances that emerge when economic and political interests converge? Or are there strategies that can overcome the trade-off so often presented between protecting jobs and protecting the environment? If political opportunities are important, how are historic developments working for or against cooperation? What can we learn from recent coalition experiences about how to build these alliances?

Competing Interests and Alliances

The debate over ANWR illustrates the triangle of competing interests among workers, environmentalists, and corporations (see figure on page 17). Each corner of this triangle represents a different social class. Unions like the International Brotherhood of Teamsters are working class in that they perform manual labor with repetitive tasks and they have little control over their work, which is closely supervised by management. Environmentalists in the mainstream organizations, by contrast, are largely middle class. Most of their members are professionals, like teachers, lawyers, or doctors and their children.[3] They do work that involves expertise and intellectual tasks, and they have more control than the working class over the pace and organization of their own work. Corporations are directed by members of the owning class and managed by their agents. They hire workers and supervise their performance on the job, and they employ or contract middle-class professionals to carry out tasks that require specific expertise.

Each class-based group has interests in cooperating with each of the other classes, and so the relations between workers, environmentalists, and corporations are politically highly contested. The possibilities for working- and middle-class coalitions need to be understood in terms of the three possible sets of class alliances and the kinds of interests that groups have in working in one of these coalitions versus another. Each of these alliances often seeks to shift the costs of change onto other parties, generally the parties that they are not allied with. These competing interests are outlined below.

First, workers and corporations have some interests in common that lead unions to side with their industries or companies on many environmental issues. The Teamsters support drilling in ANWR because they claim it would create three-quarters of a million jobs. Historically the building trades have sided with the construction industry to oppose environmental protections that limit growth. The United Mine Workers (UMW) have lobbied vigorously with the coal industry to oppose controls on carbon emissions that would protect against global warming because of the jobs that these restrictions could take from their industry. These cases illustrate that when labor and corporate interests ally, they frequently advance programs and policies at the expense of the environment.

Corporations advocate for growth and against environmental restrictions to increase profits. Workers, on the other hand, favor growth to create jobs, improve wages, or provide job security. These interests converge when workers believe that profits will translate into jobs and compensation. Since companies control jobs, they can promise real and immediate benefits to workers to gain their cooperation. However, these promises are not always carried out, and workers must assess the veracity of corporate claims. As the United Steelworkers of America observed in its environmental report "Our Children's Future" adopted in 1990:

> Steelworkers have heard the jobs argument before. For many years companies have tried to use economic and environmental blackmail on the union and its members. In every fight for a new health and safety regulation, or better wages, or improved pensions, there is a corporate economist to tell us that if we persist, the company or the industry will fold, with hundreds or thousands of lost jobs. It rarely turns out to be true.[4]

Just as new regulations do not necessarily cost jobs, corporate profits do not necessarily increase jobs.

As a second coalition, environmentalists and corporations have some converging interests. Many of the national environmental organizations have corporate executives on their boards and receive financial contributions and legitimacy from these relationships. Corporations have a similar interest in enhancing their environmental credentials and influencing the direction of environmental policies. The focus of "third-wave environmentalism" has been on making environmental protection profitable and more business friendly.[5] For example, the 1990 Clean Air Act created a market for pollution credits that allows corporations to shift pollution controls to the plants that will cost least to upgrade by buying and selling "pollution rights." Other collaborations, such as those around toxic-use-reduction policies, have focused on saving money by recycling materials or replacing costly pollutants with cheaper alternatives.

The interests of corporations and environmentalists also converge around the use of technology or expertise to solve environmental problems. Technological advances often favor both corporate profits and environmental or middle-class interests. For instance, during the Progressive Era (1880s to 1920s), middle-class reformers promoted technical solutions to urban sanitation problems such as contaminated water, garbage in the streets, air pollution, and overcrowding. Medical professionals used the new science of bacteriology and public health to shift the policy focus away from removing health threats and toward the treatment of diseases. Industry was allowed to continue to pollute the waters, for example, while reformers instituted filtration and the addition of chlorine to produce drinkable water. This solution created employment for sanitary and civil engineers in municipal water departments that came to depend on professionals to provide drinking water.[6] Expert-driven solutions to environmental problems remain a strategic focus of many of the large mainstream environmental organizations. With major corporate and foundation support, organizations such as the Environmental Defense Fund and the National Wildlife Federation have been particularly focused on finding cooperative ways to work with industry to reduce pollution and exposures rather than confront industry with new regulations.

Working-class, low-income, and nonwhite communities often bear the costs of corporate environmentalism. The environmental justice movement has loudly criticized the mainstream movement for promoting policies at the expense of low-income communities and especially communities of color. Polluting facilities and landfills often end up in their communities in the United States and also in underdeveloped countries overseas.[7] Pollution trading also means that communities around older, more costly plants will be exposed to higher pollution levels, and these communities again are often more vulnerable and less politically powerful.

Finally, labor-environmental coalitions also depend on converging interests. Often unions and environmentalists have a common enemy in corporations that are undermining both labor and environmental standards. For example, during and after the WTO protests in Seattle, unions and environmentalists joined forces against the Maxxam Corporation, which owns both Kaiser Aluminum and Pacific Lumber. Kaiser locked out striking steelworkers in 1998 in a protracted labor struggle, while environmentalists were fighting Pacific Lumber's aggressive logging of old-growth timber. When they learned of each other's struggles, both sides supported the other's campaigns—environmentalists joining protests and pickets at Kaiser plants, and steelworkers joining protests against cutting old-growth timber by Pacific Lumber. This coalition helped reach a contract settlement with Steelworkers and also contributed to the government's purchase of some of the most environmentally valuable old-growth trees in the headwaters forest. Out of this campaign grew the Alliance for Sustainable Jobs and the Environment, which stated in its founding document, the *Houston Principles*, that the coalition came together to make "corporations more accountable for their behavior worldwide."

Unions and environmentalists also share an interest in reducing pollutants in toxic industries. Workers in plants are exposed first and at higher toxic levels than the surrounding communities to chemicals, nuclear radiation, and other contaminants. Some unions in toxic industries, most notably the Oil, Chemical and Atomic Workers (OCAW) (which merged in 1999 with the paperworkers to become PACE), have allied with environmentalists to reduce pollution.[8] OCAW joined with environmentalists during a five-year struggle against BASF in Louisiana when workers were locked out of their jobs in 1984. National environmental organizations like the Sierra Club and Greenpeace joined in documenting the health hazards of spills and toxic releases from the BASF plant and joined in protests. During the struggle, the union also helped found and fund the Louisiana Environmental Action Network as an environmental justice organization in the region, which it continues to support.

Finally, the interests of unions and environmentalists converge around developing environmentally friendly jobs. For instance, in February 2002, a coalition of environmental organizations and unions issued a study, *Clean Energy and Jobs*, describing the employment benefits of shifting to industries that do not burn fossil fuels and so will not contribute to global warming. The Blue-Green Alliance that issued the study worked over five years to find common ground. The coalition grew out of a broader, more inclusive dialogue between the AFL-CIO and environmental groups initiated to bridge differences that divide the movements. But some unions, particularly the UMW, opposed regulations that might limit carbon emissions, and they blocked the AFL-CIO from developing a policy on global warming. Therefore, interested unions began to work with environmentalists to form the Blue-Green Alliance with the purpose of "seeking serious approaches to environmental protection that benefit working people and their unions." Leading groups in this sustainable-jobs-creation campaign include the Service Employees International Union (SEIU), Steelworkers, the Union of Needletrades, Industrial, and Textile Employees (UNITE), the Sierra Club, the National Resources Defense Council, and the Just Transition Alliance.

Prolabor and proenvironmental policies frequently come at the expense of corporate profits or government subsidies. Struggles with companies are often about how the costs and benefits of production will be distributed. Clearly, if corporations are forced to pay the costs of protecting the environment or to negotiate agreements with their workers, these expenses add to the costs of doing business. Others have looked to the government to cover the costs of change. OCAW, for example, developed the idea of a "superfund for workers" through which government would subsidize education and training costs for workers displaced by environmental protections. The rationale for this "just transition" policy is that society as a whole benefits from protecting the environment, so the costs should also be borne by society as a whole and not only by the workers in that industry. The key struggle in these cases is to shift the costs to government or corporations and away from workers and the environment.

This brief survey illustrates that each class-based group has multiple and competing interests. Each side has reasons to ally with the other two. In each alliance, the issues are framed differently. When labor and corporations join forces, the search for jobs and profit often means compromising the environment. And when environmentalists and corporations collaborate, the common agenda is usually efficiency as the marriage of expertise and profit. Labor and environmental coalitions unite in opposition to the inequities and excesses of the current economy and must seek positive alternatives that advance both jobs and the environment. Each side in these coalitions also faces risks if an alliance forms against it that shifts costs its way, so all sides must weigh carefully the balance of power as they negotiate their strategies and alliances. There is no inevitable or final alliance under the present economic arrangements, so both the politics and policies are ultimately contested and debatable.

Opportunities for Coalitions

The *structural problem* working against labor and environmental coalitions in a capitalist society is that the distribution of resources favors building alliances with corporations. Corporations control jobs, large quantities of funds that can be used to operate organizations, and the access to politicians that large campaign donations can buy. Unions and environmentalists cannot hope to compete with these material advantages.

However, corporate control over the economy has severe limitations. Competition often forces capitalists to shift costs onto workers or environments to cut costs. Economic contractions during the regular flow of business cycles can force even the largest corporations into crisis. In moments of change, alliances often shift as groups seek to respond to the new circumstances. This shift in loyalties was evident in the alliance that developed between the United Paperworkers International Union (UPIU) and Greenpeace in Jay, Maine, during a protracted strike in 1987 and 1988. Because of their positive relationships with the owners who employed most of the people in town, workers in the Jay paper mill and their families had long ignored the health hazards of chemicals in the plant, the stench of the air, and the toxic waste dumped on land and in local rivers. But during the strike, the town was evacuated because of a leak of chlorine dioxide that could have killed thousands of people if it had not been for the cold winter temperatures. In response, union supporters took control of the town council and, with the help of environmental supporters, began to enforce national and state environmental regulations against the company. This led to a sustained collaboration between Greenpeace and UPIU nationally.

Globalization is another source of economic crises leading to new alliances. For example, aluminum companies like Kaiser are suffering from worldwide overcapacity and falling prices. In 1998 the long-time family owned corporation of Kaiser Aluminum was purchased by corporate raider Charles Hurwitz and his Maxxam Corporation. The company had already won wage and benefit concessions from workers in order to keep the company competitive. But Maxxam immediately began to eliminate hundreds of jobs, contract out work, and propose cuts in wages, pensions, and health insurance. It wasn't long before the Steelworkers went on strike and were locked out of aluminum plants. In 1986, Hurwitz had also bought Pacific Lumber and increased cutting of old-growth timber to pay for the purchase. This decision led to dramatic protests by environmental activists. As a result, the Steelworkers found they had common interests with environmentalists in fighting Maxxam.

But coalition building is not all about circumstances and crises, since different people make different choices in the same kinds of situations. Contrast, for instance, the strategies pursued by Bob Dilger, executive secretary of the Washington State Building and Construction Trades Council, with Lane Kirkland, president of the national AFL-CIO between 1979 and 1995. In the 1970s, Dilger led the state AFL-CIO out of the Washington Environmental Council because the building trades were upset about environmental opposition to big construction projects in the state. But twenty years later, Dilger reversed course and led the unions back into an alliance with the Washington Environmental Council. Many circumstances had changed, including a booming local economy and the vicious attack on unions by the Reagan administration and contractors.[9] Construction workers, like Americans in general, were now more attuned to environmental dangers. Dilger was an environmental convert personally, and he now became a coalition leader.

Lane Kirkland, however, followed a very different course. When Reagan unleashed his attack on unions and fired air traffic controllers during the strike of the Professional Air Traffic Controllers Organization, Kirkland and the national AFL-CIO did not change their way of working. Throughout Kirkland's career, he pursued a strategy of business unionism that focused on servicing union members rather than organizing, and collaborating with government against communism abroad and militant unions in the United States.[10] He continued this strategy while union membership declined from 35 percent of the U.S. workforce to 15 percent during his tenure as head of the AFL-CIO. He did not embrace the possibility of new coalitions and alliances as Bob Dilger did in Washington state. And so, in 1995, Kirkland's hand-picked successor, Thomas Donahue, lost the election for president of the AFL-CIO, which was unprecedented in the history of the organization. John Sweeney, then head of the SEIU, ran against Donahue on a platform that included building coalitions with new allies in the community, including environmentalists. He hired Jane Perkins as environmental liaison. Perkins brought together unions and environmentalists to discuss their differences over global warming and other divisive issues with the goal of finding common ground.

So circumstances alone do not determine any individual's calculations of his or her interests. Individuals have choices, and different people will choose to see their interests in different ways. Nevertheless, the fact that activists in Washington state and Washington, D.C., went the same direction in the 1990s toward building coalitions suggests several historic trends favoring labor and environmental coalitions at this time. Globalization is propelling a new wave of mergers and acquisitions on a global scale that is creating new common enemies like Maxxam. Environmental crises are also bringing change, from the exhaustion of timber resources in the Pacific Northwest to the collapse of fish populations on both coasts to the looming dangers of global warming. These crises can be a source of labor and environmental conflict, as with the timber wars in the Pacific Northwest. But they are also opportunities for new cooperation, as with the Blue-Green Alliance.

Transitions under way within both the labor and environmental movements also favor cooperation now more than at any time since the Cold War began. The labor movement has been in decline in the United States since the 1950s, and those losses accelerated in the 1980s with the Reagan administration's attacks. Labor's losses have also worsened because of its weakened bargaining position in the global economy where corporations can escape unions by moving to countries with lower-wage, unorganized workforces. After decades of losses, there is finally widespread understanding that new strategies are needed to reverse labor's fortunes. The Sweeney leadership brought an explicit commitment to building coalitions to the AFL-CIO as a strategy to help rebuild labor.

The environmental movement has undergone a parallel transition, although with many independent organizations these trends are by no means uniform.

Environmental policies have been under assault as has labor. The success of the environmental movement in creating regulations during the 1970s and 1980s led to a hostile antienvironmental backlash, particularly with the rise of the "wise-use movement" in the 1990s. During the Reagan and Bush administrations, prodevelopment leaders have been appointed to head environmental agencies. Environmental organizations contracted in the 1990s with the election of President Clinton, as the public reaction to twelve years of hostile antienvironmental policies subsided. The issues on the environmental agenda have also grown increasingly complex and intractable. Global warming, loss of biodiversity, and global deforestation require global solutions that are harder to achieve than cleaner air and water in this country. These changes produced a broad reassessment in the environmental movement during the 1990s.

Political economic changes have also weakened the environmental movement and the security of middle-class professionals more broadly. Globalization has enabled companies to move overseas to escape environmental regulations, and the implementation of the WTO has undermined national environmental policies such as the Marine Mammal Protection Act, the Endangered Species Act, and the Clean Air Act, which are being challenged by U.S. trading partners as barriers to free trade. The middle class has similarly lost some of its autonomy relative to capital, with fewer predictable careers and more instability in many professions. Even doctors are now forming unions to protect their interests. In response to these changes, some environmentalists have begun to rethink their strategies and look for new allies.

Cultural Trends and Coalitions

Circumstances present the opportunities for change, but much more is required for leaders to take advantage of these opportunities. Leaders cannot and do not simply calculate the costs and benefits of different alliances to decide with whom to collaborate. Given that each side has multiple and competing interests that could be served by different alliances, there are reasons to pursue each path. Coalitions are not just political instruments, but also complex social relationships that emerge from historic events based on the predispositions, understandings, values, and commitments of participants. People need to know and trust each other to work together. Partners need to develop a common agenda that is convincing to their members, given how they interpret events and perceive their interests. And allies need to agree on strategies and tactics to achieve common goals. Thus, coalition organizing is deeply rooted in the cultural and historical experiences of participants.

The conflict between timber workers and environmentalists over cutting versus protecting the old-growth forests of the Pacific Northwest demonstrates the importance of relationships in determining how people make alliances.[11] Timber workers had many reasons to oppose timber corporations, which had been replacing workers with automation, exporting logs at the expense of local jobs, overcutting the resource beyond sustainable yields, shifting production to lower-cost plantations in the South, and seeking wage concessions from the unions. But when environmentalists forced injunctions through the courts that limited the sales of old-growth timber in the national forests, unions led by the National Woodworkers of America and United Brotherhood of Carpenters sided with timber companies against environmentalists. Together the unions and companies were able to block federal environmental legislation and to override court-ordered limits on timber sales on several occasions.

Relationships between timber workers and management provided the basis for an alliance. Despite their differences with the timber companies, timber workers spoke the same language, lived in the same communities, and had personal relationships with company managers. Workers and management had a mutual understanding of each other's motives. By contrast, the Sierra Club Legal Defense Fund, the Wilderness Society, and other national environmental organizations did not have personal relationships with the timber workers who were losing their jobs because of the court injunction. Environmentalists therefore were not attuned to the devastation already felt in timber communities from job loss or the desperation that the unions were experiencing as they fought for their survival in an increasingly nonunion, declining sector. To timber workers, environmentalists were outsiders imposing their interests and priorities on their communities. Environmentalists spoke of scientific research and studies about endangered species, which belied the direct experience of timber workers who saw forests regenerate because of their work planting trees. Timber workers were suspicious of the motives of environmentalists whose only direct contact with the forests was for recreation. Under these circumstances, the claims and positions of timber companies were convincing to timber workers.

The cultural differences between environmentalists and unions have their origins in the class divide between these movements. Middle-class environmentalists join their movement because they are committed to the cause. Professionals in the environmental movement are taught to use their skills and talents to contribute to careers that they are personally committed to. Just as teachers internalize the goal of educating students and doctors learn to strive for the health of their patients, so environmentalists have made a personal commitment to protecting endangered species or unique ecosystems.

This motivation by a cause that is bigger than oneself is very different from the reasons people join unions. Workers join a union to advance their bargaining power with management so they can negotiate better wages, working conditions, and dignity on the job. Working-class organizations like unions are made up of people who share immediate material interests that they seek to advance together. While environmentalists failed to address the immediate interests of timber workers in the old-growth struggle, the unions failed to understand the motivations of environmentalists.

People with relationships in both the environmental and labor movements often provide a bridge to bring together organizations that otherwise would not trust or understand each other. When the AFL-CIO wanted to improve cooperation with environmentalists, they hired Jane Perkins as their environmental liaison to serve as a bridge. She has strong ties in the labor movement, having been a union activist in Pennsylvania and a member of the staff of the national AFL-CIO, and she is the wife of the president of the SEIU. She also has deep relationships with the environmental movement, having directed Friends of the Earth.

The prospects for labor and environmental coalitions are better at the present time because the number of bridge builders with relationships in both movements has grown, and because these people are increasingly in leadership positions. Some leaders coming of age in the labor movement attended college during the 1960s and 1970s and were influenced by the proenvironmental student movements of the time. Other working-class members of this generation moved into professional jobs themselves, especially during the economic expansion after World War II, and brought their working-class experiences with them. Some activists with labor backgrounds found jobs with environmental organizations as they expanded in the 1970s and 1980s. Out of the anti–Vietnam War movement also came a cadre of politicized middle-class activists who entered unions out of a commitment to organizing. These and other personal paths have created a significant number of bridge builders who are actively building coalitions across the labor/environmental divide.

A number of important historical and generational shifts also favor coalitions at this time. Attitudes in the labor movement and in the country as a whole have become more proenvironment over the past forty years. As a sign of this change, even antienvironmental policies are now presented as considerate of the environment. As Jerry Hood, the Teamsters' special adviser for energy policy, said in a press statement, "A vote for exploration of Alaska's National Wildlife Reserve (ANWR) is a vote for environmental responsibility."[12]

The previous generation of labor members and leaders who came of age during the 1950s learned to fear any politics that seemed at all radical because of the red-baiting, blacklisting, and purging that took place during their era. They also grew up at a time when unions were strong and not inclined to work in coalitions. With the end of the Cold War and the expansion of community and middle-class organizing, coalition politics has become more and more accepted. The decline of the labor movement, greater job insecurity, and an antiunion political environment are convincing younger union activists to look for new allies out of necessity.

Generational shifts are also at work in the environmental movement. A new generation of environmentalists is incorporating social justice into their environmental advocacy, including interest in building coalitions with labor and workers. Criticisms by the environmental justice movement raised awareness of the social costs of environmental policies and forced mainstream environmental organizations to review their programs. Major battles over such issues as protecting old-growth timber and renewing the Endangered Species Act taught some environmentalists about the need to reach out to impacted communities and workers to preempt opposition. In one of the most visible battles, legislation to protect the ancient forests of the Pacific Northwest was blocked when timber unions and communities joined with corporations to oppose protections on economic grounds. During the recession in the early 1990s, this argument found sympathy among many in Congress. This experience and similar ones convinced some of the national environmental organizations to incorporate social justice into their agendas and to expand efforts to work with the labor movement. So now the Sierra Club states that the purposes of its campaign to protect national forests are "to restore healthy forest ecosystems and sustainable local economies." In this more complex and uncertain context, a new generation of environmentalists is looking for new allies with labor and community groups.

Successful coalitions contribute to future collaborations as organizations gain experience working together to build broader and deeper relationships. The first experiences with cooperation are often the most tenuous as each side tests the other to see if they can be trusted. If so, then participants gain confidence in working on more complex and risky issues. For example, when the Washington Environmental Council (WEC) and Washington building trades began to meet, they had to overcome considerable hostility on both sides. The building trades contacted the WEC first, but their leaders wanted to make the approach appear to come from the environmentalists because of skeptics in their own ranks. So the WEC wrote a letter to the trades asking for a meeting. This first meeting was extremely tense, and most of it was devoted to sharing stories about recent visits to Russia, which broke the ice for the substantive discussions. Cooperation began with small steps that were consistent with the level of trust. So each side asked the other to testify at

legislative hearings on issues important to them. As a result of this cooperation, both sides did better in the legislative session than they had in the past.
When environmentalists were attacked in the press for siding with labor,
both sides built trust by publicly defending their relationship. Based on these
experiences, labor and environmental groups cooperated to organize a major
protest against the North American Free Trade Agreement negotiations held
in Seattle in August 1991. This successful coalition developed because participants took small steps appropriate to the level of trust and expanded cooperation as groups created closer relationships and gained more experience
working together.

Finally, long-term coalitions depend on each side's learning the lessons of
past experiences and shifting strategies and practices accordingly. For instance, in the Pacific Northwest, the Alliance for Sustainable Jobs and the
Environment (ASJE) is drawing lessons from its successful collaboration
against Maxxam and during the WTO protests to develop strategies to address the simmering conflicts around timber issues. ASJE built on the relationships and cooperation it had developed in earlier struggles to articulate a
common agenda for creating jobs and protecting the environment. The result
was formation of the North Coast Initiative, whose agenda is to "create high-
skill, high-wage jobs in forest and watershed restoration on the North Coast,
beginning in Humboldt County." This collaboration around one of the most
charged environmental-labor conflicts in the country would not have been
possible without the mutual understanding that developed between cooperating organizations during previous campaigns.

Overcoming Barriers to a Sustainable
Labor-Environmental Alliance

For fifty years the Cold War defined political alliances internationally and in
the United States. But since the Berlin Wall was torn down in 1995 and the
seemingly eternal Cold War ended, the world order has been in transition.
The form that this new world order will take depends on the balance of class
power. Current arrangements like the WTO serve corporate interests by undermining labor and environmental protections at the national level. The
result has been a race to the bottom as working people in this country compete with cheaper wages overseas. And global trade agreements are undermining the ability of countries to protect their own environments.

Only a united working- and middle-class alliance, like the one that emerged
in Seattle, can provide a counter to the power of corporate-led globalization,
and labor-environmental coalitions are an important part of any such alliance. If a sustained coalition converges around the values of workers' rights

and environmental protection with the support of both the working and middle classes, then it would be possible to create a global economic system infused with these values.

The past decade has seen many promising labor-environmental coalitions at the local, state, national, and international levels, and some important social and political trends favor cooperation.[13] Alliances against common enemies or for mutual support are frequent starting points, but many of these have been short-lived issue- or event-specific collaborations. Each experience is important, however, because it builds relationships, understandings, and communication that provide a greater foundation for cooperation in the future.

Labor and environmental organizations have also learned important lessons that have produced promising directions for rethinking even the most intractable conflicts. Conflicts have been particularly dramatic around resource extraction such as timber, mining, and oil exploration as natural resources are exhausted or when the environmental costs of development are factored in. However, strategies for addressing even these tensions are emerging out of coalition efforts. Employment in environmental restoration has developed as a basis for labor-environmental cooperation by organizations like ASJE. A just transition has become part of the platform of PACE (Paper, Allied-Industrial, Chemical, and Energy Workers) International Union and the Canadian Labor Congress. These developments provide important lessons for future collaborations.

Each movement faces choices, and portions of each movement will oppose building labor-environmental coalitions. This reaction creates a major hurdle for labor, since any union now has a veto over alliances at least at the national level of the AFL-CIO. On the other hand, the lack of cohesion within the environmental movement creates other barriers since building an alliance with one environmental group does not prevent another group from opposing any agreement.

Each movement also faces challenges that present significant barriers to collaborations. The labor movement has suffered a long period of decline, and new strategies are needed to effectively organize low-wage and immigrant workers on an international scale. Unless and until labor becomes more effective at organizing, the large majority of workers will be unable to participate in coalitions of any kind. Environmentalists, too, have important work to do to bring together their splintered movement, which stretches from community-based environmental justice organizations to workplace occupational safety and health organizations to traditional preservationist groups, and from radical ecoterrorists to conservative corporate-environmentalists.

In the long run, labor-environmental coalitions need to be able to deliver visible benefits to both sides if they are to grow and be sustained. There is a critical need to develop viable ways to move toward environmentally sustainable jobs, as indicated by some of the more farsighted coalitions like the ASJE. To reach this point, organizations need to make long-term commitments to building alliances. The Sierra Club, Friends of the Earth, and Greenpeace have done this on the environmental side, as have unions such as the Steelworkers, SEIU, American Federation of State, County, and Municipal Employees (AFSCME), and PACE on the labor side. Inside these organizations and in other less sympathetic groups, a cadre of bridge builders must be nurtured to be ready to take advantage of new opportunities as they emerge on the ground.

Finally, environmental and labor organizations need to develop a learning culture where leaders and members critically rethink strategies based on experiences. This is challenging for any organization, and there is a tendency to continue to follow the same strategies and tactics year after year because these are comfortable and familiar for members and staff. But doing the same thing isn't sufficient to address the challenges of globalization that confront workers and environmentalists. Only by learning from each other's cultures, problems, needs, goals, and situations is it possible to build a broad enough movement to reorganize our economy and society in environmentally and economically sustainable ways. Recent experiments are showing that collaborations can succeed in shifting priorities and winning reforms. By drawing the lessons from both collaborations and conflicts, it is possible to build more sustained alliances in the future. Achieving this goal will require the strategic use of opportunities, building relationships and trust, a long-term perspective about costs and benefits, and the dedication of leaders at all levels.

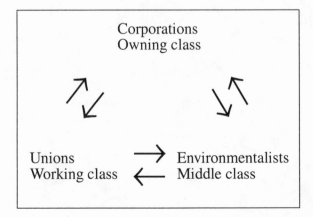

Notes

1. Washington state employee, "We Say No Because We're Fighting for Our Lives," Washington Federation of State Employees, December 1999.

2. "Teamsters Begin Paid Media Campaign to Build Support for ANWR Exploration," July 30, 2001, International Brotherhood of Teamsters (www.teamsters.org).

3. Fred Rose, *Coalitions Across the Class Divide* (Ithaca: Cornell University Press, 2000); Hanspeter Kreisi, "New Social Movements and the New Class in the Netherlands," *American Journal of Sociology* 94 (1989): 199–217; Stephen Cotgrove and Andrew Duff, "Environmentalism, Middle Class Radicalism and Politics," *Sociological Review* 28 (1980): 303–51.

4. United Steelworkers of America, "Our Children's Future, Steelworkers and the Environment," Report of the USWA Environmental Task Force, adopted at the 25th Constitutional Convention, Toronto, Ontario, August 30, 1990.

5. Mark Dowie, *Losing Ground* (Cambridge, MA: MIT Press, 1995), chapter 5.

6. Robert Gottlieb, *Forcing the Spring* (Washington, DC: Island Press, 1993), pp. 55–59.

7. Robert Bullard, ed., *Unequal Protection: Environmental Justice and Communities of Color* (San Francisco: Sierra Club Books, 1994); Richard Hofrichter, *Toxic Struggles* (Philadelphia: New Society Publishers, 1993).

8. David Moberg, "Greens and Labor: It's a Coalition That Gives Corporate Polluters Fits," *Sierra* (January/February 1999).

9. See Rose, *Coalitions Across the Class Divide*, pp. 146–48.

10. Paul Buhle, *Taking Care of Business* (New York: Monthly Review Press, 1999).

11. This analysis summarizes some of the discussion in Rose, *Coalitions Across the Class Divide*.

12. Capitol Hill news conference, July 31, 2001.

13. Brian Obach, "Labor-Environmental Relations: An Analysis of the Relationships Between Labor Unions and Environmentalists," *Social Science Quarterly* 83, no. 1: 82–100; Edward Cohen-Rosenthal, "Improving the Global and Local Environment: A Survey of International Trade Union Activity," *Work and Environment Initiative*, Cornell University, November 2001.

2

Religion-Labor Partnerships

Alive and Growing in the New Millennium

Kim Bobo

Religion-labor partnerships were instrumental in the building of the labor movement from the 1930s through the 1950s. But for a variety of reasons, the latter half of the century saw a decline in these working partnerships.

In the mid 1990s, the labor community refocused its energies on organizing low-wage workers and recognized the need to build stronger ties with the religious communities. At the same time, the religious community recognized that its twenty years of soup kitchens and shelters was not stopping the increase in poverty in society. People of faith began looking for additional ways to address economic injustice.

The National Interfaith Committee for Worker Justice emerged in 1996 to work with and help develop new religion-labor partnerships around the country. More than sixty affiliates now exist around the country rebuilding those partnerships. These groups create and implement educational programs for the religious and labor communities, mobilize religious support for workers who seek to organize a union, advocate for living wage bills and increases in minimum wage, encourage employers to negotiate contracts within a reasonable period of time, and stand with workers who are on strike or locked out. In addition, groups are finding new ways to challenge sweatshops in their own communities by developing workers' centers (the Catholic labor schools of the new millennium), creating worker-friendly partnerships with government agencies charged with protecting worker rights, training congregational worker advocates, and distributing worker rights educational materials, especially with immigrant workers.

Challenges to Religion-Labor Partnerships

Despite the dramatic growth of religion-labor partnerships, there are many challenges, some old and some new, facing the work. These are some of the most common challenges faced by religion-labor groups.

Stereotypes and Ignorance

Too many leaders in the religious community do not understand the important role that unions play in society or they have accepted the media stereotypes of unions. Thank goodness this perception is changing, but it is still a challenge and a problem. The best way to address the problem is for unions to organize workers and engage new religious leaders in supporting workers. Do not involve only the likely suspects—the religious leaders who already understand the work. Find out where workers attend religious services and engage their religious communities, regardless of their understanding or preconceptions. People change not through talk, but through active involvement.

Religious Employers

Although there have been some giant steps forward in terms of relationships with large religious employers and unions (e.g., Catholic Health Care West's partnership with Service Employees International Union [SEIU]), there remains a general "antiunion" culture among religious health care and social service employers. Union members and organizers who have experienced these antiunion cultures are skeptical about partnering with the religious community. The current crisis in health care and state social service funding creates opportunities for unions and religious employers to work together for more just federal and state public policies.

Not Enough Organizing

In some communities, there are plenty of unions organizing but that is not true across the board. The more labor organizes, the easier it is to build religion-labor partnerships because the labor movement is seen by workers and their religious leaders as a dynamic force with which to be associated.

Servicing Problems

Although some unions do a terrific job of servicing their members, others have spotty records, especially in servicing immigrant workers. This inconsistency creates problems when workers complain to their clergy about the lack of help the union is providing. Even though unions must shift resources to organizing if the union movement is to survive, it must find ways to strengthen its servicing of workers, especially immigrant workers.

Call a Collar

Even though there is much more strategic involvement of religious leaders early in a campaign than there was a few years ago, the biggest complaint from the religious community is that they get called at the last minute to show up at a rally and say a prayer. People are willing to say a prayer, but they want to be much more engaged in understanding the overall strategy and planning tactics that are appropriate for the religious community. The last-minute calls are so common that they have names: "Rent a Priest," "Call a Collar," and "Dial a Minister."

Money for Staff

The most effective interfaith religion-labor groups have staff devoted exclusively to building the coalition and reaching out to the religious community on a systematic basis. This approach requires dedicated staff, and staff cost money. If the work is to flourish, local religious and labor communities must support the partnerships.

Attacks from Large Companies

As the religion-labor work has grown stronger, so too have the attacks. Some attacks backfire: In San Diego, a hotel management told workers that the priests who had met with them were not really priests, they were just union organizers dressed up like priests. Needless to say, the priests were outraged and became even more engaged in the work.

Nonetheless, interfaith groups are receiving requests for IRS filings, calls from spies claiming they are students writing papers or freelance journalists, and even an occasional labor board charge or subpoena. Clearly, companies are beginning to take the work seriously. Such attacks require us to continue being "squeaky clean" on all legal, financial, and regulatory matters.

Opportunities for Religion-Labor Partnerships

The environment is right for strengthening religion-labor partnerships. The current public greed of corporate leaders has brought home the need for stronger worker protections. There is a growing network of people of faith engaged in the work and organizational structures through which people can work. The visibility and dynamism of some of the organizing efforts, particularly among immigrants, engages new people of faith. And increasingly, unions recognize that the involvement of the religious community really matters in worker struggles.

There are incredible new opportunities for strengthening and expanding the work. Below are descriptions of some of the programs, structures, and tactics that seem to have great potential.

Workers' Centers

Throughout the first half of the last century, there were more than 100 Catholic labor schools that taught workers their rights in the workplace and how to organize unions. Most of the workers who went to these labor schools were immigrants. Building on that tradition, interfaith groups are establishing interfaith workers' centers that create safe spaces for workers to learn about their rights, file complaints with government agencies, organize for collective action, and link with probono attorneys. These workers' centers are intentionally proworker and prounion. It is important for unions that work with immigrant workers to be active on the steering committees for the centers to ensure that the centers function well. These workers' centers are serving multiple functions such as:

Helping low-wage, primarily immigrant workers, who are not yet protected by unions. For interfaith groups, this service is incredibly important, given that clergy refer workers with workplace problems to the interfaith committee. If unions were not organizing in that sector or workplace, there was nothing that could be done to help. Now there are structures in place to provide concrete assistance. The centers help workers recover wages, get paid for overtime, address discrimination issues, and deal with health and safety problems.

Identifying leads for organizing. The first question that is asked in the workers' centers is whether the problem is an individual problem or one that is faced by many workers. Most problems are workplace-wide problems, and thus workers are urged to bring their colleagues to the centers. When workers come together, the center staff or volunteer talks about their options, including the possibility of organizing a union. Not all workers choose to organize, but some do. The workers' centers then coordinate with the central labor council to be sure that workers are put in touch with the appropriate union.

Engaging volunteers in direct contact with workers. The most effective "education" for people of goodwill is to hear the stories of workers. Workers' centers allow people of faith to meet and learn from workers and provide many volunteer opportunities to really make a difference.

Conveying to immigrant workers that both the labor and religious communities are there to support them. Many immigrants do not understand that the two communities are strong supporters of all workers, not just their members. The workers' centers help both the religious and labor communities to get in touch with workers' issues and to be seen as strong supporters.

Interfaith workers' centers are currently operational in Miami, Chicago, Madison (Wisconsin), in northwest Arkansas, western and eastern North Carolina, and the Twin Cities. Plans are under way to create centers in Mississippi and other places. In San Diego, the interfaith committee actively collaborates with a secular workers' center.

Sanctuary Congregations

Clergy and Laity United for Economic Justice (CLUE), the religion-labor interfaith group in Los Angeles, has developed a new initiative called the Worker Sanctuary Program, which integrates some of its most effective ongoing strategies with new program components that are designed to specifically overcome the obstacle of worker fear. All the groups in California plan to develop congregation worker sanctuary programs and collectively revive the spirit of the sanctuary movement of the early 1980s, which defended the rights of Central American refugees. That spirit will be sought in defending the rights of workers.

CLUE's Worker Sanctuary Program organizes individual religious leaders and congregations to sign a pledge to accompany the workers in their struggles. The pledge describes five ways to accompany workers:

1. "Make visible" low-wage workers who are struggling for their rights. Carry out ongoing educational activities that provide opportunities for the workers to address the congregation.
2. Inspire and encourage the workers through special services, home visits, presence at actions, and so on.
3. Provide sustained advocacy.
4. Facilitate funding to support workers who lose their income as a result of their organizing.
5. Participate in public policy campaigns that advance workers' struggles and protect their rights.

CLUE's Worker Sanctuary initiative began in Los Angeles on March 17, 2002, in response to workers at the Doubletree Hotel in Santa Monica who were ready to go public with an organizing campaign in an environment in which it was clear that they would encounter serious retaliation. The first sanctuary service involved thirty clergy and seventy lay leaders as well as fifty workers involved in various campaigns. During the service, religious leaders (workers and nonworkers together) formed a circle with the Doubletree workers in the center and everyone else around the outside, and the inner group and outer circle blessed one another. The service was followed by ten days of sustained advocacy and delegations of clergy and lay leaders and other community members to the Doubletree management. Even though two workers received warnings, no worker was fired or demoted. When the delegations ended, the management called CLUE's bluff by giving the top worker leader an indefinite suspension for her organizing activities. Within two days, CLUE held an action at the Doubletree restaurant with twelve clergy and thirteen lay leaders—the participants were thrown out for praying for the workers and the management and demanding the worker's reinstatement. By the next day, CLUE had letters of support from the bishops of four major protestant denominations and the Muslim Public Affairs Council, and more than 100 lay and community leaders had called the hotel. The worker was reinstated with a week of back pay.

CLUE leaders then expanded the initial sanctuary focus to include employees at three Santa Monica hotels that retaliated against workers who were participating in organizing drives. The hotels also opposed a pioneering living wage ordinance. CLUE organized monthly rotating vigils, highlighting each hotel's workers whose rights were violated, and advocated for these workers with management. The vigils also provided an opportunity to encourage the workers involved in the campaign and for congregational leaders to bring donations and food for workers who lost wages as a result of their organizing activities. CLUE chose the Santa Monica living wage campaign as the first public policy focus of the Worker Sanctuary and became committed to involving sanctuary signatories and their congregations in active support of the campaign.

Although it is not called a formal sanctuary program, the Chicago Interfaith Committee and the Hotel Employees and Restaurant Employees International Union (HERE) built similar congregational support for hotel workers. The interfaith committee recruited more than 100 congregations to support the possibility of 7,000 hotel workers' going out on strike. Before the strike vote, congregations collected and contributed eight tons of food goods for the workers, "just in case" the workers had to go out on strike. The food ensured that workers could vote their conscience without worrying about feeding their families. Approximately 100 workers on the religious outreach committee worked with a Chicago interfaith staff person and two seminary interns to build the support among congregations. Building a base of congregations that support workers is essential for protecting workers and educating more people in the congregations.

Future Religious Leaders

Close to 100 seminary and rabbinical students have participated in the Seminary Summer program, jointly sponsored by the AFL-CIO and the National Interfaith Committee for Worker Justice. The students have gone back to their schools and on to congregations with proworker and prounion perspectives. In Chicago, a group of Seminary Summer graduates organized a group called "Seminarians for Worker Justice" that engaged students from seven different seminaries in supporting laundry workers at Carousel Linens who were seeking a contract. The seminarians led prayer vigils with the workers, organized delegations to talk with catering companies that rented Carousel Linens, and participated in events sponsored by the Union of Needletrades, Industrial, and Textile Employees (UNITE) to support the workers. Within a few years, most of these students will be in leadership in congregations. They are and will be creating new relationships between labor and religion.

Every union that wants to build ties with the religious community should sponsor a Seminary Summer intern or recruit field placement students from seminaries or rabbinical schools in its area. These students are on the cutting edge of building religion-labor partnerships. In Collins, Mississippi, two seminaries worked with the Laborers' International Union of North America (LIUNA) in supporting poultry workers and reaching out to the local religious community for support. According to Regina Botterill, National Interfaith's Seminary Summer coordinator, "In Chicago, two seminarians at UNITE helped organize laundry workers by planning actions, mobilizing clergy, and putting pressure on customers of the laundry owner. In Georgia, a seminarian at SEIU helped organize state workers in Atlanta, Macon, and Milledgeville and began building a clergy network to form the Atlanta Interfaith Committee for Worker Justice. In Los Angeles, two rabbinical students and a seminarian worked with HERE to coordinate a local faith-labor conference, support the Santa Monica living wage campaign, and plan a powerful prayer vigil in front of the Doubletree Hotel." (Personal communication)

Public Policy

As the interfaith religion-labor groups around the country have developed their capacity, they have become more engaged in public policy issues. This trend is likely to increase significantly over the next few years.

Some of the religion-labor groups formed around local living wage campaigns. Others have played or are playing the lead roles in mobilizing religious support. In San José, the Interfaith Council on Race, Religion, Economic and Social Justice collected 5,000 postcards from congregations as part of its living wage campaign. The New Orleans Interfaith Committee, although staffed completely by volunteers, provided a consistent religious voice to support the ACORN-led (Association of Community Organizations for Reform Now) citywide vote on a living wage. Almost all the religion-labor groups in New York State have mobilized religious support for living wage campaigns, and some groups, like the Coalition for Economic Justice in Buffalo and the Central New York Labor-Religion Coalition, have spearheaded the campaigns (Buffalo successfully, and Central New York still working!).

The New York State religion-labor groups have been the most involved in statewide public policy. The groups passed a historic antisweatshop bill that allows schools to select ethical uniform producers, not just the lowest-cost producer (possibly a sweatshop factory). This past year, the groups have worked tirelessly on a statewide farmworker bill. Next year, the California groups are considering support changes to the statewide Medi-Cal program because of the potential for raising wages and benefits for thousands of health care workers. Groups in several states are joining forces with the American Federation of State, County, and Municipal Employees (AFSCME) and state social service providers to explore state "justice budgets" that do not balance the state fiscal crises on the backs of social service clients and workers.

Nationally, the National Interfaith Committee for Worker Justice is developing its capacity to engage in selected worker-justice public policy debates. The organization worked diligently to raise the minimum wage. As the immigration reform efforts accelerate, it will be mobilizing religious support for a rational immigration policy. And over the next few years, the organization will seek to work in partnership with the labor movement to develop a comprehensive reform/improvement package for the Fair Labor Standards Act.

Chaplaincy Program

In Los Angeles, CLUE has developed an innovative chaplaincy program. The premise of worker-justice chaplaincy is to give area clergy uncomfortable with activism an opportunity to lend their pastoral skills to the movement, strengthening the resolve and supporting the souls of those workers most vulnerable on the front lines. Many Latino pastors have become engaged in the work through this program. Pastors accompany workers in their struggles for justice in the workplace. Pastors meet with workers, pray with workers, encourage them about God's presence in justice work, and stand with them in struggles for justice.

In Christian seminaries, most students are required to take a clinical pastoral education (CPE) program. Most students do a chaplaincy internship in a hospital, prison, or nursing home. Over the next few years, groups will be exploring the potential of worker chaplaincies as part of the seminary curriculum. Please note that these chaplaincies are not to be confused with the chaplains hired by poultry companies and other employers. True worker chaplains are not on the payroll of employers.

Government Partnerships

Over the last few years, the National Interfaith Committee for Worker Justice has developed strong partnerships with the agencies charged with protecting worker rights, such as the Wage and Hour Division of the Department of Labor (DOL) and the Equal Employment Opportunity Commission (EEOC). Although the organization and the government agencies do not always see eye to eye, the basic commitment to protecting workers and enforcing the law is the same. Most of the rank-and-file investigators and the regional administrators are truly doing herculean work and deserve our support and partnership. Too often, these government staff have felt all alone in requiring that unethical employers follow the laws and treat workers decently.

The Chicago Interfaith Committee on Worker Issues organized a collaboration of government agencies, religious groups, and community organizations to develop better outreach mechanisms and complaint-filing procedures for low-wage workers. A joint complaint form was developed that is accepted by staff at the DOL Wage and Hour Division, Occupational Safety and Health Administration (OSHA), the EEOC, and the Illinois State Department of Labor. The complaint form is used by staff and volunteers. More than 120 worker-rights advocates from congregations and community organizations have been trained to help reach out to workers and fill out the complaint forms. The collaboration is creating a network of eyes and ears in the community for protecting worker rights.

In Houston, the EEOC, the DOL Wage and Hour Division, the archdiocese, and the Mexican consulate partnered to reach out to workers via billboards and information at the offices of the Mexican consulate. Additional religious partners are being sought to strengthen this partnership.

In 2001, the DOL Wage and Hour division created a terrific worker-rights advocate manual called the *AWARE Resource Handbook*. This is a fabulous resource for helping religious advocates, business representatives, and social service staff to understand and wade through the complexities of many U.S. labor laws.

Although partnerships with government agencies alone are not the answer to a more just society for workers (we still need a strong labor movement), they are important in finding additional avenues for protecting and enforcing workers' rights.

Islamic Participation

The fastest-growing segment of the religious community is the Islamic community. Increasingly, Islamic leaders are getting actively involved with interfaith religion-labor groups. Unions are recognizing the importance of developing ties with the Islamic community, given the growing number of Muslim workers they represent or seek to represent.

The National Interfaith Committee for Worker Justice had a conference on "Islam and Worker Justice" scheduled for September 12, 2001, in Washington, D.C. That conference had to be postponed, but it and three more similar ones have been held around the country helping unions and people of faith understand Islam's commitment to justice for workers. Two new resources have been developed to support groups: *The Holy Qur'an and Worker Justice* and *Understanding Islam* (both available at www.nicwj.org).

Making the Connections

Religion-labor partnerships are growing and flourishing across the country, but given the crisis for workers in the society, the partnerships must be expanded and deepened. Everyone in the faith community and everyone in the labor community can help. The coming years will require a new level of partnership, commitment, and courage to bring forth justice in today's world. Alone, it is hard to make a difference. Together, we can bring about lasting changes.

To learn more about religion-labor partnerships, visit the National Interfaith Committee website at www.nationalinterfaith.org and join the organization to receive its resources in Faith Works. Contact a local interfaith group or Kristi@nicwj.org about forming a new one.

3

ACORN's Experience Working with Labor

Steve Kest

Since the Association of Community Organizations for Reform Now (ACORN)'s beginnings in Arkansas in 1970, we have enjoyed a mutually beneficial partnership with organized labor.[1] ACORN members (many of whom are themselves union members) have long believed that an alliance between organized community members and organized workers is a critical component of any effective strategy for social change. As ACORN president Maude Hurd has stated often, "ACORN builds powerful organizations in the community, and unions build powerful organizations in the workplace. Let's unite these two people's organizations into a powerful movement that can deliver victories for all our members."

Over the years, ACORN has built formal partnerships with unions and central bodies and has entered into shorter-term coalitions on a wide range of issues, including living wage and minimum wage campaigns, efforts to improve public schools, and fights for better housing. Equally important, ACORN has provided critical support to local union-organizing campaigns.

Two of the most significant ACORN-labor partnerships exist in Louisiana, Arkansas, and Texas, and in Illinois, where ACORN organized independent unions of low-wage workers in the 1980s, which then affiliated with Service Employees International Union (SEIU). Both of these unions—SEIU Locals 100 and 880—remain closely allied with ACORN and serve as models for the type of collaborative campaigns that we have promoted elsewhere.

A couple of recent victories won by Chicago ACORN, SEIU Local 880, and other labor allies suggest the power of these collaborations. In May 2003, nearly a half million workers learned they would get a raise when the Illinois legislature voted to increase the state minimum wage from $5.15 to $5.50 on January 1, 2004, and to $6.50 on January 1, 2005. In January 2003, the Coalition to Reward Work had begun promoting a minimum wage bill. The coalition was put together by ACORN, Local 880, and the Illinois AFL-CIO. Following months of demonstrations, calls, faxes, rallies, negotiations, and lobby visits, on May 27, with five days left in the legislative session, the votes were lined up in the House Labor Committee and on the floors of the House and Senate, and the governor's pen was at the ready. But the Speaker of the House was refusing to call the bill up for a vote. ACORN staged rallies at the capitol in support of the increase every day of the last five days of the legislative session.

On May 29, the Labor Committee chair announced that the bill would not be called for a vote. For what happened next, here is the Springfield, Illinois *Journal Register's* account from May 30, 2003:

> That's when members of the Chicago community activist group ACORN rose from their seats and began verbalizing their disgust with the process. "How do normal working-class people like ourselves get heard? We know how the suits get heard, but how do we get heard?" said ACORN member Toni Foulkes. Three members from the group were allowed to formally address the committee. Several members of the committee commended the group on its actions and promised to do what they could to help. When their time was done, the group began protesting and shouting slogans such as, "We can't survive on five-one-five." After the protest went on several minutes, Illinois police were poised outside the committee room, ready to confront the group. Just then, AFL-CIO President Margaret Blackshere interrupted the protest and announced that an agreement had been made and that the bill will be called in the committee today.

The bill passed less than two hours before the legislative session ended on May 31.

Blackshere had played a central role, initiating the campaign and persuading the governor to support $6.50 when he was a candidate. She had worked with ACORN on drafting the bill and had handled most of the inside game.

Tom Balanoff, Illinois president of SEIU, and Henry Tamarin, president of Hotel Employees and Restaurant Group (HERE) Local 1, both brought up the minimum wage issue to Speaker Madigan in personal meetings during the last four days of the session. Tim Drea, legislative director for United

Food and Commercial Workers (UFCW) Local 881, was very helpful with behind the scenes maneuvering in Springfield. Jackie Gallagher and Deborah Lynch (president) of the Chicago Teachers Union were also helpful throughout.

ACORN, for its part, persuaded the University of Illinois at Chicago to produce a study of the wage law's likely impact, put pressure on key state senators, built the coalition, provided major turnout for the governor's minimum wage increase rally in Chicago, and traveled to Springfield twenty times to support the bill, including bringing nine busloads on the last five days of the session and threatening civil disobedience if the bill was not called for a vote.

Two days after this victory, SEIU Local 880 won a major victory of its own. Local 880 has 20,000 members in a unit made up of personal assistants to elderly and disabled persons who are paid with state vouchers. On May 31, 2003, these workers won the right to negotiate a contract with the state when the Illinois House passed HB 2221 by a vote of 115 to 0. On the same day, they won passage of a bill calling for a $2 per hour raise, boosting pay to $8 effective July 1, 2003, and to $9 on January 1, 2004. The Senate did not vote to allocate the necessary funds, however, and Local 880 hopes to win that in negotiations or when the governor signs the bill. Both recent votes came with Local 880 members packing the chambers. Chicago ACORN members had supported Local 880 in this long campaign, turning out members for numerous actions, including acts of civil disobedience for which members were arrested.

These victories could not have happened without years of collaboration. ACORN alliances with labor unions are unique in their focus on building long-term power for our constituency. ACORN does not just deliver our leaders to union-sponsored rallies in support of organizing drives or contract campaigns (although we do in fact regularly turn out for these events). More important, we look for ways to involve our membership and union members in joint campaigns that strengthen both types of organizations. ACORN members and union members work together on campaigns for affordable housing, living wages, and better schools, knowing that these issues affect our entire constituency and that victories on these issues help both ACORN and our union partners deliver for their members.

In addition, ACORN members understand the value of organization and are often active in their neighborhoods encouraging their neighbors to vote "yes" in a union drive. Similarly, ACORN's union partners have encouraged their members to join the ACORN chapter in their neighborhood, knowing that strong organizations of working people are in the interests of our entire constituency.

When the South Bay AFL-CIO Labor Council (SBLC) and San Jose ACORN signed a memorandum of understanding on March 26, 2003, it began with these words:

> The underlying philosophy of the partnership between the SBLC and ACORN is one that is founded upon the belief that institutional power must be built in order to advance the political, economic and social interests of working families. The SBLC and ACORN have unique capacities that together allow working families to advocate for their interests in the community, workplace, and halls of government. Those actions not only achieve immediate outcomes but also strategically position these organizations to advocate for working families on an on-going basis, building lasting, meaningful power.

Prior to the memorandum, this partnership had already realized significant results. ACORN made a significant contribution to a SBLC-led San Jose City Council campaign that yielded the first majority labor-friendly council in city history. Other political victories include state and federal races, giving Silicon Valley one of the most working-families-oriented elected delegations in the nation. The SBLC and ACORN have also partnered to establish new eviction protection laws in San Jose; a landmark for a city with a notoriously powerful landlord lobby.

California ACORN chapters have also worked very closely with affiliates of the National Education Association (NEA) to block school budget cuts. In June 2003, ACORN national president Maude Hurd and NEA president Reg Weaver signed a memorandum of understanding putting in place plans to collaborate in a range of areas, including encouraging collaboration between state and local chapters on public education advocacy.

Critical Elements of the ACORN Community-Labor Alliances

Here are four rules that have guided ACORN's work in building alliances with organized labor:

1. Alliances are first and foremost about building power for working families. We recognize that power comes from the unity of organized workplaces and organized neighborhoods fighting together.

In Arkansas, for example, ACORN and the Central Arkansas Labor Council established the Central Arkansas Labor Council/ACORN Partnership whose explicit goal is to advance the interests of both organizations. The partnership is a model for how membership-based community and labor organizations can combine their members, resources, and agenda to increase the participation and power of working families in politics and public policy.

The partnership has embarked on a program of joint membership-training sessions, joint voter registration projects, and precinct network development to build the two organizations' grassroots electoral capacity and long-term political clout. Working together, ACORN and the labor council are promoting living wage ordinances, supporting organizing drives, and working to elect candidates who back our community and labor policy agenda. Two members of ACORN in November 2002 were elected to their second terms on the Little Rock Board of Directors.

This partnership has become a powerful force in the politics of Little Rock, Pine Bluff, and the state of Arkansas. As a direct result of the partnership's work, in April 2003 Arkansas governor Mike Huckabee signed into law a bill placing some basic restrictions on predatory lending abuses. In June 2003, the partnership's "Raise Taxes; Fund Medicaid" campaign won an increase in taxes on tobacco and a 3 percent surcharge on income taxes to help cover the cost of Medicaid. During a special legislative session in May, ACORN, SEIU Local 100, Arkansas Advocates for Children and Families, and other allies planned and carried out a "health–care-a-van," which made stops at small towns and held press conferences. The last stop was in Pine Bluff where ACORN organized a rally on the steps of the courthouse. The next day, the coalition held a press conference at the state capitol and presented to legislators a banner signed by people at rallies during the health–care-a-van tour. The legislature then voted for the tax increases. The next victory these activists have in their sights is winning a living wage ordinance for the city of Pine Bluff.

2. Alliances need to be explicit about mutual support for organizing: community members help unions sign up members and win contracts, and union members help community organizations sign up members and win campaigns.

ACORN members regularly support local labor efforts. Here are a few recent examples from Chicago: ACORN organizers and members signed up more than 300 parent workers in the schools in an SEIU Local 73 campaign and then turned them out to vote for the union in an August 2002 union-recognition election. An ACORN campaign assisted by the American Federation of State, County, and Municipal Employees (AFSCME) in the Chicago Mexican immigrant neighborhood of Little Village in the fall of 2001 successfully stopped the privatization of a city health clinic where AFSCME members were employed. The initiative won a commitment to continue the clinic as a public facility, with all benefits and services maintained and even enhanced. ACORN is also working with unions that are facing major contract fights (suburban janitors, supermarket workers) to use the living wage campaign to win broad public support for significant wage increases. ACORN is working with SEIU to address discriminatory pricing by hospitals that charge much higher prices for care to the uninsured, while deeply discounting charges to the insured. Both groups are also addressing predatory collection practices by hospitals.

Just as important, many of ACORN's union partners encourage their members to join their local ACORN chapter. In Baltimore, for example, ACORN, AFSCME, and several other unions formed a partnership called CLUB (Communities and Labor United for Baltimore) to fight the city's cutbacks and privatization of services. AFSCME has aggressively encouraged its members to join ACORN, arguing that a strong community-based ally is critical to their overall strategy.

On November 5, 2003, CLUB placed an initiative on the ballot and passed it with 65 percent of the vote, replacing six large three-member city council districts in Baltimore with fourteen small single-member districts. The population of each city council district will now be reduced from 108,000 to 46,500. Under the old system, all three people representing a given district tended to live in the wealthiest part of it and would each refer matters to the other two. Under the new system, a city council member will have to live in an area of 46,500 people and be uniquely accountable to those people. Campaigning for election in these new smaller districts will cost less money, opening up the possibility of candidates who are not wealthy or beholden to the wealthy.

In Tampa, SEIU has given the local ACORN chapter its membership lists so that ACORN can match them with neighborhood chapter boundaries and approach union members about joining ACORN. The Stamford Organizing Project in Connecticut has assigned an organizer to do house visits with an ACORN organizer to sign up families as ACORN members. And in New Jersey, ACORN is working with the building trades on a campaign to hire local residents to work on publicly subsidized jobs. The residents are joining both the local ACORN group and the union.

3. *Alliances have to deliver victories to their members on campaigns that address critical issues that face the constituency: living wages, better health care, affordable housing, improved schools, safer neighborhoods.*

The living wage movement, with its 100-plus victories to date, is an obvious example. But take a look at the work ACORN is doing with labor unions in California for a broader picture of joint campaigns on issues that are important to the membership. In 2001, for example, the state AFL-CIO joined ACORN in mobilizing support for a far-reaching bill that outlaws many predatory lending practices that have victimized community and union members alike. The bill passed in the legislature and was signed into law by the governor after an aggressive grassroots campaign. The following year, ACORN and SEIU, along with other allies, launched a multiyear campaign for renters' rights in California that has won significant state and local protections against abuses by landlords. Among the campaign's victories: in 2003 the governor signed a bill to make it easier for tenants to collect their security deposits and a bill increasing from thirty to sixty days the notification requirement for mass evictions. In addition, ACORN and labor allies succeeded in getting the San Jose City Council and Oakland voters to pass just-cause eviction laws, and voters statewide passed the biggest housing bond in state history. And in July 2003, the governor signed an ACORN- and SEIU-sponsored bill that provides renters with the means to force landlords to make needed repairs by withholding rent and/or filing suit without fear of being evicted.

Among the many other collaborations with labor in California, ACORN's work with the teachers' unions and school employees' unions in 2003 is one of the most exciting. On February 5, the California legislature voted to keep in place a class size reduction program after the California Teachers' Association (CTA) lobbied for it with assistance from ACORN and other organizations. ACORN and the CTA organized rallies around the state to oppose budget cuts and demand "Schools, not Jails." In May, California ACORN members gathered in Sacramento for a state convention, which included a 450-person rally at the state capitol to stop education budget cuts and a 300-person sit-in in the office of the secretary of education, who agreed to oppose the cuts. Participating were members and officials from the California Labor Federation, CTA, United Teachers of Los Angeles, California School Employees Association (CSEA), Los Angeles County Probation Officers Association, SEIU Local 790, and AFSCME. In San Diego, ACORN teamed up with the San Diego Education Association and the CSEA to win the right for parents and the PTA to participate in budget negotiations, and to block proposed layoffs. In Oakland, as part of a national pilot project of the NEA, ACORN worked with the Oakland Education Association (OEA), CTA, and others to stop massive layoffs and help lobby for a record $100 million loan from the state to the school district. To make this happen, members of ACORN and the OEA marched into a School Board meeting chanting "No Cuts! No Layoffs!" Four of ten board members signed ACORN and OEA's demands, and the next evening the board decided to ask for the loan. San Jose ACORN and labor allies prevented the closure of Miller Elementary in June, and the South Bay Labor Council honored San Jose ACORN with its annual organizational award at a dinner attended by over 1,000 and featuring AFL-CIO Vice President Linda Chavez-Thompson as keynote speaker.

In early February 2002, ACORN, SEIU Local 100, and the Greater New Orleans AFL-CIO won a huge precedent-setting victory to raise the minimum wage for all workers in New Orleans. By a vote of 63 percent to 37 percent, New Orleans voters approved the measure, which was placed on the ballot through petitions circulated by the three organizations. The newly passed ordinance increased the minimum wage for any worker employed in the city (not just those working for companies that receive public benefits) to a dollar above the federal minimum—providing a raise for an estimated 80,000 workers. Unfortunately, the Louisiana State Supreme Court later overturned the vote, ruling in favor of a coalition of low-wage employer organizations. But ACORN and SEIU are pressing ahead with campaigns at the state and city levels to pass additional minimum wage and living wage measures.

Other cities have followed New Orleans's lead. In San Francisco, ACORN, together with labor and other groups, have formed the "$6.75 Is Not Enough" coalition, which on July 7, 2003, turned in over 20,000 signatures in an attempt to put an initiative on the ballot in November 2003 that would create a city wide minimum wage standard of $8.50.

In Paterson, New Jersey, ACORN, the Passaic County Building Trades, and the North Jersey Regional Council of Carpenters worked together for months to win in April 2003 a breakthrough project labor agreement with the New Jersey Schools Construction Corporation, including a provision that contractors hire apprentices to fill up to 25 percent of their positions, and a provision that 50 percent of the apprentices be women, minorities, or economically disadvantaged members of the community. The agreement also allows graduates of training programs to begin work prior to passing a union test. The Building Contractors Association and local unions have committed to maximizing the number of apprentices and reserving apprenticeship positions for community residents. In June, the Paterson city council passed an ordinance requiring that any company doing $1 million or more of construction work for the city hire from local preapprentice training programs. It requires that at least 20 percent of the work hours on those projects be done by apprentices, and that half of these come from a locally based training program. The labor force must also be 20 percent women or minority group members. The ordinance establishes a local board, the Paterson Community Apprenticeship Initiative, which will designate local training institutions, monitor contractors' compliance, and be composed of a range of appointees representing labor, community, and public entities like the board of education. Other cities, including Jersey City, Newark, and New York, are now considering similar laws.

ACORN chapters from around the state of New Jersey have also joined with the New Jersey Education Association and other allies in the Fairness Alliance to promote a "millionaire tax" to help avert planned budget cuts to housing and schools. The proposal calls for a tax increase for the wealthiest in the state, about 2 percent of the population, while decreasing taxes for people who make the least money. Four hundred and fifty ACORN members participated in an alliance rally at the state capitol in May 2003. Between

2,000 and 4,000 people were estimated to have participated in the May 31 rally. The alliance did not succeed in passing a millionaire tax, but as a result of these and other actions, millions of dollars for housing, low-income families, and urban schools that were slated to be cut were saved.

4. *Alliances must be politically active: Joint voter registration, voter education, candidate recruitment, and voter-participation campaigns are crucial elements of a power-building strategy.*

Unlike most community groups, ACORN members, through the ACORN Political Action Committee, get involved in partisan political activity—often in alliance with local unions. In New York, for example, ACORN and many of the largest unions in the state formed the Working Families Party (WFP) to promote worker- and neighborhood-friendly candidates and policies. As the *New York Times* reported on April 8, 2002:

> The Working Families Party and ACORN, one of its largest affiliated groups, have emerged as a significant policy-making force on the [New York City] Council, working with a loose coalition of about two dozen [city council] members. . . . They have nudged members to propose laws that would raise to $8.10 an hour the minimum wage that companies receiving public money through subsidies or contracts must pay their employees, regulate training and education for welfare recipients, and prohibit the city from doing business with banks that engage in predatory lending. . . . Several proposals to generate additional revenue, developed with the help of the Working Families Party, are supported by at least half of the Council's 51 members. They include reviving taxes on stock transactions and on commuters, and raising the personal income tax for the wealthiest New Yorkers.

The *Times* went on to point out that "the proposals are the result of a coordinated effort to influence the makeup of the new Council. The party supported 29 candidates, 15 of whom won."

As a result, ACORN and labor, through the WFP, passed New York City laws on predatory lending, living wage, and education and training for workfare participants, overriding the mayor's vetoes on these bills. They also passed a New York State law on predatory lending, and passed revolutionary city and state measures that tax the rich to pay for schools—the latter over the veto of the governor!

Why ACORN and Labor Are Natural Allies

ACORN, unlike "advocacy" or "policy" groups, is a membership organization, with deep roots in low- and moderate-income communities. With more than 150,000 dues-paying family members organized into 700-plus neighborhood chapters in 60 cities, ACORN has the ability to move large numbers of community residents on the issues that affect them. We have 300 full-time paid organizers in the field, who talk one-on-one, in person, to more than 15,000 families each week. Our neighborhood chapters meet monthly, and our block captains reach thousands more in their communities.

This powerful base in low- and moderate-income communities means that ACORN shares a set of values and common interests with most labor unions:

1. ACORN, like labor, is a membership organization that is accountable to the interests and issues of its members.
2. ACORN is around for the long term: Arkansas ACORN, where ACORN first began, is still going strong after thirty-three years. ACORN's reliance on membership dues provides financial stability, and it means that we are not dependent on the whims and interests of outside funders and that we can be a reliable long-term partner to unions.
3. ACORN members look like union members (and in many cases are union members): Our membership is low income and moderate income, African American, Latino, white, and Asian. Many are immigrants, and some are undocumented workers struggling to support their families. ACORN members are home health care workers, retail clerks, factory employees, hospital workers, and government employees. Some receive welfare, some unemployment insurance, and many social security.
4. ACORN members join their organization because they are "mad as hell" and want to take action. They fight for living wages, for better schools, for affordable homes, for better city services, for an end to corporate abuses. They are on the streets, in the halls of city councils and state legislatures, and in church basements and union halls, working for a fair and just society.
5. ACORN understands power, and that power comes from the numbers an organization can deliver. As *New York Daily News* columnist (and union leader) Juan Gonzalez wrote on March 13, 2001, in the context of New York ACORN's fight against the Edison company's attempt to privatize five New York public schools,

    Luckily, one of the city's most vocal community groups, ACORN, got involved. When it comes to mobilizing large numbers of poor people in this town around bread-and-butter issues, few can match ACORN. . . . For the Edison folks to win over the parents would be hard without opposition. But ACORN has far more ties in the

neighborhoods than do outsiders with grand schemes for making a
buck out of educational failure. Even in a rigged contest, I wouldn't
bet against ACORN.

All of this means that ACORN is a reliable ally—an organization that can
support unions in their organizing drives and contract campaigns, join together in policy campaigns on issues of mutual interest to union and ACORN
members through the ACORN Political Action Committee, and collaborate
on political campaigns to ensure that worker- and community-friendly candidates are elected to office.

Potential Problem Areas and Concerns

What are the drawbacks or issues to watch out for? From ACORN's perspective, we have run into a number of problems in building coalitions with labor
unions, including:

Coalitions as one-way streets: Too often union partners are quick to request
community support for an organizing drive or a contract campaign, but are
unwilling to utilize their power to support a community organization's goals.

Examples are too numerous to list. Local ACORN operations get calls all
the time from unions asking them to produce leaders or 20, 50, or 100 members at a press conference, "street heat" action, or some other event in support of worthy labor struggles. ACORN organizers sometimes resent this
"rent-a-community-leader" syndrome, and, more important, they are angered
by the presumption that turnout just happens, that it is cost-free to produce
twenty or fifty ACORN members, and that somehow the labor struggle in
question is more important than the priorities that the ACORN membership
themselves have set for their own campaign activities. In one city, an ACORN
organizer, when asked once too often to produce members for a union event,
invited the union leader to attend an ACORN community meeting and listen
in as the members planned an elaborate schedule of actions and events in
support of an ACORN priority. He came away from the meeting with an
appreciation for the fact that ACORN members have more to do than wait
around for another call from the union. In other cities, ACORN organizers
have utilized "count-on-me" forms to engage unions in discussions about
reciprocal turnout: We will produce for your rally if you will get your members to our event.

Confusion about advocacy versus community organizing: Unions sometimes do not understand the differences between their various partners and
allies and view the various players on the progressive scene as indistinguish-
able from one another. As a result, unions can overvalue the contributions of

public interest or advocacy organizations that have no base, and undervalue the role of a community organization that has actually built real power.

Many unions support public-interest organizations and join coalitions put together by advocates—and then wonder why the labor members of the coalition are the only ones pulling any weight. When ACORN or other community organizations with a base ask unions to join a coalition, union leaders sometimes ask why, since all of their previous experience has been with coalitions that cannot deliver. Chicago ACORN had a good solution to this problem in the context of its living wage coalition: The price of admission to join the coalition's decision-making structure was the ability and commitment to fill a bus with members for the campaign's various actions and rallies. The unions understood right away: This was a coalition that valued organizations that had a base and it was not going to get hijacked by groups that had no ability to deliver.

Race and gender: Not surprisingly, some union leaders are still caught in an older world and are more comfortable dealing with white males—while community organizations like ACORN more often than not are led by African-American and Latino women.

In one city, for example, a trades-dominated central labor council (CLC) was initially hesitant about joining an ACORN-led living wage coalition— largely because in that city ACORN was seen as an African American organization that had been on the opposite side of many local political battles. Nonetheless, mutual allies brokered a relationship, the organizations joined together in a successful living wage fight, and the presidents of the two organizations over time developed a relationship of respect. The head of the CLC now refers to the local living wage law as the "Davis-Bacon law for the service sector" and has joined with ACORN in a continuing series of campaigns on issues of interest to both organizations.

Examples of ACORN-Labor Alliances

Beyond the examples described above, the following ACORN-labor collaborations are worth noting. These examples point to the variety of relationships that local ACORN groups and labor unions have developed, and indicate the wide diversity of issues and projects that ACORN and unions have collaborated on.

Arkansas

Arkansas ACORN and the Arkansas state AFL-CIO, together with unions throughout the state, have worked together on virtually every critical issue facing low- and moderate-income Arkansans since ACORN's founding in 1970. ACORN and labor have led fights to repeal the state right-to-work laws, and for lower utility rates, a more progressive tax structure, and living wages.

In addition to the Central Arkansas Labor Council/ACORN partnership mentioned above, at the statewide level, ACORN, the Arkansas AFL-CIO, and the Arkansas Education Association created in 1999 the Arkansas State Electoral Coalition, a permanent statewide coalition of membership organizations that is working together on state legislative issues and is identifying, recruiting, and helping elect candidates for public office, including active members of the participating groups.

Illinois

Chicago ACORN and SEIU Local 880 jointly organized a broad community-labor campaign that was successful in winning both a Chicago living wage ordinance over the mayor's opposition, and then a second living wage ordinance that covers Cook County. This campaign was characterized by dozens of joint labor-community events in individual aldermen's wards, along with major rallies that involved over 1,000 union and community members. Since then, Local 880 and ACORN have organized the Chicago Grassroots Collaborative, which has carried out campaigns for immigrant rights and the expansion of the Children's Health Insurance Program.

At the statewide level, ACORN, SEIU, and other unions have organized an ongoing living wage campaign that succeeded in winning wage increases for 15,000 home-care workers and increases for 40,000 nursing home workers. ACORN played a critical role in these campaigns by turning out hundreds of ACORN members for rallies and direct lobbying of state legislators.

Massachusetts

Massachusetts ACORN, the Greater Boston Labor Council, and the Massachusetts AFL-CIO have worked as a powerful team over the past five years, starting with their joint campaign to pass the Boston Jobs and Living Wage Ordinance in 1997. The three organizations then worked together over the next two years to win passage of a state law raising the state minimum wage to $6.75 and to increase the state earned income tax credit. ACORN and labor then turned their attention back to Boston, and in 2001 won an expansion of the Boston living wage ordinance to cover more workers at a higher wage level. In all of these campaigns, the three organizations conducted regular leadership and strategy meetings, jointly approached allies, and took responsibility for turning out their members for lobbying and critical mass rallies.

ACORN, the central labor council, and the state AFL-CIO are committed to continuing joint campaigns on a variety of issues that are of common concern to our membership.

Louisiana

Anchored in the long-term SEIU Local–100 Louisiana ACORN partnership, Louisiana ACORN has worked closely with Louisiana labor unions on a long list of campaigns, including canvassing ACORN members and turning out community support for SEIU's campaigns to organize hotel workers and secure "labor peace" agreements from the city. ACORN is also working with SEIU to help guide the creation of one of the first Union Community Funds in the country, and serves on the board of the New Orleans fund.

On April 30, 2003, ACORN members from New Orleans, Lake Charles, and Baton Rouge attended committee hearings in the state legislature, together with allies from United Teachers of New Orleans, to express opposition to four bills that would have created school voucher programs. The bills were defeated. ACORN and allies are planning forums to educate the public on this issue and mobilize statewide opposition to any future voucher proposals.

New York

New York ACORN's extensive work with organized labor includes:

- The formation of the WFP, a joint effort of ACORN, other citizen organizations, and most of the largest labor unions in the state. The WFP has an aggressive program to promote worker-friendly policies at the state and local levels, and to recruit and support worker-friendly candidates for public office.
- The Alliance for Quality Education, a collaborative effort involving ACORN, the unions representing teachers and other school employees, and other parent and community organizations, which is working statewide to promote higher teacher salaries, smaller class size, universal pre-K, and new school construction.
- Organizing the New York Living Wage Coalition, with the participation of most of New York City's unions, to promote the most comprehensive living wage ordinance in the nation.
- Working closely with the United Federation of Teachers to improve school performance throughout New York City, and to successfully prevent the privatization of New York City public schools.

- With the support of several city unions, conducting a first-ever organizing drive among the city's 35,000 workfare workers, and winning passage of a grievance procedure that provides significant on-the-job protections to these welfare recipients, who are required to work off their benefits at city worksites.

New Jersey

New Jersey ACORN has been a consistently reliable partner in many of northern New Jersey's union organizing drives over the past several years. At the request of Local 1199J, ACORN field organizers carried out home visits in ACORN neighborhood turf in connection with a representation election, and used ACORN neighborhood leaders to convince undecided workers to vote "yes." Similarly, New Jersey ACORN has been working with SEIU's Justice for Janitors campaign and the Passaic County Building Trades Council by turning out members to rallies, meetings with public officials, and so on.

Having established a track record of support for union-organizing drives, most of the major unions in northern New Jersey are now supporting ACORN's campaign to pass a linked-development ordinance in Jersey City that would require developers of luxury housing and commercial space to build affordable housing. In particular, SEIU, the Laborers, the Carpenters, and 1199J have turned out members who live in Jersey City in a joint grassroots campaign with ACORN to fight for the linkage ordinance. SEIU leaders know that the value of their members' wages is eroding as housing costs in gentrifying Jersey City skyrocket, and they are committed to working with ACORN in the fight for affordable housing.

Missouri

Missouri ACORN's history with labor dates back to the late 1970s, when ACORN joined the state AFL-CIO in mounting a successful campaign to defeat a statewide ballot measure that would have legalized right-to-work legislation. Since then, ACORN and local unions, led by SEIU Local 880, have worked together on a long list of joint campaigns, including a statewide ballot fight to raise the minimum wage (which was unsuccessful), and a follow-up citywide ballot fight in St. Louis to pass a living wage ordinance, which passed overwhelmingly. ACORN and local unions also worked together in 2001 to successfully pass a bond issue to increase funding for affordable housing and health care in St. Louis.

Texas

Texas ACORN, SEIU Local 100, and the Harris County Labor Council have been the driving forces behind the Houston living wage campaign, which put a living wage ordinance on the ballot in 1996 and has continued to press the issue. And, similar to New Orleans, ACORN serves on the board of the newly formed Houston Union Community Fund and is helping to set direction for this new labor initiative.

Maryland

Baltimore ACORN has joined with AFSCME to lead a campaign to prevent the privatization of city work, stop layoffs of critical city workers, and promote broad-based opposition to antiworker, antineighborhood city policies. In addition, ACORN, AFSCME, and a broader group of additional unions have initiated a campaign to change the city charter by ballot initiative to create single-member city council districts that will be more responsive to voters than the current system is.

New Mexico

The Central New Mexico Central Labor Council, the state AFL-CIO, and AFSCME Council 18 have been working with New Mexico ACORN on its Living Wage for State Employees campaign, which is seeking state legislation to raise wages of workers employed by the state. Also, ACORN and the Albuquerque Teachers Federation are working together on a campaign to increase the number of well-trained permanent teachers who work at public schools in low-income neighborhoods, as well as on a campaign to keep the Edison company from taking over a cluster of Albuquerque public schools.

Connecticut

Connecticut ACORN, working closely with United Auto Workers Region 9A, the Teamsters, the Communications Workers of America, United Food and Commercial Workers, and AFSCME, has begun the development of a new ballot line political party modeled on the New York WFP. This new organization will promote candidates committed to establishing corporate responsibility standards for businesses receiving state economic assistance; giving agricultural workers the right to organize; and supporting a broad platform of community and labor issues. Meanwhile, ACORN, the AFL-CIO's Stamford Organizing Project, and SEIU Local 32BJ are collaborating on a campaign to stop the state's plans to restrict immigrants' access to driver's licenses.

Florida

ACORN and SEIU have recently initiated the Florida Community-Labor Organizing Project, an ambitious long-term plan to develop a collaborative organizing and campaign program in Tampa and St. Petersburg. With financial and staff support from both organizations, Florida ACORN and SEIU plan to assist each other in organizing drives in the community and the workplace; to carry out joint campaigns on health care, immigrant rights, education, housing, and predatory lending issues; and to conduct joint voter registration and voter participation projects.

Note

1. ACORN is one of the nation's largest and most successful networks of community organizations, with more than 150,000 low- and moderate-income members organized into 700 neighborhood chapters in 60 cities across the country. Since 1970 ACORN has been building solidly rooted and powerful community organizations that are committed to social and economic justice and that have taken action and won victories on thousands of issues of concern to our members. Its priorities include: better housing for first-time home buyers and tenants; living wages for low-wage workers; more investment in our communities from banks and governments; and better public schools. We achieve these goals by building community organizations that have the power to win changes—through direct action, negotiation, legislation, and voter participation.

4

Labor-Community Coalition Strengths and Weaknesses

Case Study Evidence

Bruce Nissen

Some academics and observers have called on the U.S. labor movement to adopt "social movement unionism" as a way to revitalize itself (Moody 1988; Turner and Hurd 2001; Johnston 2001, 2002; Robinson 2002). While definitions of social movement unionism vary, virtually all of them require that unions make alliances with social movements and community forces struggling to wrest concessions from corporations and corporate-dominated governments. If indeed coalitions in and with the community are critical elements of social movement unionism revitalization, it is worth examining the question in some detail. Are labor-community coalitions being attempted? Are the experiences of those attempting them positive? What factors make a labor leader, or a union, likely to attempt coalitions? What factors inhibit coalition building? In short, what are the potentials and the limitations of labor-community coalitions for U.S. unions in the current period? The remainder of this chapter will first examine the literature on this topic and then examine recent union experiences with this approach in south Florida to provide evidence for tentative answers to some of the questions enumerated above. (Because of the emphasis on local communities, union coalitions across national boundaries will not be considered in this chapter, important though that topic is in its own right.)

Literature on the Topic

A "classic" of the literature on this topic is the book *Building Bridges: The Emerging Grassroots Coalition of Labor and Community*, edited by Jeremy

Brecher and Tim Costello (1990). This book contains short case studies of coalitions concerning labor struggles, jobs and economic development struggles, electoral coalitions, and issue campaigns, as well as interpretive essays. While the range of coalitions and examples is wide, the cases are by now rather dated, and the chapters are only intermittently scholarly research—many are closer to journalism. Despite these limitations, this book has been one of the very best resources on labor-community coalitions for quite some time. A similar journalistic article by Acuff (1993) places coalitions at the center of a call for mass action as a way forward.

Much of the earliest work on labor-community coalitions centered on struggles to prevent plant closures. Haines and Klein (1982) detail labor-community coalition efforts against deindustrialization in Philadelphia in the late 1970s and early 1980s. Lynd (1983) analyzes the labor-community struggle to prevent the shutdown of the steel plants in Youngstown, Ohio. Issue 19 of *Labor Research Review* (1992) analyzes labor and community efforts to "save manufacturing." Hathaway (1993) analyzes plant closing struggles in the Pittsburgh area in the 1980s. The volume edited by Craypo and Nissen (1993) contains numerous case studies of attempts to forge union-community alliances in (usually futile) efforts to save jobs in times of deindustrialization. Nissen (1995) details and analyzes northwest Indiana labor-community efforts to confront and reverse plant closings. Swinney (1999) describes a labor-community alliance to save jobs in the candy industry in Chicago.

Some have analyzed labor-community coalition efforts in union contract campaigns. Green (1990) analyzes the unsuccessful struggle of United Food and Commercial Workers (UFCW) Local P-9 and allies to resist concessions at the Hormel company. Kingsolver (1989) and Rosenblum (1995) analyze the 1983 Phelps-Dodge strike in Arizona, where a labor-community effort was ultimately unsuccessful. Sciacchitano (1998) details a successful first contract campaign involving extensive community participation. Juravich and Bronfenbrenner (1999) relate the victorious struggle by the United Steelworkers and community allies against the Ravenswood Aluminum Corporation. Bronfenbrenner and Juravich (2001) explore increasingly successful coordinated campaigns by the United Steelworkers involving community alliances from 1983 through 2000. Franklin (2001) covers the (mostly losing) major struggles in Decatur, Illinois, pitting union-community forces against three employers determined to wrest concessions from their workers.

Other literatures look at the utility of labor-community coalitions in organizing the unorganized. Banks (1991–92) analyzes the Service Employees International Union (SEIU)'s Justice for Janitors (JfJ) experience, and the growth of Jobs with Justice (JwJ), arguing for "community unionism" in organizing efforts. Greer (1996) shows how community-labor alliances aided multiple union organizing drives in South Carolina. Needleman (1998) analyzes California garment worker and health care organizing experiences to draw out the potentials and pitfalls of coalitions between unions and low-wage communities. A portion of Janice Fine's excellent article (2000–01) on community unionism in Baltimore and Stamford concerns the decisive advantage community alliances gave to hospital workers organizing in Stamford, Connecticut (a revised version is included in this book).

Some literature concerns coalitions built around broader "community" concerns that may not be thought of as directly "union issues." One such concern is accountability by corporations who take public subsidies for allegedly saving or creating jobs. Nissen (1993) describes and analyzes successes in northwest Indiana, where pioneering legislation was won in Gary by a labor-community coalition. Peterson (2001–02) gives a detailed analysis of similar efforts in the state of Minnesota (a revised version is included in this book).

In a similar vein, there is a somewhat lengthy literature on living wage campaigns, perhaps the most successful sustained labor-community coalition movement in the United States today. Reynolds (1999) provides a broad survey of earlier living wage efforts. Nissen (2000) uses a south Florida example to evaluate the potential of living wage efforts to build genuine social movements. Nissen (2001) makes a broader assessment of living wage movements from a social movement analytical perspective. A portion of Fine's article (2001–02) analyzes the Baltimore alliance that kicked off the modern living wage movement. Luce (2001, 2002) analyzes the role of organized labor in living wage campaigns. Reynolds and Kern (2001–02) provide an analysis of similar issues (a revised version is included in this book). Reynolds (2002: 145–72) provides an overview of living wage issues, as do Levi, Olson, and Steinman (2002–03).

Others focus on the role of central labor councils (CLCs) in providing coalitions between organized labor and communities. Dean (1996) details Working Partnerships USA, a pioneering and innovative effort by a California CLC. Sneiderman (1996) shows how the national AFL-CIO began efforts to revitalize CLCs as community-based institutions in the mid-1990s. Gapasin and Wial (1998) make alliances with community forces a central criterion for determining which CLCs are "transformative" ones capable of playing a major role in organizing. Acuff (1999) uses Atlanta as an example to show the potential power of CLCs when alliances are made with community forces, especially minority communities. McLewin (1999) analyzes community fragmentation and labor efforts to build CLCs in the modern era. Kriesky (2001) gives a scholarly analysis of the structural and functional changes being attempted in recent efforts to rebuild CLCs embedded in communities.

A few articles explore the potential of labor-religious coalitions. Bole (1998) traces the reawakening of a religion-labor alliance that had fallen into abeyance. Peters and Merrill (1998) show the important role played by people of faith in organizing drives at Chicago's O'Hare airport and a local hospital. Russo and Corbin (1999) look at potential for coalitions between the Catholic Church and labor.

Alliances between organized labor and environmentalists have also received some coverage. Leonard and Nauth (1990) detail a successful labor-environmentalist alliance that humbled the BASF corporation, which was attempting to break a union in Louisiana. Braden (1993) relates southern environmental-labor alliances in organizing drives. Kellman (1994) analyzes union involvement in environmental protection in a strike situation in Jay, Maine. And a journal, *New Solutions,* was founded to find methods of uniting, rather than dividing, labor and environmentalists.

There are also numerous articles and books looking at relations between, and possible coalitions between, organized labor and minorities and immigrants. The entire literature is too broad to include here, but *Labor Research Review 20* (1993), Kelley (1999), and Blackwell and Rose (1999) give a flavor of some of the recent issues and debates.

Since the "Battle in Seattle" in 1999, some literature has analyzed a possibly emerging coalition between organized labor and the new global justice movement. Three reflections on the Seattle event are Fraser and Lichtenstein (2000), Acuff (2000), and Crosby (2000). Neumann (2002) is a thoughtful reflection on the difficulties facing this fragile, emerging coalition.

A book that has been unjustly neglected explores lessons from attempts to build coalitions between organized labor and the environmental and peace movements. Fred Rose's *Coalitions across the Class Divide: Lessons from the Labor, Peace, and Environmental Movements* (2000) focuses on cultural differences between working class organizations like unions and middle-class institutions such as peace and environmental groups. An in-depth insightful analysis of class cultural characteristics complements an astute reading of historical conjunctures in this book. Rose pays special attention to "bridge builders" who operate in progressive movements on both sides of the class divide. This book has a deep analytic structure missing from much of the literature on labor-community coalitions.

A recent paper by Frege, Heery, and Turner (2003) provides an excellent analytical framework through which labor-community coalitions can be evaluated. They define labor-community coalitions as follows:

> Union coalitions involve discrete, intermittent or continuous joint activity
> in pursuit of shared or common goals between trade unions and other non-
> labor institutions in civil society, including community, faith, identity, ad-
> vocacy, welfare and campaigning organisations. (p. 2)

This definition excludes union-union coalitions, or coalitions with government structures, politicians, or political parties. But it broadly covers all other
kinds of community coalitions into which unions may enter. This paper cata-
logues five types of resources coalitions may bring to unions: (1) financial
and physical resources, (2) communications, (3) expertise, (4) legitimacy,
and (5) mobilization of popular support. It also identifies four types of coalitions: (1) vanguard coalitions, where coalition partners simply support labor-
defined and -led activities; (2) common-cause coalitions, where separate but
associated interests coalesce; (3) bargained coalitions, where explicit bargaining defines the parameters of the coalition; and (4) integrative coalitions, where unions offer unconditional support to coalition partners.

This chapter will follow Frege, Heery, and Turner's definition of what
constitutes a labor-community coalition, and it will also use their distinc-
tions between types of coalition as analytical tools. In addition, Rose's concept of the "bridge builder" will be employed to analyze the dynamics of the
various coalitions.

The South Florida Case

The labor movement in south Florida engaged in very few coalition efforts
with community forces in the mid-1990s. Although Miami had been the birth-
place of the JwJ movement in 1987 at a rally of 11,000 in the Miami Arena
supporting the Eastern Airlines workers, by the mid-1990s there was no JwJ
chapter in the area. Virtually all other forms of labor-community coalition
were also extinct. This may have been due to the massive defeat of the Machinists union and its community allies in the Eastern Airlines struggle (out
of which the national JwJ grew), when the company was stripped of its assets by owner Frank Lorenzo and ultimately put out of business. Sometimes
massive labor defeats dampen further efforts for years. This may have happened in Miami.

Whatever the reason, the labor movement by the middle of the decade
was mostly disconnected from community activism. The central labor council considered itself connected to the community through its community services liaison at the United Way, but this connection was entirely focused on
charity rather than social activism. When I moved to Miami in 1997, there
was not a single labor-community coalition visible.[1] This changed in that

year, when the central labor council joined with a local human services coalition to explore the idea of pushing for a living wage in Miami-Dade County. The Community Coalition for a Living Wage (CCLW) was born.

From the beginning, this labor-community collaboration exhibited both positive features and problematic ones. The positive features were continued collaboration that eventually resulted in passage of a county living wage ordinance in 1999, a Miami Beach living wage ordinance in 2001, and ongoing efforts in several other south Florida towns. The problems were many. Aside from a couple of building trades leaders who intermittently attended CCLW meetings, organized labor's official presence in coalition meetings was almost entirely through one individual, the secretary-treasurer of the central labor council. This individual made no effort to actively involve other leaders of local unions. He made periodic reports to central labor council meetings on the CCLW's progress, but the entire effort was totally "top-down."[2]

The secretary-treasurer was totally committed to the cause of winning a living wage ordinance, but he exhibited a number of problematic attitudes. First, since he was originally from an airline Transport Workers Union local, he appeared to care almost exclusively about coverage of (union and nonunion) airport baggage handlers. At one point he argued that if they weren't covered the ordinance would be worse than nothing, since virtually all county contractors were nonunion, and winning wage increases for their nonunion workers would be a step backward. A coalition, he argued, was "you scratch my back; I'll scratch yours"; if union members weren't directly winning pay increases, organized labor had no stake. He refused to concede that a broader, integrative goal like "raising the floor for all workers" (and thus lessening the impetus for the county to privatize the American Federation of State, County, and Municipal Employees [AFSCME]-represented county jobs), was desirable.

Aside from the personal orientation of the individual involved, the broader labor movement's involvement in the living wage movement is revealing. Virtually all unions sympathized with the living wage effort, but until the final week before passage, none of them played an active role in the CCLW. They considered the individual participation of the central labor council's secretary-treasurer to be sufficient. Some union leaders saw the issue as one of helping unfortunate fellow employees, not a cause in the direct self-interest of local unions. Thus, their role was to passively watch the campaign unfold, until the final point of passage. That said, it is important to emphasize that the labor movement did provide most of the bodies in the mass mobilization of approximately 500 attending the county council meeting where the ordinance was passed. While the understanding of some (but not all) was limited (somewhat closer to "charity" than "solidarity"), it remains true that the south Florida labor movement's coalitional efforts did grow in both understanding and practice in this initial living wage campaign.

The next coalitional effort revealed a split within the ranks of organized labor. In 1998, an individual with long experience in community organizing in the area began to create a local chapter of the Interfaith Committee for Worker Justice (IFCWJ). Once the committee was established, a conflict erupted. Some of the more activist local unions, including SEIU and Union of Needle Trades, Industrial, and Textile Employees (UNITE) affiliates, began bringing organizing and contract battle requests for assistance to this committee. The central labor council secretary-treasurer, at the insistence of the council's president, demanded that locals not be allowed to bring requests to the IFCWJ. He argued that *all* requests could be channeled only through the central labor council to IFCWJ, not directly from a union local. If the IFCWJ accepted and acted upon requests for assistance from a union local, he threatened that the central labor council would refuse all cooperation with IFCWJ, and treat it as an unfriendly organization. He further demanded that an African American pastor who had taken a position favoring school vouchers be removed from IFCWJ leadership, since the local teacher's union opposed vouchers.

These demands reveal three things about the attitude of the central labor council's leadership at that time (the leadership has since changed). First, all coalitions between unions and community forces were to be controlled by the council. Any efforts outside of this unitary "official" channel were to be suppressed. Second, community allies (in this case, religious allies) were not to be allowed to act as an independent body—they were to operate only as a labor support group unconditionally supporting whatever the central labor council wished. Third, individuals involved in coalition efforts were not to be allowed to take a position in opposition to positions taken by the central labor council's largest affiliate, the teacher's union. Intimidated, the fledgling IFCWJ voted to deal exclusively with the central labor council, and to never take a position different from that taken by the AFL-CIO.

Under these conditions, the IFCWJ failed to grow beyond the initial group of about a half dozen prolabor clergy and laity who had originally set up the group. As a captive labor support group, it was unable to develop its own internal life or to move beyond the most dedicated initial founders. Subsequently, the president and the secretary-treasurer of the central labor council moved to different positions. This enabled the IFCWJ to become a more independent organization, with its own part-time staffing, independent decision-making leadership body, and ability to relate to whatever unions come to it for assistance. Given this greater freedom and ability to develop "ownership" of the organization from people in the faith community, the organization has grown enormously, and has become one of the most important and active IFCWJs in the United States.

A final coalitional effort was to reveal even greater splits within the labor movement itself. In late 1999, community and union activists who were unhappy with both the lack of activism in the central labor council and the weak mobilizational capacity (and narrow focus) of the CCLW decided to recreate a JwJ chapter in south Florida. The union component of the newly formed JwJ chapter was composed of the most activist unions in the area, primarily local affiliates of SEIU, UNITE, and AFSCME. (A Transportation Workers Union [TWU] local and a Communication Workers of America [CWA] local also supplied leadership individuals for the new JwJ chapter.) The prechangeover central labor council leadership was highly suspicious of the JwJ chapter from the beginning, because it felt that some of the union locals putting most energy into JwJ were not active or energetic enough participants in the central labor council.

The tensions broke into open warfare when the central labor council secretary-treasurer disrupted a JwJ meeting by getting into a shouting match with an AFSCME local president, accusing this president of lowering his labor council affiliation numbers at the same time he was supporting JwJ. He shouted that JwJ was a "dual union" phenomenon that the central labor council would treat as an enemy. The council subsequently wrote a letter to AFL-CIO president John Sweeney demanding that he intervene and force the JwJ chapter to disband. The "dual unionist" accusations to the national AFL-CIO were persistent, not simply one letter. Eventually the AFL-CIO national office called both the central labor council president and the cochair of the local JwJ chapter (who is the leader of an SEIU local) to Washington, D.C., for a meeting with AFL-CIO vice president Linda Chavez-Thompson. Much to the surprise of the central labor council leader, Chavez-Thompson defended the right of JwJ to exist, and instructed the local central labor council to cooperate with it. Because of the post–1995 leadership of the AFL-CIO, bureaucratic sanction was given to the activists in the labor movement, not to those attempting to suppress local activism.

As noted before, leadership in the central labor council has since changed. Both the new president and secretary-treasurer of the council now support the existence of the JwJ chapter, and the council actively publicizes JwJ activities. On the broader issue of coalitions in general, the new leadership is also much more expansive in attitude, supporting any coalitions that are prolabor. There is still some unease within the labor council about whether JwJ is attempting to encroach on council "turf," or perhaps creating multiple organizations that are unnecessary. But on the whole, the "official" labor body's attitude toward coalitions, and its understanding of their nature is much more positive than it had been earlier.

It remains true that most of the "in the streets" activism of the labor movement in south Florida is channeled through the JwJ chapter, not the central labor council. As long as there are positive relations between the council and the JwJ chapter, this division of labor is probably for the best, because the council contains a large number of union locals whose leadership outlooks (and internal cultures) are not oriented toward either coalition building or confrontational activism. Given this, the labor council would have a hard time carrying out the activist program pursued by JwJ. An alliance between the two organizations allows the labor council to lend support to left progressive activism, without having to carry out the work entirely on its own.

Of the approximately eighty union locals in south Florida, approximately 10 percent participate actively in JwJ, with maybe another 10 percent occasionally relating to the organization and its activities. The JwJ chapter is currently recruiting members aggressively, and may be able to double these numbers. This is an impressive number of labor organizations—far beyond anything that would have been conceivable in the past—but it also indicates that most unions are not oriented toward activist coalitions. This is of course not surprising, given that the post–World War II U.S. labor movement almost never engaged in such coalitions prior to the 1980s.

Reasons for the indifference of most unions are not hard to find. First, in most unions (but not all) the demand for coalitions is not coming spontaneously from the rank-and-file. Most members, familiar with the traditional role played by U.S. unions in the immediate past, seldom think of unions as coalition partners in activist formations (Nissen 2003). Thus they look to the union only for contract negotiations and servicing.

Given this, the likelihood that a union will proactively enter into coalitions usually is highly dependent on the attitudes of the leaders toward coalitions. When south Florida union leaders do enter into coalitions, their ability to get members actively involved depends heavily on the composition of the membership. The south Florida unions most easily able to mobilize members for coalition efforts have at least one of two characteristics. They are overwhelmingly composed of people of color and low-wage workers; or their members work in one of the service or helping industries (nursing homes, blue collar school employees), or both. Other JwJ member unions, such as the Ironworkers local in the area and the author's union of university professors, have been able to induce small-scale participation in JwJ events, but the membership has not easily embraced this type of coalition work as a natural thing to do.

Whatever the degree of mass participation, the most critical variable determining whether a south Florida union will participate in the local coalition opportunities available is the presence (or absence) of a union activist or leader with a strong ideological motivation to connect his/her union with the coalition. Most often, this is someone in a leadership position within the union. Such people are what Rose (2000, 167–80) calls "bridge builders" who fuse labor with other progressive organizations. Virtually every instance of strong union involvement in the local JwJ chapter exhibits such a bridge builder (or builders) from the union. South Florida union leaders and activists who are bridge builders often have a background of involvement with some other social movement or campus-based movement. This is not universally true, but it is in a majority of cases. A couple of bridge builders were also introduced to the idea of coalitions as "a union way of life" in labor education classes from the local university-based labor center.

The other characteristic of south Florida bridge builders that is nearly universal is that they have a leftist political ideology that views the world in class terms, and in terms of struggle. South Florida union leaders who have a clear political perspective of this nature are a minority, but they are the same minority as those who have chosen to involve their unions in the local JwJ chapter. Leaders with this perspective see organized labor as part of a larger social movement for social and economic justice, so coalitions seem to be a natural thing from this perspective. In south Florida, the most prominent bridge builder is Monica Russo, leader of SEIU 1199-Florida. Other "bridge builder" union leaders and staffers have also played a major role in building a JwJ chapter and other labor-community coalitions: Dave Gornewicz of Ironworkers Local 272, Sherman Henry of AFSCME Local 1184, John Ratliff of SEIU Local 1991, J. W. Johnson and Dorothy Townsend of TWU Local 291, Maria Revelles of UNITE, and others.

The more a labor leader's vision is focused on simply members or simply economic gain for the members, the less likely he or she is to engage in coalitional activities. And to the extent that a narrowly focused leader does undertake coalitional activities, he or she is likely to view coalition partners from only an opportunistic perspective. Coalitions are seen as merely a tactical device for immediate gain. A coalition can be only a *labor support group*, from this perspective. In the language of Frege, Heery, and Turner (2003), they confine themselves to "vanguard" coalitions whose sole purpose is for coalition partners to unconditionally support a union. Coalitions never progress to the "common cause" stage, much less a bargained agreement or an integrative state. Consequently any coalitions tend to be small, intermittent, and short-lived. More frequently, no coalition efforts are attempted at all.

Among labor leaders with a wider vision, there still exists a tension over how far afield coalition efforts can go. All unions, including those led by progressives with a left-leaning vision, are under tremendous pressure to attain short-term results as the labor movement continues its slow decline in numbers and influence. Direct institutional gains in the form of a better union contract, union recognition in an organizing battle, obtaining a first contract, or a political objective, have to be a part of the thinking of all leaders when considering where to put time and resources. Thus even the most progressive leader has to concentrate on only those coalitions most likely to bring about union victories in the near term.

The ability of south Florida labor-community coalitions to deliver such gains varies from circumstance to circumstance. For example, the CCLW hoped that its living wage victories would result in some union-organizing victories. Yet, only one organizing victory at the airport (for a Teamsters local) resulted from passage of the Miami-Dade ordinance. Whether this is the fault of unions for not aggressively attempting to organize workers of county contractors winning living wage increases, or whether it is because the living wage movement was not enough to convince these workers to overcome their fear and organize, is not clear.

Other examples of little apparent gain include the struggle by UNITE to organize workers at a facility of Goya foods. Despite support from coalition allies, the union has been stymied by employer intransigence. A group of workers organized by the Ironworkers has never obtained a first contract, despite active support from JwJ and the IFCWJ. The Carpenters organized a lumber yard and eventually lost the unit in a decertification election four years later due to unfair labor practices and employer intransigence despite rallies and interventions by the IFCWJ and JwJ. In other words, coalitions do not *consistently* deliver sufficient "clout" to turn the tide for unions facing obstinate employers.

On the other hand, nursing home workers at Mt. Sinai/St. Francis nursing home won an SEIU 1199-Florida union contract after several JwJ and IFCWJ support activities, including a widely publicized "Workers Rights Board" hearing into the nursing home's behavior featuring actor Danny Glover. And workers organized by UNITE at a Point Blank bullet-proof vest plant clearly have been aided (both materially and in terms of morale) by the south Florida JwJ chapter in their struggle, which is ongoing.

This question of how often, and how visibly, labor-community coalitions can "tip the balance" enough to deliver victories for labor unions is important, because it may determine the degree to which unions with less ideologically committed leadership are likely to be pulled into coalition efforts. In south Florida, the record is mixed. The combination of living wage movements, an active JwJ chapter, and an active IFCWJ is resulting in enough victories to bring ever more attention and respect to the coalition idea, but progress has been only partial.

Two points are crucial here. First, local coalitions have had to struggle to obtain sufficient resources to be adequately staffed and developed. The CCLW has had to operate with either no staffing or intermittent very part-time staffing of ten hours a week after a local foundation grant was obtained. The local JwJ chapter has been more fortunate; thanks to support from the national JwJ and national foundations, it has operated with one or two staff in the past few years. The IFCWJ started with no staffing but evolved into a part-time staff position for a very talented individual able to offer more than half-time work for only half-time wages. These low levels of staffing have been enough to keep the organizations functional, but much more could be done with more support. Especially the JwJ chapter and the IFCWJ are striving hard to become more self-sufficient with local support from member organizations.

Second, the real power of labor-community coalitions lies not only in immediate victories for labor that they are able to deliver, but also in their ability to achieve broader, and longer term, goals. Properly built labor-community coalitions build credibility for organized labor among potential allies. This can be critical for long-term political power, community support over time, and the like. For example, the south Florida JwJ organized and cosponsored in October 2002 an early vote rally and march. This coalition effort united unions, gay and lesbian organizations, Haitian activists, civil rights organizations and leaders, rappers, students, and others. The chapter also worked hard on a Florida constitutional amendment to mandate smaller class sizes in the public schools. It also supported a "People's Transportation Plan" to raise the taxes necessary for better public transportation in the county. All of these were successful, and organized labor gained in credibility with a number of organizers and community leaders with whom it had limited contact before.

The biggest task for organized labor in this country is to change the cultural climate of the country so that union rights become a *cause* to which large percentages of the population are dedicated. As the AFL-CIO notes, labor rights must be made into *human* rights. If the cultural climate could be changed decisively in this way, the size of the labor movement could grow enormously in short order because union-busting employer behavior would not be tolerated. As Nelson Lichtenstein notes (2002), violation of union rights must be made just as shameful and unacceptable as denial of rights due to racism. If this type of cultural change is ever to occur, it is hard to see how it could happen in the absence of extensive labor-community coalitions throughout the country.

Long-term goals like this are equally relevant with short-term gains when appraising the importance of labor-community coalitions to unions in this country. But long-term goals that may or may not be realized are difficult to induce labor leaders to embrace as a high priority. This is perfectly understandable at a time when unions are struggling for their very survival in a hostile environment. Thus, commitment to labor-community coalitions in south Florida is only partial, even among some of the most progressive unions. Despite this qualification, the idea is gaining more and more adherents, thanks to what has been accomplished through coalitions to date.

To a large degree, it seems that the future of labor-community coalitions in south Florida depends on the prospects for social movement activism on a broader scale. This too has been improving in the Miami area. An active and energetic Miami Workers Center has been set up in the heart of the African American community. Several activists have set up a "Power University" at a local university that trains neighborhood activists in leadership. A well-established affiliate of the church-based Direct Action Research and Training (DART) community organizing network exists, and it has been establishing some ties with the living wage movement. Thanks to the success of the living wage movement, the community organizing group, The Association of Community Organizations for Reform Now (ACORN), has established a local chapter in both Miami and neighboring Broward County. All of these are recent developments, occurring within the past five years. If such social movement activism continues to grow, it will increase the potential power of community allies, making labor-community coalitions more appealing and likely in the future.

Summary and Conclusion

In south Florida, labor-community coalition efforts have grown enormously in the past six years, although they are still definitely the exception rather than the rule. In this particular locale, the following factors have influenced developments:

1. A widely resonant initial issue—a living wage—began the process of initial formation of labor-community coalition groups. Success on this issue inspired the formation of other labor-community coalition groups.

2. Problematic attitudes from the central labor council leadership made initial efforts difficult, but a turnover in council leadership has removed that obstacle. Proprietary attitudes that attempt to monopolize all union activity and a "vanguardist" attitude toward all community partners (forcing them to make no decisions, but to merely support unconditionally a union) are very detrimental to effective development of a labor-community coalition.

3. The coalitions that have grown and prospered have not been "vanguard" coalitions where community partners are asked to be nothing more than a labor support group unconditionally supporting decisions made by a particular union. Instead, the most successful have been "common cause" coalitions focused on converging interests. These coalitions have been allowed to

develop their own leadership and decision-making bodies, and have allowed participating organizations and individuals to "buy in" to the mission of the coalition through active participation in group decisions.

4. All coalitions have depended heavily on "bridge builders" who share both labor and community viewpoints, and who actively work to bring labor together with nonlabor potential partners. Bridge builders from within organized labor are often labor leaders or staff with a broadly left-leaning working class perspective on the world; frequently they have had previous experience in other social movements.

5. Effectiveness of the coalitions depends heavily on their ability to mobilize enough resources to have adequate staffing. All-volunteer, or virtually all-volunteer, organizations, never develop beyond a low level of effectiveness. The quality of the staffing is also critical—fortunately, south Florida labor-community coalitions have had high-quality levels of staffing.

6. The likelihood that coalition-building will spread to broader sections of the local labor movement depends a lot on the degree to which labor-community coalitions are able to demonstrate concrete results for achieving union goals. So far, the record is mixed, although enough results have been achieved to give the idea growing appeal within south Florida unions.

7. Coalitions most easily attract large-scale membership participation from south Florida unions whose membership is either heavily minority and/or immigrant, or in the public service or helping industries. Unions with more skilled and more "white" memberships draw more limited mass participation.

8. Future growth of labor-community coalitions appears to depend on growth of social movement activism on a broader scale. In the Miami area, such activism has been growing, making for a cautious optimism about future prospects.

Whether these conclusions are generalizable beyond the south Florida area is of course subject to debate. But my reading of the entire range of literature cited earlier leads me to believe that they are broadly applicable. When enough case studies are consulted for congruence with the conclusions drawn, we can be relatively confident about those conclusions. In this case, the general factors and influences cited in the above eight conclusions appear to have fairly wide applicability. Scholars and activists around the country can probably reliably utilize the above conclusions in analyzing the prospects for labor-community coalitions in their local community.

Notes

1. The following account of the growth of labor-community activism in south Florida in the years between 1997 and 2003 is based on my participation in, and observation of, the organizations covered.

2. For a fuller explication of the problems with the CCLW from a social movement perspective, see Nissen, 2000.

References

Acuff, Stewart. 1993. "The Right Thing, the Smart Thing: A Call for Mass Action." *Labor Research Review* 21, XII, no. 2 (Fall/Winter): 97–104.

———. 1999. "Expanded Roles for the Central Labor Council: The View from Atlanta." In *Which Direction for Organized Labor? Essays on Organizing, Outreach, and Internal Transformations,* ed. Bruce Nissen, 133–42. Detroit: Wayne State University Press.

———. 2000. "The Battle in Seattle and Where We Go From Here." *New Labor Forum* 6 (Spring/Summer): 30–34.

Banks, Andy. 1991–92. "The Power and Promise of Community Unionism." *Labor Research Review* 18, X, no. 2 (Fall/Winter): 17–31.

Blackwell, Angela Glover, and Kalima Rose. 1999. "Overcoming the Obstacles: Forging Effective Labor-Community Alliances." *New Labor Forum* 5 (Fall/Winter): 59–67.

Bole, William. 1998. "Religion and Labor: Reawakening the Alliance." *WorkingUSA* 2, no. 4 (November/December): 42–49.

Braden, Anne. 1993. "Environmental Justice = Social Justice." *Labor Research Review* 20, XII, no. 1 (Spring/Summer): 63–69.

Brecher, Jeremy, and Tim Costello, eds. 1990. *Building Bridges: The Emerging Grassroots Coalition of Labor and Community.* New York: Monthly Review Press.

Bronfenbrenner, Kate, and Tom Juravich. 2001. "The Evolution of Strategic and Coordinated Bargaining Campaigns in the 1990s: The Steelworkers Experience." In *Rekindling the Movement: Labor's Quest for Relevance in the 21st Century,* ed. Lowell Turner, Harry C. Katz, and Richard W. Hurd, 211–37. Ithaca, NY: Cornell University Press.

Craypo, Charles, and Bruce Nissen, eds. 1993. *Grand Designs: The Impact of Corporate Strategies on Workers, Unions, and Communities.* Ithaca, NY: ILR Press/ Cornell University Press.

Crosby, Jeff. 2000. "The Kids Are Alright." *New Labor Forum* 6 (Spring/Summer): 35–39.

Dean, Amy. 1996. "Working Partnerships USA: The Latest Initiative for a Council on the Cutting Edge." *Labor Research Review* 24 (Summer): 43–48.

Fine, Janice. 2000–01. "Community Unionism in Baltimore and Stamford: Beyond the Politics of Particularism." *WorkingUSA* 4, no. 3 (Winter): 59–85.

Franklin, Stephen. 2001. *Three Strikes: Labor's Heartland Losses and What They Mean for Working Americans.* New York: Guilford Press.

Fraser, Steve, and Nelson Lichtenstein. 2000. "Teamsters and Turtles." *New Labor Forum* 6 (Spring/Summer): 23–29.

Frege, Carola, Edmund Heery, and Lowell Turner. January 2003. "Comparative Coalition Building and the Revitalization of the Labor Movement." Paper presented to the Industrial Relations Research Association Conference, Washington, DC.

Gapasin, Fernando, and Howard Wial. 1998. "The Role of Central Labor Councils in Union Organizing in the 1990s." In *Organizing to Win: New Research on Union*

Strategies, ed. Kate Bronfenbrenner, Sheldon Friedman, Richard W. Hurd, Rudolph A. Oswald, and Ronald L. Seeber, 54–67. Ithaca, NY: Cornell University Press.

Greer, Simon. 1996. "Community-Labor Alliance Sparks South Carolina." *Labor Research Review* 24 (Summer): 87–91.

Haines, Pamela, and Gary Klein. 1982. "Citizens and Unions Respond." In *Community and Capital in Conflict: Plant Closings and Job Loss*, ed. John C. Raines, Lenora E. Berson, and David Gracie, 234–54. Philadelphia: Temple University Press.

Hathaway, Dale. 1993. *Can Workers Have a Voice? The Politics of Deindustrialization in Pittsburgh*. University Park: Pennsylvania State University Press.

Johnston, Paul. 2001. "Organize for What? The Resurgence of Labor as a Citizenship Movement." In *Rekindling the Movement: Labor's Quest for Relevance in the 21st Century*, ed. Lowell Turner, Harry C. Katz, and Richard W. Hurd, 27–58. Ithaca, NY: Cornell University Press.

———. 2002. "Citizenship Movement Unionism: For the Defense of Local Communities in the Global Age." In *Unions in a Globalized Environment: Changing Borders, Organizational Boundaries, and Social Roles*, ed. by Bruce Nissen, 236–63. Armonk, NY: M.E. Sharpe.

Juravich, Tom, and Kate Bronfenbrenner. 1999. *Ravenswood: The Steelworkers' Victory and the Revival of American Labor*. Ithaca, NY: Cornell University Press.

Kellman, Peter. 1994. "Jay, Maine Fights for Jobs and the Environment." *Labor Research Review* 22, XIII, no. 1 (Fall/Winter): 21–27.

Kelley, Robin D.G. 1999. "Building Bridges: The Challenge of Organized Labor in Communities of Color." *New Labor Forum* 5 (Fall/Winter): 42–58.

Kingsolver, Barbara. 1989. *Holding the Line: Women in the Great Arizona Mine Strike of 1983*. Ithaca, NY: ILR Press/Cornell University Press.

Kriesky, Jill. 2001. "Structural Change in the AFL-CIO: A Regional Study of Union Cities' Impact." In *Rekindling the Movement: Labor's Quest for Relevance in the 21st Century*, ed. Lowell Turner, Harry C. Katz, and Richard W. Hurd, 129–54. Ithaca, NY: Cornell University Press.

Leonard, Richard, and Zack Nauth. *Labor Research Review* 16, IX, no. 2 (Fall): 35–49. 1990. "Beating BASF: OCAW Busts Union-Buster."

Levi, Margaret, Davaid J. Olson, and Erich Steinman. 2002–03. "Living-Wage Campaigns and Laws." *WorkingUSA* 6, no. 3 (Winter): 111–32.

Lichtenstein, Nelson. 2002. *The State of the Union*. Princeton, NJ: Princeton University Press.

Luce, Stephanie. 2001. "Building Political Power and Community Coalitions: The Role of Central Labor Councils in the Living Wage Movement." In *Central Labor Councils and the Revival of American Unionism*, ed. Immanuel Ness and Stuart Eimer. Armonk, NY: M.E. Sharpe.

———. 2002. "Life Support: Coalition Building and the Living Wage Movement." *New Labor Forum* 10 (Spring/Summer): 81–92.

Lynd, Staughton. 1983. *The Fight Against Shutdowns*. San Pedro, CA: Singlejack Books.

McLewin, Philip J. 1999. "The Concerted Voice of Labor and the Suburbanization of Capital: The Fragmentation of the Community Labor Council." In *Which Direction for Organized Labor? Essays on Organizing, Outreach, and Internal Transformations*, ed. Bruce Nissen, 113–32. Detroit: Wayne State University Press.

Moody, Kim. 1988. *An Injury to All: The Decline of American Unionism.* New York: Verso.

Needleman, Ruth. 1998. "Building Relationships for the Long Haul: Unions and Community-Based Groups Working Together to Organize Low Wage Workers." In *Organizing to Win: New Research on Union Strategies,* ed. Kate Bronfenbrenner, Sheldon Friedman, Richard W. Hurd, Rudolph A. Oswald, and Ronald L. Seeber, 71–86. Ithaca, NY: Cornell University Press.

Neumann, Rachel. 2002. "Out of Step: Labor and the Global Social Justice Movement." *New Labor Forum* 11 (Fall/Winter): 38–47.

Nissen, Bruce. 1993. "Successful Labor-Community Coalition Building." In *Grand Designs: The Impact of Corporate Strategies on Workers, Unions and Communities,* ed. Charles Craypo and Bruce Nissen, 209–23. Ithaca, NY: ILR Press/Cornell University Press.

———. 1995. *Fighting for Jobs: Case Studies of Labor-Community Coalitions Confronting Plant Closings.* Albany, NY: State University of New York Press.

———. 2000. "Living Wage Campaigns from a 'Social Movement' Perspective: The Miami Case." *Labor Studies Journal* 25, no. 3 (Fall 2000): 29–50.

———. 2001. "The 'Social Movement' Dynamics of Living Wage Campaigns." *Proceedings of the 53rd Annual Meeting of the Industrial Relations Research Association,* January 5–7, 2001, New Orleans, Louisiana, 232–40. Champaign, IL: Industrial Relations Research Association.

———. 2003. "Alternative Strategic Directions for the U.S. Labor Movement: Recent Scholarship." *Labor Studies Journal* 28, no. 1 (Spring): 133–55.

Peters, Ron, and Theresa Merrill. 1998. "Clergy and Religious Persons' Roles in Orgizing at O'Hare Airport and St. Joseph Medical Center. In *Organizing to Win: New Research on Union Strategies,* ed. Kate Bronfenbrenner, Sheldon Friedman, Richard W. Hurd, Rudolph A. Oswald, and Ronald L. Seeber, 164–77. Ithaca, NY: Cornell University Press.

Peterson, Erik. 2001–02. "Coming Together: Promises and Pitfalls of Minnesota's Corporate-Accountability Campaigns." *WorkingUSA* 5, no. 3 (Winter): 46–80.

Reynolds, David B. 2002. *Taking the High Road: Communities Organize for Economic Change.* Armonk, NY: M.E. Sharpe.

Reynolds, David, and Jen Kern. 2001–02. "Labor and the Living-Wage Movement." *WorkingUSA* 5, no. 3 (Winter): 17–45.

Reynolds, David. "The Living Wage Movement Sweeps the Nation." *WorkingUSA* September/October 1999.

Robinson, Ian. 2002. "Does Neoliberal Restructuring Promote Social Movement Unionism? U.S. Developments in Comparative Perspective." In *Unions in a Globalized Environment: Changing Borders, Organizational Boundaries, and Social Roles,* ed. Bruce Nissen, 189–235. Armonk, NY: M.E. Sharpe.

Rose, Fred. 2000. *Coalitions Across the Class Divide: Lessons from the Labor, Peace, and Environmental Movements.* Ithaca, NY: Cornell University Press.

Rosenblum, Jonathan D. 1995. *Copper Crucible: How the Arizona Miners' Strike of 1983 Recast Labor-Management Relations in America.* Ithaca, NY: ILR Press/ Cornell University Press.

Russo, John, and Brian Corbin. 1999. "Work, Organized Labor and the Catholic Church: Boundaries and Opportunities for Community/Labor Coalitions." In *Which Direction for Organized Labor? Essays on Organizing, Outreach, and Internal Transformations,* ed. Bruce Nissen, 95–111. Detroit: Wayne State University Press.

Sciacchitano, Katherine. 1998. "Finding the Community in the Union and the Union in the Community: The First-Contract Campaign at Steeltech." In *Organizing to Win: New Research on Union Strategies*, ed. Kate Bronfenbrenner, Sheldon Friedman, Richard W. Hurd, Rudolph A. Oswald, and Ronald L. Seeber, 150–63. Ithaca, NY: Cornell University Press.

Sneiderman, Marilyn. 1996. "AFL-CIO Central Labor Councils: Organizing for Social Justice." *Labor Research Review*, no. 24 (Summer): 39–42.

Swinney, Dan. 1999. "Early Warning Systems: A Progressive Economic Strategy for Labor." *WorkingUSA* 3, no. 2 (July/August): 9–18.

Turner, Lowell, and Richard W. Hurd. 2001. "Building Social Movement Unionism: The Transformation of the American Labor Movement." In *Rekindling the Movement: Labor's Quest for Relevance in the 21st Century*, ed. Lowell Turner, Harry C. Katz, and Richard W. Hurd, 9–26. Ithaca, NY: Cornell University Press.

II

Areas of Common Ground

5

Labor and the Living Wage Movement

David B. Reynolds and Jen Kern

The State of the Movement

Begun in 1994 with Baltimore's pioneering ordinance, the living wage movement has spread to every part of the country (see Table 5.1). By early 2004, 119 local living wage laws had been passed, the result of impressive grassroots campaigns by community and labor coalitions in cities large and small—from Boston to Miami, Duluth to San Antonio, Portland to Tucson. In addition, active campaigns are organizing in about seventy-five other communities, including Atlanta, Santa Barbara, Indianapolis, Phoenix, and Miami. Most notably, the ranks of active campaigns include the antiunion South—with local campaigns in Louisiana, Kentucky, North Carolina, Arkansas, Alabama, Georgia, Tennessee, Texas, Florida, and Virginia. The living wage movement has also planted firm roots in American higher education. The dramatic 2001 Harvard University living wage sit-in represented only the most publicized of over fifty campus campaigns for worker justice active across the country. The track record of the past nine years reveals the living wage as a compelling issue with remarkable staying power.

In short, living wage campaigns seek to require private businesses that benefit from public money to pay their workers a living wage (usually defined as at least enough to bring a family of four to the federal poverty line, currently $8.85 an hour). Commonly, the ordinances cover employers who hold large city or county service contracts or benefit from public tax dollars

Table 5.1

Living Wage Wins as of July 2003

Listed below are places that have enacted living wage laws.

Lakewood, OH (July 2003)
Dayton, OH (July 2003)
Arlington, VA (June 2003)
Ingham County, MI
  (June 2003)
Prince George's County, MD
  (June 2003)
Santa Fe, NM
  (February 2003)
Bellingham, WA
  (November 2002)
Louisville, KY
  (November 2002)
Cincinnati, OH
  (November 2002)
Westchester County, NY
  (November 2002)
Taylor, MI (November 2002)
New York City, NY
  (November 2002)
Broward County, FL
  (October 2002)
Watsonville, CA
  (September 2002)
Fairfax, CA (August 2002)
Southfield, MI (July 2002)
Oxnard, CA (July 2002)
Montgomery County, MD
  (June 2002)
Port of Oakland, CA
  (March 2002)
Santa Fe, NM
  (February 2002)
New Orleans, LA
  (February 2002)[a]
Hazel Park, MI
  (February 2002)[b]
Marin County, CA
  (January 2002)
Pima County, AZ
  (January 2002)
Salem, OR (2001)
Santa Cruz County, CA
  (December 2001)
Bozeman, MT
  (December 2001)
New Britain, CT
  (December 2001)
Cumberland County, NJ
  (December 2001)
Camden, NJ
  (December 2001)

Burlington, VT
  (November 2001)
Charlottesville, VA
  (November 2001)
Richmond, CA (October 2001)
Washtenaw County, MI
  (October 2001)
Hempstead, Long Island, NY
  (October 2001)[c]
Monroe County, MI
  (October 2001)
Ashland, OR (September 2001)
Oyster Bay, NY (August 2001)
Gloucester County, NJ
  (August 2001)
Suffolk County, NY (July 2001)
Pittsburgh, PA (May 2001)[d]
Santa Monica, CA (July 2001)[e]
Ventura County, CA (May 2001)
Miami Beach, FL (April 2001)
Pittsfield Township, MI
  (April 2001)
Eastpointe, MI (March 2001)
Missoula, MT (March 2001)
Ann Arbor, MI (March 2001)
Ferndale, MI (February 2001)
Rochester, NY (January 2001)
Meriden, CT (November 2000)
Santa Cruz, CA (October 2000)
Berkeley, CA & Marina
  (October 2000)
Eau Claire County, WI
  (September 2000)
San Francisco, CA
  (August 2000)
St. Louis, MO (August 2000)[f]
Cleveland, OH (June 2000)
Alexandria, VA (June 2000)
Toledo, OH (June 2000)
Omaha, NE (April 2000)
San Fernando, CA (April 2000)
Denver, CO (February 2000)
Warren, MI (January 2000)
Corvallis, OR (November 1999)
Hartford, CT (September 1999)
Tucson, AZ (September 1999)
Buffalo, NY (August 1999)
Los Angeles County, CA
  (June 1999)
Ypsilanti, MI (June 1999)
Ypsilanti Township, MI
  (June 1999)

Somerville, MA (May 1999)
Miami-Dade County, FL
  (1999)
Cambridge, MA (May 1999)
Hayward, CA (1999)
Madison, WI (March 1999)
Dane County, WI
  (March 1999)
Hudson County, NJ
  (January 1999)
San Jose, CA
  (November 1998)
Detroit, MI (November 1998)
Multnomah County, OR
  (October 1998)
Boston, MA (September
  1998; expanded
  October 2001)
Pasadena, CA
  (September 1998)
Cook County, IL
  (September 1998)
Chicago, IL (July 1998)
San Antonio, TX (July 1998)
Portland, OR (1996,
  amended 1998)
Oakland, CA (March 1998)
Durham, NC (January 1998)
West Hollywood, CA
  (October 1997)
Duluth, MN (July 1997)
Milwaukee County, WI
  (May 1997)
New Haven, CT (April 1997)
Los Angeles, CA
  (March 1997)
Minneapolis, MN
  (March 1997)
St. Paul, MN (January 1997)
New York City, NY
  (September 1996)
Jersey City, NJ (June 1996)
Milwaukee, WI
  (November 1995)
Santa Clara County, CA
  (1995)
Baltimore, MD
  (December 1994)
Gary, IN (1991)
Des Moines, IA (1988,
  amended 1996)

School Boards	Universities
Milwaukee Public Schools (January 1996)	Wesleyan University April 2000)
Richmond, VA School Board (March 2001)	Stanford University (2002)
	Harvard University (February 2002)

Source: ACORN Living Wage Resource Center, 1486 Dorchester Avenue, Boston, MA, 617–740–9500, www.acorn.org.

[a] Overturned by Louisiana Supreme Court, September 2002.

[b] Repealed June 2002 in reaction to state threat to cut revenue sharing to living wage cities.

[c] Repealed before implementation, December 2001.

[d] Implementation on hold as of March 2003.

[e] Repealed before implementation, November 2002.

[f] Overturned by lawsuit, July 2001; amended and reinstated by Board of Aldermen, July 2002.

in the form of tax abatements or other economic development subsidies. Over the years, however, the phrase "living wage" has been adapted to a range of campaigns around working conditions, workers' right to organize, and corporate accountability. As such, the living wage concept now usefully frames efforts to raise state and even city minimum wages just as well as campaigns to demand that public money not be used for union-busting or that subsidized companies return public money if they fail to meet established standards. Here we discuss the more strictly defined efforts to enact living wage ordinances.

As the living wage movement has matured, it has grown more sophisticated and aggressive. The wage levels have grown from the early days of $6.25 an hour to an average of $9.80 among ordinances passed in the last year. Nearly all campaigns require even higher wage levels for companies that fail to provide any health benefits to their workers. The typical required living wage runs at least $8.85 an hour if the employer provides some health benefits, or roughly $10 if no health benefits are provided. Capitalizing on high living expenses in the area, the Fairfax, California living wage campaign won a record $13 an hour with health insurance or $14.75 without.

Many ordinances mandate additional standards such as paid vacation time and local hiring. Living wage advocates have also inserted language designed to protect workers' jobs when city contracts change hands and to prohibit employer retaliation against employees for asserting their rights under the ordinance. Still other ordinances require companies to report to the public on their hiring, wages, and benefits and obligate cities themselves to detail public spending on service contracts and economic development incentives. Less common, but perhaps most promising, a handful of living wage ordinances include language designed to protect the rights of workers to join unions. In various ways, these laws either attempt to weed out antiunion employers or encourage companies that fall under the ordinance to recognize a union through a card-check process. This process is strongly favored by unions, as it allows for recognition when a majority of workers sign cards indicating their desire to join the union—rather than requiring a notoriously slow and often coercive National Labor Relations Board election process. Unfortunately, this more pointed card-check language walks a thin legal line and is vulnerable to challenge under the National Labor Relations Act.

Campaigns have also sought new ways to broaden the reach of living wage ordinances. While many of the early ordinances limited coverage to those employed by city contractors, now almost one-fourth of the living wage laws on the books cover both city service contractors and companies receiving economic development assistance from the city. A handful of these laws go one step further, extending living wage requirements to the tenants and contractors of these subsidized companies (think the Gap in a mall built with public subsidies or a janitorial contractor in a tax-abated office tower). In recent years, campaigns in Berkeley and Santa Monica have extended the concept of living wage even further, requiring living wage compliance from large employers located in highly developed waterfront tourist zones. These zones, which are home to the area's most profitable hotels and restaurants, have benefited from substantial taxpayer investment and intense tourist promotion while harboring thousands of low-wage housekeepers, busboys, dishwashers, and parking attendants, many of whom remain poor enough to qualify for government assistance. Most recently, voters in New Orleans and San Francisco and the city council in Santa Fe, New Mexico have gone even farther—establishing a citywide minimum wage that applies to most private employers in the city. These area-wide laws face fierce opposition. Santa Fe is fending off legal challenge from business opposition, while the cutting edge laws passed in Santa Monica and New Orleans have been repealed. However, the Berkeley law has withstood legal challenge and the San Francisco law—passed in November 2003—is unlikely to be challenged.

The Opposition

As organizers have begun to push further and further, the opposition pushback has grown increasingly fierce. The main players among the vested anti–living wage interests will come as no surprise. They are the restaurant and hospitality industries that profit from low-wage labor—including the National Federation of Independent Business, the National Restaurant Association, and the U.S. Chamber of Commerce—as well as the local chambers of commerce. Their policy ringleader, the Employment Policies Institute, maintains its own anti–living wage Web site and has even published an anti–living wage "guide" available in bookstores (*Living Wages: The Basics*).

What *is* surprising, though, is that after years of living wage organizing, these captains of low-wage industry have presided over very few living wage setbacks. And, in some cases, initial setbacks were overcome, as in Chicago where the Association of Community Organizations for Reform Now (ACORN) and the Service Employees International Union (SEIU) forced Mayor Richard Daley and the city council to revive a defeated living wage ordinance before raising their own salaries. Initial ballot defeats were parlayed into local legislative victories in St. Paul, Minnesota, and Missoula, Montana. In other campaigns, legislative council defeats seem only to have inspired and energized campaigns, such as Knoxville, Tennessee.

In Santa Monica, a cabal of large hotels sought to crush the initial living wage effort by promoting a bogus "living wage" ballot measure that would have covered almost no workers and included fine print prohibiting future living wage ordinances. Thanks to an ambitious counter campaign, voters rejected the measure in an 80 percent to 20 percent vote. Campaign-spending reports revealed that the hotels spent over a million dollars to keep from paying their workers enough to survive.

Admittedly the battle has intensified in recent years. In just the last four years, living wage opponents have repealed eight laws—New Orleans in court, Santa Monica at the ballot, and the rest through the same city councils that had originally passed them. Perhaps most disturbing, the opposition's strategy to enact state laws prohibiting local wage action appears to be gaining ground. Such laws now exist in Arizona, Louisiana, Missouri, South Carolina, Utah, Oregon, Colorado, Texas, and Florida and have been proposed in several other states. These strategies threaten to put on the defensive what has thus far proved a rare example of successful offensive progressive policy making.

Clearly, the anti–living wage forces and the tactics they employ are also familiar foes of union organizing. We now turn more directly to a discussion of the connections between the labor movement and the living wage.

The Labor Movement and the Living Wage

In 1997, the national AFL-CIO passed a resolution at its convention committing itself to supporting local living wage campaigns. Almost all living wage campaigns witness some form of union involvement. For many campaigns, organized labor is an important coalition partner. Typically a few key labor bodies prove to be the active drivers of labor's involvement in the local living wage battle. The key players may be one or two union locals (for example, SEIU Local 880 in Chicago or Ironworkers Local 5 in Alexandria, Virginia) or the central labor council—a city or metro-wide coordinating body to which locals may voluntarily belong. In some cases, labor's state structures—state labor federations—support local living wage efforts.

Below we discuss four strategic interests that foster union participation in living wage campaigns: (1) revitalization of central labor councils, (2) direct links to organizing, (3) political action, and (4) building community alliances. While, for our purposes here, examples fall into one of the four categories, in practice most labor leaders are driven by a combination of concerns and the categories themselves certainly overlap.

Central Labor Council Revitalization

The change in leadership of the AFL-CIO in 1995 signaled a renewed focus on organizing. This focus included organizing new union members, mobilizing existing members, and promoting the community partnerships and campaigns that would foster this work. Central labor councils (CLCs) were seen as vital to these efforts. In the past, many CLCs were ineffectual, and those that did have an agenda and some capacity to carry it out traditionally confined their activities to narrow electoral politics and sporadic displays of cross-union solidarity. With AFL-CIO president John Sweeney's new priorities, these bodies were being asked to do more. In fact, CLCs were positioned as the linchpin of the AFL-CIO's "Union Cities" program, which encourages new alliances between labor and community allies as well as commitments to build support for union organizing through public education, mobilization, and political action.

Enter living wage campaigns. With obvious potential for alliance building, mobilization, and political work, these local campaigns have been regarded as an important opportunity by many CLCs and their local affiliates. They offer a popular and winnable reform that both taps labor's core concerns for the overall wage environment and draws the active interest of a wide range of community organizations, religious leaders, progressive policy makers, and other potential partners. The legislative lobbying aspect of living wage activism allows CLCs to draw on the connections already established by their traditional electoral work, but also challenges them to engage in more aggressive political action—including worker-to-worker mobilization, developing leadership and running union members for local office, and committing to a more proactive and ongoing local legislative agenda.

The San Jose living wage campaign offers one of the most developed examples of the link between central labor council revitalization and living wage campaigns. Like most central labor bodies across the country, the South Bay Labor Council was a modest organization with a staff of two that maintained a low profile in the community. Following the 1994 election of new leadership, the council began aggressive efforts to strengthen its political work and to build alliances between labor and the community. In 1995, it established Working Partnerships USA (profiled by Bob Brownstein's contribution in this volume) as a nonprofit policy and research institute to foster labor-community ties.

It is within this broader movement-building context that the San Jose living wage campaign developed. The first round took place in 1995, when the labor council put together a coalition to attach living wage standards to a county tax incentive program. The 1998 San Jose living wage campaign provided a robust channel for the central labor council and Working Partnerships to further expand their work. The first Labor/Community Leadership Institute classes used the living wage as their group project. The new Interfaith Council on Religion, Race, Economics, and Social Justice used the issue to build and mobilize its membership. In the end, the effective labor-community campaign succeeded in passing what was then the highest living wage in the country—$9.50 an hour with health insurance or $10.75 without (the wage requirements have since increased to $10.10 with health insurance or $11.35 without).

The most obvious signature of labor's strong involvement in crafting the San Jose ordinance can be found in its "labor peace" and worker retention provisions. The ordinance created an involved bid review process that discourages the city from contracting with companies that cannot demonstrate good labor relations and therefore ensure "labor peace." Arguing that companies vulnerable to labor disputes may be incapable of delivering uninterrupted quality services to the city, the ordinance obligates city staff to consider a company's record of labor standards—such as worker retention, paid time off, and general vulnerability to strikes and other "labor unrest"—before granting the contract. This provision intends not only to favor companies that agree to card-check recognition of the union but also to discourage would-be city contractors from mounting aggressive antiunion campaigns at any time, as it might hamper their ability to win a lucrative city contract in the future. Since passage of the living wage, the South Bay AFL-CIO and its local affiliates of SEIU, Hotel Employees and Restaurant Employees (HERE), Teamsters, United Food and Commercial Workers (UFCW), American Federation of State, County, and Municipal Employees (AFSCME) and others have used these provisions—combined with political leverage and solid organizing—not only to raise wages for union workers, but also to win union recognition, secure new collective bargaining agreements, settle new contracts, and retain union jobs. In 2002, labor council president Amy Dean estimated that more than 7,000 workers have benefited from these policies and the strategies they spawned. So, both through the relationships it built and the organizing-friendly language it won, the San Jose living wage campaign contributed to the revitalization of the South Bay Labor Council.

Similarly, the active involvement of central labor councils in places such as Tucson; Miami-Dade County; Madison, Wisconsin; Cleveland; Omaha; Albuquerque; Rochester, New York; Santa Cruz, California; and Detroit, has benefited the campaign while serving to elevate the profile of the CLC and deepen its community alliances and political power.

Direct Links to Organizing

Some of the most extensive living wage efforts have come from unions in industries directly affected by living wage ordinances. The SEIU is a prime example. A leader in these campaigns, SEIU represents workers in many low-wage industries that are common targets of living wage ordinances, such as janitorial firms, garbage hoppers, security guards, and home health care workers. Typically, unionized firms in these industries must directly compete with nonunion companies. To the extent that such firms compete for public funds—such as lucrative city or county service contracts—living wage ordinances have the potential to even the playing field between union and nonunion firms. Setting wage and benefit standards for the expenditure of public money helps head off a race to the bottom of the wage scale—perpetrated by low-wage firms intent on submitting low bids—that undermines the ability of unionized firms to compete in a local industry and the ability of unions to organize and win good labor contracts. In raising the wage floor, living wage ordinances have the potential to help unions raise the wage standards for their industry.

Ongoing activism in Los Angeles illustrates well the way living wage organizing can be linked to the agenda of specific unions while building a local movement for economic justice. The Los Angeles area has led the country in the growth of low-wage jobs. Unions organizing in these industries are challenged by a diverse workforce growing through steady streams of immigration. Both factors favor community-based organizing strategies.

Within this context, the Los Angeles living wage effort grew out of a battle to defend the jobs of 1,000 unionized workers at the city's main airport. Three hundred of these jobs were lost when the city brought in nonunion concession contractors, such as McDonald's, to replace unionized firms. The remaining 700 jobs were similarly threatened. A core group from HERE and SEIU joined with several community groups and religious leaders to map out a response. They devised a three-tier strategy connecting public funds to community standards. The first was a worker retention ordinance inspired by the union busting at the airport. Passed in 1995, the ordinance set standards for city service contracts to provide for the retention of service workers when contracts change hands. The second was the 1997 living wage law.

The third major part of the strategy involves the ongoing battle to protect and promote workers' right to organize.

The eighteen-month battle to win Los Angeles's living wage ordinance produced a broad alliance of more than 100 labor and community groups. It overcame the mayor's veto and concerted opposition from the chamber of commerce. Activists tapped grassroots energy through a series of actions such as a Thanksgiving mailing to city councilors of more than a thousand decorated paper plates symbolizing the struggle to feed a family on poverty wages. The campaign also made a deliberate effort to recruit and involve workers affected by the ordinance. This time-consuming task reflected the leadership's desire to build relationships with potential union members.

Most significantly, the living wage campaign was conceived and is being carried out as one part of an ongoing strategy to use community alliances, economic development issues, and public policy to support union organizing and contract bargaining. In 1998, the Los Angeles living wage coalition became a key component of a multiunion organizing drive at the Los Angeles airport that sought to secure living wages and union protection for thousands of low-wage airport workers, such as security guards and fast-food employees. With those workers in mind, the campaign successfully pushed to amend the city's living wage ordinance to make clear its application to workers at the airport. The impressive San Francisco living wage campaign pursued a similar strategy, linking its work closely to union organizing efforts at the airport. The strategy paid off, resulting not only in a living wage and health benefits for an estimated 8,500 airport workers (and an estimated 21,000 citywide), but also a card-check rule for the airport that led to nearly 2,000 workers joining the SEIU, Teamsters, International Association of Machinists, and others before it was overturned by the courts.

Through the Los Angeles Alliance for a New Economy (LAANE), the Los Angeles living wage campaign maintains an active database on city contract and subsidy decisions. The information allows LAANE and area unions to be active players in the contracting and subsidy process—upholding community standards. Most recently, Los Angeles activists won three precedent-setting agreements with developers of the massive new entertainment facilities. The agreements call for many community and job benefits that will reduce the harm and increase the benefits of the projects for local residents, including 20 percent affordable housing set-asides, 70 percent living wage job targets, open-space subsidies, parking set-asides, and monetary assistance to local nonprofit development corporations. These landmark agreements represent the further fruition of living wage-related activism as labor movement revival becomes increasingly linked with community revitalization and the development of a progressive agenda for economic development shared by ever more diverse segments of the community.

In Santa Cruz, living wage organizers worked closely with the central labor council to ensure that the broader community fight for a living wage effectively advanced worker organizing. As a result, the living wage law that was passed in 2000 not only delivered the highest living wage in the country, it also required that covered employers remain neutral during union-organizing elections and agree to card-check recognition of a bargaining unit. Literally days after the living wage law went into effect, it was used to persuade a nonprofit agency with a history of antiunion behavior to agree to card check and neutrality for a unit of paratransit workers. Those workers have since negotiated a union contract that uses the impressive $11-an-hour Santa Cruz living wage as its wage floor. The living wage campaign also paved the way for SEIU Local 415—a driving force in the campaign—to organize the city's temporary workers. Rather than contracting out work, the City of Santa Cruz had hired up to 650 "temporary" employees who were paid less and offered fewer benefits than the city's 450 unionized workers—members of SEIU Local 415. Supporting these workers' right to organize was an explicit goal of the campaign. Temporary workers themselves were brought into the campaign as active members, and the coalition's public message and lobbying strategy reflected this organizing priority. Following the living wage victory, the city council passed a resolution recognizing the right of temporary employees to organize and agreeing to card check and neutrality.

A living wage law on the books can provide fuel for broader wage demands or unionization. After the Tucson law was passed, direct city workers demanded that they receive a living wage along with the contracted service workers whom the ordinance technically covered. Working with the Communications Workers of America, the city workers organized and won recognition and then a first contract, covering 1,200 workers, earlier this year.

In Chicago, SEIU Local 880 effectively mobilized its own home health care members in the successful fight for a local living wage law from 1995 to 1998. As a result, hundreds of SEIU members received raises, even checks for back pay. In the fall of 2002, the union and close ally ACORN led another successful campaign when they pushed the city to expand its four-year-old living wage, raising the wage by $1.50 an hour and indexing it permanently to inflation. What is more, the union's high-profile organizing on the campaign generated new organizing leads. "You can bet that every time we do any action around living wage, we get calls," said Keith Kelleher of SEIU Local 880. According to Kelleher, Local 880 has won two union elections, representing almost 800 workers, as a direct result of contacts made during the living wage campaign.

In some cases, a union's direct self-interest is less obvious. For example, the United Auto Workers (UAW) has, on the surface, little direct connection to the living wage. Its core industry, automobiles, is far removed from local public contracting. And, while many Big Three auto plants receive local subsidies, their highly unionized workers are paid well above the living wage. However, management's policy on outsourcing—to a largely nonunion auto parts industry—has become a major issue in collective bargaining negotiations. Supplier firms can pay as low as seven and eight dollars an hour with no benefits. Even when the union organizes individual supplier firms, the bargaining team can face tough opposition from employers who cry competitive pressures from their nonunion counterparts. To the extent that many supplier firms receive local public subsidies and are therefore subject to living wage requirements, the living wage may prove a potent antioutsourcing tool. At the same time, the union is a major political player in both Ohio and Michigan. Its social democratic tradition has faced a tough road in today's conservative political climate. Several UAW regions have used living wage organizing as a way to enhance their mobilizing capacity and to hold officials that they helped elect accountable to a working people's agenda.

Faced with continued threats of privatization, AFSCME has also been a leader in local living wage campaigns. Public contracts to low-wage private-sector employers may well have once been public jobs paying union wages. The living wage helps to level the playing field by eliminating poverty jobs as a source of competition. Not surprisingly, therefore, AFSCME was one of the two central players in winning Baltimore's pioneering living wage law, as well as a driving force in other successful campaigns, including Duluth, Minnesota, and Pasadena, California. The possibilities of direct connections between a local union's core agenda and the living wage does not always produce strong union involvement, however. The privatization connection, for example, has not always meant strong local AFSCME leadership. Where the local union's vision does not afford a view beyond the bread-and-butter tasks of collective bargaining, some campaigns have struggled for an AFSCME endorsement.

In an exciting new development, some unions have begun to use living wage enforcement as an additional tool to pressure companies in recognition and/or contract fights. In Baltimore, HERE Local 7 was heading into negotiations with concessions giant Aramark when they discovered both wage and overtime violations of Baltimore's living wage law among both union members and other temporary workers at the local convention center. The union helped three workers file complaints with the city's wage commission. If the violations on the four-year-old contract are confirmed, Aramark faces the prospect of owing four years of back pay to workers as well as possible fines of $50 per day per worker from the city—not to mention the bad PR that violating the nation's first living wage law could bring! The union plans to use this leverage to push the company in contract negotiations on a range of demands including wages and benefits, adding subcontracted workers to the bargaining unit, and card-check recognition of workers at another stadium.

Across the country in Hayward, California, the Union of Needle Trades, Industrial, and Textile Employees (UNITE) has unearthed living wage violations by Cintas Corporation—the biggest uniform supplier and industrial launderer on the continent—which has apparently been underpaying workers as well as flouting the 1999 law's provision for paid days off. UNITE is assisting two workers to bring what could expand into a class action suit against the company. The living wage lawsuit came just days before Cintas was named the target of an historic joint organizing campaign of UNITE and the Teamsters in June 2003.

Political Action

With the national AFL-CIO pressing the labor movement to rethink and reinvigorate union political action, living wage campaigns present useful political opportunities. Increasingly, these campaigns are being used effectively by community and labor activists as litmus tests for candidates for office, as tools to measure the accountability of elected representatives, and as training grounds to prepare our own grassroots leaders to run for office. The broad appeal of the living wage also promises to bring new and underrepresented voices into the democratic process.

In Detroit, for example, the Metropolitan AFL-CIO placed the living wage on the 1998 November ballot, in part as a way to raise voter turnout in the city by offering voters a compelling issue. The living wage won with a stunning 80 percent of the votes cast. In Madison, Wisconsin, the living wage campaign of 1997–99 brought labor and progressive community forces together in a way that helped build Progressive Dane, the county's New Party chapter. In Santa Monica, the hard-fought living wage battle helped build the Green Party and elect a Green Party mayor sympathetic to the proposed ordinance.

Shaking up local politics was almost an explicit goal of Chicago's feisty living wage effort, led by organizers from ACORN and SEIU Local 880 and joined by the Chicago Federation of Labor. In the home of the last great urban political "machine," the campaign activists knew they faced an uphill battle. However, the living wage issue also promised to provide a wedge issue for breaking up politics as usual. Mayor Daley's consistent opposition and his tight control over the board of aldermen propelled the campaign into escalating grassroots mobilization. By the end of the two-and-a-half year campaign, the city had witnessed several large living wage demonstrations and marches, accountability sessions with members of the board of aldermen, the picketing of the mayor as he welcomed delegates to the Democratic National Convention, a "Tour of Shame" highlighting low-wage blight, an effective media campaign, the arrest of six living wage activists, and countless hours of door knocking, flyer distributing, and phone banking.

While Daley won a "no" vote from the board of aldermen in the summer of 1997, the political pressure eventually proved too strong. Following the defeat, living wage activists began organizing in the districts of anti–living wage aldermen and publicizing the names of aldermen who had retreated from their living wage commitments when confronted with Daley's arm twisting. Organizers from ACORN and the Chicago New Party began moving symbolic living wage ballot resolutions in a ward-by-ward strategy designed to pressure aldermen who had voted against the measure by reminding them where their constituents stood on the issue. When a proposal by the mayor and aldermen to grant themselves hefty raises prompted living wage demonstrations outside city hall, city officials decided to offer a deal. While the living wage ordinance enacted in 1998 was narrower than the original proposal, the fact and form of its passage demonstrated the power of the living wage as a political wedge issue. To immediately capitalize on the new political power and momentum afforded by the victory, ACORN, SEIU, and their allies began an all-out grassroots political campaign to elect Ted Thomas—Illinois ACORN president, Chicago New Party chair, and living wage leader. That Thomas won election to the Board of Aldermen despite never having held elected office was only the most immediate sign of how the campaign had begun to reshape local politics.

Building Community Alliances

> I'm tired of being called a labor boss, and told that we're only
> interested in collecting dues. [The living wage campaign] was
> an opportunity for labor to be a community partner.
> —*Ian Robertson, president, Southern Arizona Labor Council*

One of the noticeable characteristics of living wage campaigns is the broad range of local groups that it brings together. Not only does the typical living wage coalition involve leadership from labor, community, and faith-based groups; it frequently pulls in the endorsement and participation of groups beyond the "usual suspects" of progressive activists. The strategic importance of some coalition connections can provide a direct motivation for union leadership to take an active role in a living wage campaign.

Some segments of the building trades unions in the Washington, D.C., area, for example, faced the challenge of a building industry that was become steadily more nonunion. As part of this transition, some employers were using ever-growing numbers of Latino workers. Changing demographics provided employers a weapon to pit the unions against the Latino community. Ironworkers Local 5, however, realized the need for the building trades to build connections to that community. The living wage served that purpose. It fit with the general goals of organized labor while at the same time having direct implications for low-wage Latino workers. Joining with a local low-income organization, the Tenants and Workers Support Committee, the unions helped launch the Northern Virginia Living Wage Coalition. The campaign was characterized by an impressive coalition of local labor, low-income, and religious activists and a disciplined campaign that combined public pressure tactics with grassroots lobbying. By the time the campaign snatched a living wage victory in Alexandria in June 2000, the Ironworkers were not the only union that understood the benefits of such coalition work. In exchange for active labor participation in the living wage fight, the coalition turned out 150 activists in major solidarity actions for a Teamsters local (and living wage endorser). The public show of support and pressure from the living wage coalition helped the union win an incredible new contract for its workers.

In New Orleans, SEIU Local 100 was a key player in ACORN's successful campaign to raise that city's minimum wage by ballot initiative in 2002. At the same time, ACORN's grassroots neighborhood base has been essential in a campaign by SEIU and other labor allies to win card-check and neutrality agreements from local hotels and restaurants that will allow them to unionize. Indeed, it is a natural partnership, as many of the low-wage employees in these nonunion tourist traps reside in the low-income neighborhoods in which ACORN organizes.

Growing student activism around a living wage on campus is leading to promising student-labor alliances. These relationships have already delivered benefits to unionized campus workers at Johns Hopkins, Harvard, Stanford, the University of Connecticut, the University of Tennessee, the University of California–San Diego, and many others. Student agitation around worker issues and outreach to local unions has also laid the groundwork for new union organizing on several campuses.

On another front, the growing sophistication with which living wage campaigns have approached the question of nonprofits that receive public funds has provided unions a new way to relate to such employers. According to a study of nonprofit employers covered by Detroit's living wage law, the majority of nonprofits are actually capable of complying with living wage requirements with minimal financial impact. However, the researchers also found that a clear minority did face significant financial obstacles. Over the past twenty years the state has increasingly shifted the burden of social service provisions onto the nonprofit sector while not always providing the level of resources needed to do the job. The total additional funds needed to cover the costs to such financially constrained employers, however, was quite modest when compared to the total public funds granted to nonprofits. The ideal solution, therefore, is to enact a living wage ordinance that covers nonprofits, but with government providing additional funds explicitly for wages.

Such an approach provides an opportunity for a living wage campaign and its participating unions to build alliances with nonprofit agencies, associations, and clients. Unable to keep quality staff when wages are low, many nonprofit heads have already had to confront the issue of poverty pay. By seeking financial assistance for those organizations most in need, living wage activists become allies for nonprofits that understand the benefits of raising salaries. Thus, the Western Pennsylvania Living Wage Campaign built connections with nonprofit staff willing to speak out on the need for living wages to provide quality services. In addition to a living wage ordinance, the campaign fought to increase county investments in nonprofit social services as well as a county commitment to join in lobbying efforts to increase state funds. In Duluth, Minnesota, union bargaining committees had a history of negotiating with nonprofit child-care providers whose response to union contract demands was to cry poverty. Following the passage of a living wage law in 1997, the unions and community groups involved in the campaign began to develop an alliance with nonprofit child-care providers to lobby the state legislature for increased allocations reserved explicitly for wage increases.

What Unions Bring to the Table

While living wage coalitions benefit from the participation of all kinds of organizations, labor brings some specific strengths.

First, unions can bring their political connections. Even through the traditional candidate-endorsement/get-out-the-vote model of union political activity, labor has been able to influence local elections. Typically, some local Democrats, and sometimes even a few Republicans, seek endorsements from labor when running for office. Thus, organized labor can offer a certain level of access to local elected officials. Ideally, union political activity has produced labor-friendly officeholders willing to champion the living wage.

Second, as serious local organizations, unions can add to a local campaign's legitimacy. In certain circles, the participation of key unions can help a campaign draw in other community players. Unions can increase the perceived legitimacy and influence of the campaign in the minds of local media. Union credibility can also help gain the support of funders. Obviously, given the beating that organized labor's image has taken over the past three decades, union involvement can also work against a campaign. Some community groups hold a negative view of unions, the media may decry the living wage as a union plot, and some funders of antipoverty work may steer clear of efforts connected to organized labor.

Finally, unions can contribute specific resources to a campaign. These assets can include money, staff, and volunteers. To be on the Chicago campaign's steering committee, for example, organizations had to contribute an initial $1,000 and commit to turn out a busload of people to living wage actions. Several unions also contributed part of their staff's time to work on the campaign. The western Pennsylvania living wage campaign enjoyed sustained regular monthly contributions from a handful of committed labor partners. Central labor councils in Madison, San Jose, and other places have designated staff specifically to work on the living wage campaign. In countless campaigns, labor has paid for mailings as well as the printing of brochures, flyers, and yard signs.

Access to union resources can be especially significant when a campaign directly overlaps with labor's traditional electoral work. For example, during the San Jose living wage campaign, the central labor council mounted an elaborate and labor-intensive effort to elect the council's political director, Cindy Chavez, to the city council against Tony West, a chamber-of-commerce-supported, Harvard-educated federal prosecutor. Despite a last minute flood of business-driven pro-West mailings, Chavez won the election by 200 votes following one of the strongest labor-community get-out-the-vote drives in the city's history. The living wage had been a central wedge issue during the campaign. During the 1998 Detroit ballot drive, the living wage campaign itself was a rather modest undertaking—with the campaign's staff focusing on outreach to area churches. However, the campaign was also able to tap into the labor movement's coordinated get-out-the-vote drive. As a result, 300,000 living wage flyers made it out into the community. The results were obvious on election day when more than 150,000 voters went to the end of a long paper ballot to vote yes for the living wage.

Limitations of Union Involvement

While organized labor has been a necessary and key player in living wage activism, campaigns can also demonstrate the limitations of union involvement.

Most unions today have a limited grassroots mobilization capacity. Some unions, such as SEIU through its Justice for Janitors campaign, have built a mobilization structure linked to community action. These unions typically are the ones most readily attracted to the living wage model. Others may have developed an ability to initiate workplace actions through prior contract campaigns. Most labor organizations, however, have little or no structure in place to turn out their rank-and-file members for living wage events such as rallies and marches, direct actions, grassroots lobbying, door knocking, flyer distributing, and public hearings. More often than not, the involvement of local labor unions that have endorsed the living wage campaign is limited to staff or a couple of key leaders with no broader rank-and-file mobilization.

With the national AFL-CIO taking the lead, unions have begun to change the way they conduct electoral action to bring the campaign into the workplace. In theory, unions build a network of worker-to-worker volunteers so that during an election season, each individual worker receives direct and repeated one-on-one contact from an active member publicizing the various issues of the campaign. State labor federations, central labor councils, and a growing number of individual unions have officially endorsed the worker-to-worker idea. On the ground, however, the practice varies widely from local to local. Some have quite developed networks, many have none, and the rest lie in between. Furthermore, the notion of using a living wage mobilization to strengthen a worker-to-worker network is often not an obvious connection that a union's leadership, busy with a range of concerns, will automatically make. At the central labor council level, there is also the AFL-CIO's "Street Heat" initiative in which councils are challenged to mobilize a pool of 1 percent of local union membership into grassroots action. Once again, the actual practice varies enormously. The notion that a living wage campaign could help start or expand such a network is one that campaign organizers need to actively promote—rather than assume that a link will be made by labor leaders.

Labor's political connections, which are a source of strength, can become a limitation if they are advanced as an exclusive strategy. While officeholders elected with labor's support are often willing to champion the living wage, campaigns intent on building real power are not served by "insider-driven" legislative victories. This tension sometimes emerges inside coalition strategy discussions. Well-connected union leaders may press for quieter "power lobbying" strategies, while other grassroots groups call for picketing city hall, public hearings, identifying workers themselves to lobby council, targeting low-wage workplaces, and the like. In the end, most campaigns negotiate this tension, and, indeed, successful campaigns benefit from both tracks—a combination of insider lobbying and a larger, more confrontational public fight.

In addition to different perspectives on the process of legislative change, coalition members can also differ widely in the resources they bring to the table. A union, for example, may make a serious financial contribution to the campaign and pull in valuable political contacts. On the other hand, a community group, while small, may provide a significant pool of volunteers as most of its active membership take on the living wage as their main cause. Such differences can become friction points when a campaign faces key decisions that have concrete implications for different member groups' resources, prestige, energy, or political clout. Ideally, campaigns have developed a structure and culture of decision making in which groups with different resources, constraints, and perspectives can learn to appreciate each other and make decisions that balance different needs.

Finally, despite our earlier discussion, it should be noted that the apparent connections between a local union's core agenda and the living wage do not always produce strong union involvement. In fact, in some cases, unions whose workers could directly benefit from living wage coverage opt out of the campaign altogether. In rarer cases, local unions have been hostile to local campaigns. For some, this reaction is a result of a general disinterest in new organizing. Others argue that living wage laws hinder rather than help unions grow their membership. Nor does labor's financial and political backing of candidates necessarily guarantee support for living wage measures or other issues of importance to working families. As Stephanie Luce notes in an insightful article on the involvement of central labor councils in the living wage movement:

> In short, without the power to hold candidates accountable, the labor movement has no political independence and is tied to "politics-as-usual": supporting candidates you think will win and hold power in the city rather than supporting those who most closely represent a labor platform.[1]

To illustrate this idea, she notes that the narrow political vision of some labor councils has led them to remain neutral in local elections that pitted pro– and anti–living wage candidates against each other—or even to endorse living wage opponents. She argues—correctly, we think—that in order to translate living wage campaigns into lasting political gains, labor must see these efforts as one part of a broader strategy to build real political power. Such a strategy must include new alternatives to improve accountability of leaders, such as campaign finance reform, new political organizations, and proportional representation.

Organizational change is always slow. The American labor movement has only just begun a long-term process of change. Living wage campaigns tend to attract union leaders and activists who are farther down this road than the movement as a whole. As one state AFL-CIO official who actively supports the living wage commented: "Most labor leaders in this state do not see the living wage as one of their active concerns." He added, however, that while they are a minority in the labor movement, union organizers of living wage campaigns represent an important active element that is having a significant impact on local and state politics and the regional labor movement.

Union Transformation

The living wage offers an issue that has proven an ideal tool for pulling groups into an expanding battle. On one hand, the living wage is a cause with popular appeal that ultimately has a good track record of prevailing in the end. On the other hand, the campaigns are not cakewalks. Living wage proposals typically draw enough opposition that some elected officials will show their true colors and even some supporters will get cold feet, often backtracking on pledges to support living wage laws. Passage of an ordinance is rarely as straightforward as is assumed—testing the accountability of our elected officials and our resolve as organizers. By the same token, then, the road to victory may be paved with opportunities for progressive organizing beyond what the campaign endorsers originally hoped for or expected.

The Boston living wage campaign provides a good example. Because the campaign was launched during an election cycle, the Massachusetts AFL-CIO, while supportive, was focused elsewhere. However, when labor-backed elected officials seemed not to be taking the campaign seriously, the Greater Boston Labor Council and the Massachusetts AFL-CIO took notice—and jumped headfirst into the fight, developing a close relationship with Massachusetts ACORN, the campaign's driving force. That fight led to a local living wage ordinance, and so much more. After the initial victory, the ACORN-labor partnership continued. The partners teamed up to successfully push the state legislature to raise the state's earned income tax credit for working poor families and to raise the minimum wage to $6.75, the highest in the nation at the time. Building on what appears to be a permanent, strategic relationship, ACORN and the state AFL-CIO have suceeded in expanding the local living wage law as well as introducing state minimum wage and corporate accountability legislation.

The Michigan living wage movement is another excellent illustration of the living wage's ability to grow beyond initial expectations. As mentioned earlier, the 1998 Detroit ballot campaign developed out of a focus by key labor leaders on raising voter turnout for the November election. Few plans existed for implementation after the election. Yet, the stunning 80 percent victory launched what has proven to be ongoing and mushrooming living wage activism. Following the Detroit win, local supporters carried the living wage into the suburbs—passing laws in Warren, Ferndale, Eastpointe, Southgate, Taylor, and Southfield, by mid-2003. Similarly, the Detroit win prompted an aggressive effort in nearby Washtenaw County that scored victories in Ann Arbor, Ypsilanti, three townships, the county road commission, and the county government. Living wage activism also spread to Kalamazoo, Grand Rapids, Lansing, and other parts of the state.

These developments prompted the Detroit Regional Chamber of Commerce and the Michigan Chamber of Commerce to lobby the Republican-controlled state legislature to pass a law banning governments from passing wage requirements that conflict with the state's minimum-wage statute. Although coming close, they repeatedly failed to pass the same law in both houses of the legislature before the election of a Democratic governor in late 2002. This state opposition helped make the living wage a key wedge issue that drew in more organizations. The Michigan State Democratic Party formally endorsed the living wage, while the state AFL-CIO became a central force in blocking efforts to pass the state pre-emption law.

State and local leaders also found themselves jumping into a battle to save Eastpointe's living wage law. In April 2001, the Libertarian Party of Macomb County decided to "save" the people of Eastpointe by collecting the 287 signatures needed to place the living wage ordinance before voters—despite the fact it had already passed the city council unanimously. With a popular vote in this small community having implications for the state anti–living wage legislation, both sides appear to be geared up for an intense election battle. On election day, the people of Eastpointe affirmed the vote of council and upheld the living wage by 55 percent majority. Similarly, in Detroit, efforts by the regional chamber of commerce to "amend" the city's living wage ordinance sparked a significant labor-community mobilization that resulted in the city council's allocating $70,000 for two new city positions dedicated to enforcing the living wage. In subsequent city and suburban elections, candidates seeking labor's endorsement had to pledge to defend or support passage of living wage laws.

Without any grand self-conscious design, a single Detroit-focused living wage get-out-the-vote effort grew in five years to become the focus of an expanding grassroots agenda and a wedge issue in Michigan politics. Labor leaders and activists who had never heard of the living wage in 1998 now champion it as one of their central causes. In May 2003 key partners held a statewide gathering of living wage activists to launch a formal effort to promote living wage campaigns across the state.

The lesson can be generalized. When unions join active living wage campaigns, not only do they help change public policy, they transform themselves. They join efforts that involve many of the core aspects needed to revitalize organized labor as a progressive social force. As living wage campaigns become more ambitious and as they spread into more conservative areas of the country, they will offer even greater promise as seedbeds of progressive transformation. The future of living wage organizing is part of the future of American unionism.

Note

1. Luce, Stephanie. 2001. "Building Political Power and Community Coalitions: The Role of Central Labor Councils in the Living-Wage Movement." In *Central Labor Councils and the Revival of American Unionism: Organizing for Justice in Our Communities*, ed. Immanuel Ness and Stuart Eimer, 140–160. Armonk, NY: M.E. Sharpe.

6

Coming Together

Promises and Pitfalls of Minnesota's Corporate Accountability Campaigns

Erik Peterson

In 1994, when Minnesotan activists first began working on corporate accountability issues, any discussion of what constituted a "living wage" was far from front-page news, and the term "corporate welfare" had just been coined. Over the next nine years, Minnesota became a national leader in pushing for corporate accountability. I have been directly or indirectly involved in many of these campaigns, sometimes in a consulting role, sometimes in a legislative role, sometimes as an organizer directing the campaign itself. Minnesota's experience offers a way to see living wage and corporate accountability campaigns not simply as ends in themselves, but as means for building progressive coalitions that can challenge corporate power, change our political culture, and open new opportunities for workers to organize.

Shifting Politics

Across the nation, corporate accountability campaigns have responded to a political climate where worker wages have stagnated at the same time corporate profits and government subsidies to private businesses continue to grow. Minnesota is no different. Although Minnesota has long enjoyed a national reputation for progressive politics, over the past several years, its political climate has shifted. Minnesota still has one of the least regressive tax structures in the nation, but in recent years the state legislature has increasingly focused on cutting business taxes to "improve" Minnesota's business climate. These tax cuts have shifted costs to workers and individual property owners. The wealthiest families in Minnesota, following national trends, have seen their incomes grow at the same time their overall tax burden has shrunk.[1] Despite our reputation as a "different kind of state," Minnesota is increasingly looking like the rest of the country.

Minnesota Alliance for Progressive Action

In response to these shifting priorities, the Minnesota Alliance for Progressive Action (MAPA) formed in 1988. Dave Mann, one of MAPA's founders and its former executive director, describes MAPA responding to a "growing frustration with the unwillingness of 'friends' in the legislature . . . to take difficult votes" and set a progressive political agenda.[2] MAPA is the only permanent, progressive, multi-issue, multi-constituency coalition in Minnesota and currently has twenty-eight member groups representing labor unions, seniors, environmentalists, women, consumers, affordable-housing and low-income advocates, peace and social justice activists, communities of color, and gay/lesbian advocates. All of these groups are committed to "the long-term work of building progressive power." MAPA works only on issues that cut across many different constituencies, all that define and implement a progressive political agenda, build political power, and increase citizen participation and voice in the political process. Over the past several years, MAPA has increasingly "focused on the power of large corporations to influence elections and public policy and how they benefit from these policies." It was out of this philosophical and political position that MAPA began to focus on corporate accountability measures in the mid 1990s.

Changing the Debate

The mid 1990s were not good years for progressive politics. The national debate over raising the minimum wage had collapsed into a debate over "one dime versus three dimes." Universal health care was effectively derailed. In November 1994, Newt Gingrich and the Republicans ignited a new "Republican Revolution" when they took over both the U.S. House and Senate in the largest midterm political shift in U.S. history. For progressives, this glum political outlook took a turn for the worst when President Bill Clinton began "triangulating" his way to reelection by making "ending welfare as we know it" his top domestic priority.

In Minnesota, as elsewhere, progressives felt (and were clearly put) on the defensive. "It felt like all we were doing was rushing around putting out fires," recalls Alexa Bradley, who codirected MAPA with Dave Mann at the time.[3] As a way for progressives to insert their agenda back into the political debate, MAPA began self-consciously searching for issues that would re-focus the debate away from the problems of "big government" to the problems of "big corporations." At the time there were few models. One of the few available was Greg LeRoy's *No More Candy Store*, a compilation of laws from around the country that held corporations accountable for government subsidies.[4]

LeRoy's focus on corporate accountability offered a whole different way of talking about who was benefiting from the New Economy. MAPA had been working on income inequality issues for many years. They had received some attention for their "4% Solution"—a four percent increase in the income tax rate for the top four percent of Minnesota wage earners with the additional revenue going to strengthen the state's social infrastructure and lower taxes for lower-income taxpayers. But in the face of the Republican "Contract for America," MAPA needed a "hook" to grab media and public attention. They found that hook in the term "corporate welfare" just as the welfare reform debate began heating up.

The media quickly adopted the term "corporate welfare" as a rhetorical label for taxpayer subsidies to private businesses.[5] "If we had done a press conference on corporate subsidies or business accountability, the press would have said, 'A story on taxes, what a snooze,'" Bradley recalls. "But 'corporate welfare' got the media's attention because it was current and it seemed like a contradiction in terms." It also offered a way of taking the hot topic of welfare reform and turning it upside down to ask who, in fact, controls and benefits most from public resources: single mothers or wealthy corporations? Equally important, it became a way to mobilize progressives and their allies to go back on the offensive in "a politically bold way to confront corporate power that was both fun and serious at the same time."[6]

Building a Movement: Baby Steps

Duluth's 1995 Corporate Accountability Policy

In Duluth, the Northeast Minnesota Senior Federation also began looking for ways to shift the debate over taxes. Founded in 1975, the Senior Federation is the oldest, largest, and most significant organization representing seniors in Duluth, with over 4,000 dues-paying or affiliated members. The organization has always worked on issues that benefit people of all ages, not just seniors, and has an impressive record of accomplishment. A consistent theme over the years has been tax policy, particularly how property taxes, as a regressive tax, hurt low-income people, who disproportionately include seniors.

In 1995, the Senior Federation's Tax Committee began looking for "meaningful ways to act locally to reduce property taxes that also challenged the state's shift from more progressive income taxes to more regressive property taxes," recalls to Buddy Robinson, staff director for the Senior Federation.[7] The Senior Federation asked Alexa Bradley from MAPA to present a tax workshop for their group, and Bradley linked tax increment financing, or TIF, and individual homeowner property tax bills.[8] At the time, TIF claimed nearly 20 percent of Duluth's entire tax capacity.

The Senior Federation used the 1995 city elections to secure pledges of support from the mayor and from several city councilors running for election. After the election, they were able to pass Duluth's first corporate accountability measure—a modest requirement that the Duluth Economic Development Authority (DEDA) hold public hearings for subsidies over $50,000 in tax increment financing and report on the number and quality of jobs created (including wages paid) from such subsidies. Although modest, this resolution represented the beginning of what has become an eight-year debate in Duluth over corporate accountability.

Minnesota's 1995 Corporate Welfare Law

In 1995, MAPA also began working at the state legislature to pass a law making corporate welfare more accountable. MAPA drafted a bill that required businesses receiving more than $25,000 in public money to create a net increase in jobs in Minnesota within two years of receiving the assistance, pay a "living wage" of at least 110 percent of the federal poverty line for a family of four for all new jobs created, or repay the subsidy if job and wage goals were not met. It further directed the Department of Trade and Economic Development (DTED) to prepare a report for the legislature each year evaluating business assistance programs, the number of jobs proposed, the number of jobs created, and the wage and benefit distribution for those jobs.[9]

The living wage requirement began as a tactic to gain public attention. According to Alexa Bradley, "Living wages became a way of directing public scrutiny toward public subsidies of private businesses to raise the question of 'Why are we subsidizing a private enterprise in the first place if the public doesn't get something from it?'"[10] But what began as a "tactic" quickly became the focus of the legislative battle. On one side, living wage proponents argued that public dollars should be held accountable to higher standards, and, at a minimum, jobs created at public expense should pay wages above the poverty line. On the other side, the Minnesota Chamber of Commerce and other business groups argued that government had no business interfering in the marketplace and "artificially" setting wage rates. They claimed that such interference deterred economic development, and that any new reporting requirements would be too burdensome and place Minnesota at a competitive disadvantage with other states. Ironically, this debate occurred at a time when Minnesota's economy was booming and the state was routinely outperforming the nation and surrounding states in job creation and income growth. Nevertheless, in the end, the living wage provision was stripped out of the final bill, and all that passed were rather innocuous wage and job goal requirements and an annual report compiling this information. "We thought we had lost," recalls Bradley, "but what we didn't at first realize is that we had stumbled onto something much bigger than we had originally thought."[11] By passing this simple measure, Minnesota became the first state in the nation to systematically account for public subsidies provided to corporations.[12] It was the data collected from this first Corporate Welfare Reform Law that became the basis for five years of organizing, culminating in 1999 when Minnesota passed the strongest corporate accountability law in the country.

In 1998, Greg LeRoy and Tyson Slocum of Good Jobs First went through the initial rounds of 1996 and 1997 data. Of the 553 economic development disclosure reports examined, in 123 deals corporations received more than $35,000 per projected new job. Yet, three-quarters of the subsidized jobs were paying wages below the state average for their industry; fully half paid 20 percent or more below the state industry wage. In interviewing more than 100 local economic development officials, LeRoy and Slocum found a significant number either indifferent or poorly informed about attaching basic standards to financial assistance deals. More than three-quarters of the subsidies were approved despite projecting wages that would qualify a family of three for Medicaid. In a large number of approved cases, local officials had set job targets at one new job per firm. In nearly all cases using the state's Tax Increment Financing Program, the public had ended up subsidizing "new jobs" that simply involved the relocation of a company from one part of the state to another.[13]

Building a Movement: The Debate over Living Wages

Over the next several years, attention remained focused on trying to pass significant legislation that required a living wage for all jobs created through corporate welfare. While this focus narrowed the debate over corporate accountability to a relatively small group of workers and specific types of economic development, it also provided a hot issue to organize diverse community coalitions in ways that a broader corporate accountability agenda could not.

Focusing efforts on winning living wage legislation also created a political context for groups across the state to work together and to begin to play off of each other's efforts.

St. Paul Living Wage Referendum Crushed

During the summer of 1995, the Association of Community Organizations for Reform Now (ACORN) launched a series of living wage campaigns across the country. In St. Paul, it helped create the Campaign for Jobs and a Fair Wage, which collected thousands of signatures to put a living wage ordinance on the November ballot. The proposed ordinance would have required all businesses receiving more than $25,000 in public subsidies to pay their employees at least a poverty-level wage for a family of four—defined as $7.21 per hour in 1995.[14] It would have also required businesses receiving public assistance to create a net increase of jobs within two years after receiving the subsidy and to hire a certain percentage of city residents through a "community hiring hall."[15] St. Paul mayor Norm Coleman deployed his communications director, Erich Mische, to lead the effort to defeat this initiative. Coleman called the living wage a noble cause but a "job killer," and in November, after a blistering campaign, the initiative went down in a landslide defeat.

The reasons for defeat were many, not the least being that living wage opponents outspent supporters nearly seven to one.[16] But this imbalance of resources was not the only reason for the ordinance's defeat. While proponents effectively gathered signatures to put the measure on the ballot, they did not begin building the coalition necessary to withstand fierce anti–living wage opposition until relatively late in the campaign. The Democratic Farmer Labor Party (DFL), which is the dominant party in St. Paul politics, was never seriously brought into the coalition. Key labor groups, including the St. Paul Trades and Labor and the American Federation of State, County, and Municipal Employees (AFSCME) were not consulted on the law's residency requirements, an issue they had opposed for public employees for many years. There may have also been some internal tensions within the labor movement. As one St. Paul labor organizer recalls, "The perception by the labor bureaucracy was that [the living wage ordinance] would lessen their power."[17] The ordinance itself also had "political problems," principally that it covered *all* businesses receiving subsidies, regardless of size, making it possible for the opposition to cherry-pick individual "ma and pa" minority businesses that could be held up as potential "victims" of the ordinance. In short, the campaign did not successfully demonstrate to many constituencies why passing a living wage requirement should be a key issue.

Despite this setback, the St. Paul referendum thrust public subsidies and corporate accountability into the center of political debate and effectively made the case that the community was owed something for investing taxpayer money in private businesses.

Twin Cities Joint Living Wage Task Force

Although the November election set back living wage efforts, living wage supporters secured commitments from the St. Paul and Minneapolis city councils to form a Twin Cities Joint Living Wage Task Force. This task force was composed of representatives from economic development agencies, labor, and other community groups from both cities and had the purpose of making recommendations for a living wage policy.

Strategically, forming the task force kept the living wage debate alive after a stunning defeat, but as a serious venue for finding "common ground," the results were more mixed. Some task force members, like MAPA's Bradley, look back on the experience as perhaps "our biggest mistake," because it drew attention away from building grassroots power and support in the community to fighting an insider's game among sometimes hostile constituencies. Although progressives effectively organized to have living wage supporters appointed to the task force, they could not always count on support from their presumed allies. One key building trades representative and statewide labor leader came into the discussions stating, "Some jobs don't deserve a living wage." Another concern arose when, for political reasons, the heads of the Minneapolis Community Development Association (MCDA) and the St. Paul Port Authority—the two largest economic development authorities in the Twin Cities—cochaired the task force. These cochairs effectively controlled the debate and threatened to oppose any final recommendation that didn't include certain provisions.

After nearly eight months of bimonthly meetings, the task force arrived at an uneasy consensus. Living wage supporters secured a living wage requirement of 110 percent of the federal poverty wage for a family of four—$8.25 an hour in 1996. They were also able to include labor peace language, which made "responsible labor practices" a condition for receiving a subsidy, and a requirement that 60 percent of all new employees be city residents. But living wage opponents exempted key types of business subsidies, including "redevelopment assistance," which accounted for nearly 75 percent of all economic development assistance given. In late 1996 Minneapolis passed its living wage policy, including some labor peace provisions, and at the beginning of 1997 St. Paul passed its policy. The final resolutions were weaker than even the task force recommendations, because living wage activists had not "built a base of community support sufficient to fight the claims of living wage opponents and force councilors to pass stronger measures." Two years after passage, not a single worker in either St. Paul or Minneapolis came under the resolution's requirements, and even after Minneapolis strengthened its policy a few years later, only a few hundred workers have seen wage increases.[18]

Duluth's Grassroots Coalition

In early 1997, Duluth activists learned from the Minneapolis and St. Paul experience, as well as other living wage campaigns around the country like Baltimore and Los Angeles, and began organizing. Duluth has a rich history of organized labor, and with nearly 40 percent of all Duluth workers represented by unions, it ranks among the top cities in the country with high union density. Yet, despite this labor heritage, Duluth's politics has long been controlled by "old money" and business-oriented conservatives. Like many industrial cities, Duluth was ravaged by deindustrialization in the 1970s and early 1980s and lost nearly 20,000 residents, or about one-fifth of its population. In the mid 1980s, a billboard on the hill leading out of town read: "Would the last person out please shut off the lights?"

This history is important for understanding Duluth's obsession with recruiting new businesses and its paranoia that any restrictions placed on development will result in further job loss. This obsession has not always served Duluth well. In the late 1980s, Duluth grabbed national headlines when Diamond Tool, a leading manufacturer of quality tools, used $10 million in low-interest City of Duluth bonds to purchase new equipment, only to move that equipment to plants in the south and close down its Duluth facility. This experience sparked some brief interest in new accountability safeguards, but it did not result in any serious challenge to the city's prodevelopment, propublic subsidy approach to economic development. Since the mid-1980s, Duluth's economy has shifted increasingly to part-time and low-wage tourism and other service-sector jobs. By the mid-1990s Duluth was known for its low wages, and between 1994 and 1996, city officials, through the DEDA, put together several large tax increment financing subsidies to telemarketing firms and three hotels on Duluth's waterfront. Most of the jobs created through these subsidies paid wages just above minimum wage.

In January 1997, several Duluth progressive activists came together to build a coalition willing to challenge this approach to economic development. Duluth's Living Wage Coalition became the most diverse of any in the state, and the ensuing eight-month campaign was one of the most dynamic grassroots organizing efforts in the country. In the end, the coalition included groups as diverse as the Central Labor Council, the Senior Federation, and the International Workers of the World (IWW), the DFL Party, the Green Party and key environmental groups, the Catholic Diocese, the local gay/lesbian organization, students, teachers, and community clubs. In all, fifty-seven groups eventually endorsed the living wage ordinance and joined the coalition.

There were many reasons community groups joined. The Senior Federation had a long interest in tax increment financing and corporate accountability issues. They also had strong support among their members who had watched their children and grandchildren leave during the economic downturns of the 1970s and 1980s. Groups like Churches United in Ministry (CHUM), which organizes the food shelf, saw the living wage as a way of making the case that not everyone was benefiting from the booming economy. Groups such as Low Income People Organizing for Power (LIPOP), which was organizing against welfare reform, saw in the living wage campaign a way to create more living wage jobs and draw a contrast between public assistance to corporations and public assistance to individuals. The most active union in the coalition was the public employee union, AFSCME, which has had a long commitment to supporting basic economic justice issues in Duluth. AFSCME also saw in the living wage debate a way to frame the privatization of public services in a different way: that public money should not go to create low-wage, low-benefit jobs for workers doing the public's work. Several churches saw the campaign as a way to enact the social ministry statements of their various denominations. Neighborhood community groups often responded to the way public subsidies to businesses diverted city resources away from supporting neighborhoods. What united these fifty-seven diverse groups was a common goal that government has a responsibility to use public money to create jobs that pay wages above the poverty line and that private businesses that receive public money should be accountable to some public good. Most of the groups were also committed to building individual and institutional relationships that might strengthen a progressive challenge to Duluth's business-oriented political culture on other issues.

Duluth's organizing efforts were strengthened when the Minnesota Twins tried to lobby the state legislature for a new taxpayer-financed stadium. This proposal ignited a firestorm of public opposition. On the day of the vote, the capitol's switchboard crashed for the first time in history under the volume of spontaneous citizen calls of opposition. In Minnesota, corporate welfare had a new face in the Twins owner, billionaire Carl Pohlad. And yet, in March 1997, when the Living Wage Coalition announced its intention to pass a living wage ordinance in Duluth, Mayor Gary Doty, backed by the Duluth Chamber of Commerce and all but two city councilors, pledged to veto "any living wage policy" that might be passed.

Three months later, the Duluth City Council passed by a five-to-four margin the strongest living wage law in the country at that time. Mayor Doty, who had opposed the ordinance at every turn, felt compelled to make a midnight appeal before a packed city council chamber to living wage opponents pleading that they "had to swallow hard and pass something." The reason for this turnabout was due to a massive grassroots mobilizing effort. By the time the ordinance passed, coalition members had door-knocked nearly one-third of Duluth's households, mailed out more than 10,000 leaflets, dropped literature in key precincts, generated more than 1,000 postcards to each targeted city councilor, and dominated the local and regional news for weeks. Internal polls done by a sympathetic telemarketing firm showed 75 to 80 percent public support for the ordinance. Unfortunately, in the end, councilors stripped the provisions affecting the most workers out of the final ordinance, and the wage rate of $7.25 an hour indexed to inflation was too low to make a meaningful difference for most workers.[19] Nevertheless, Duluth became the smallest city in the country with a living wage law and one of the first to apply a living wage standard to corporate welfare.

Putting It All Together: Building a Movement Long Term

Keeping the Issue Alive

As in any organizing campaign, the Minnesota campaign to pass a significant corporate accountability law developed through a series of steps. It would be nice to think that these events were carefully planned and coordinated, but any real coordination between statewide corporate accountability efforts and local living wage efforts did not begin until late 1997. This creative collaboration emerged as the most remarkable piece of Minnesota's experience: The ultimate goal shifted from passing specific pieces of legislation to creating new ways to challenge corporate power and open new opportunities for organizing.

Minnesota's Legislative Commission on Business Subsidy Reform

Legislators often use legislative commissions to kill grassroots activism without actually having to vote against whatever measure is being championed. In this case, however, the Legislative Commission of Corporate Subsidy Reform became a way to unite various living wage and corporate accountability efforts from around the state and begin building bipartisan legislative support. For the Duluth legislative hearing, the Duluth Living Wage Coalition mobilized nearly 200 supporters, and the hearing made front-page news. In Minneapolis and St. Paul, ACORN and other groups mobilized more than 150 citizens to attend the hearings. MAPA also drew on its relationships with corporate accountability campaigns around the state to recruit credible and diverse supporters to serve as commissioners. Art Rolnick, director of research for the Minneapolis Federal Reserve Bank, had worked with MAPA to fight the Twins stadium deal; he brought extraordinary credibility in the media as an informal spokesperson for the commission. I also served as a commissioner because of my experience working on the Duluth living wage campaign.

After a year of meeting, commissioners drafted a consensus document that made strong recommendations to the legislature and had a degree of bipartisan buy-in.[20] Contained in the commission's final report were many of the provisions that had earlier been introduced through Duluth's living wage ordinance. In 1998, a new corporate subsidy reform bill was introduced in the legislature based on the commission's report. This 1998 bill died in a rules interpretation fight between the House and Senate, but it was reintroduced in 1999 and, except for the removal of the living wage proposal, was passed largely intact.

Minnesota's 1999 Corporate Subsidy Accountability Law

In 1998, there was a sea change in Minnesota politics that ushered in a "tripartite government" with Reform Party governor Jesse Ventura, a Republican-controlled House, and a Democrat-controlled Senate. During his campaign, Ventura regularly railed against big corporations and tax subsidies for a stadium. But although Ventura wanted corporate accountability, he was philosophically opposed to living wage mandates. Furthermore, the Republican House was strongly opposed not only to any living wage requirement but also to any "government burdens" on economic development or business. The Senate was supportive of further accountability measures, but split on the living wage requirement. What had been a dynamic grassroots organizing effort now became a very insular process of closed-door negotiations between bill supporters (chiefly MAPA and AFSCME), key legislators, and opponents of the bill (chiefly the Association of Minnesota Cities and the Minnesota Chamber of Commerce). The "living wage piece was what caught people's attention and was what we could organize around," said Beth Fraser, the lead lobbyist for the bill in 1999. But faced with certain defeat if the living wage provision was kept in the bill, MAPA agreed to drop it, and once that rallying point was gone, negotiations "got into details and it got harder and harder to get people out and get them excited."[21]

The 1999 law was possible because of five years of organizing and building awareness among the media, the public, and legislators. In the end, however, the key to passing the bill had less to do with citizen mobilization than with skillful insider politics and the careful selection of the bill's authors. When the House killed the bill without a hearing, the Senate countered by dropping the living wage requirement and passing the rest of the bill as part of the Senate tax bill. This action ensured that it would go intact to conference committee, where differences in the House and Senate tax bills would be reconciled. During the conference committee, the Senate's chief author of the bill, Senator John Hottinger, managed to secure commitments to keep the corporate subsidy reforms in. On the afternoon before the final day of session, MAPA lobbyist Beth Fraser, the key lobbyist for the cities, and the key House Republican sat in a room behind where the conference committee was meeting and "cut the deal." This final agreement passed the conference committee, won a majority in the legislature, and was signed by the governor without further comment.

Ironically, Minnesota's corporate accountability legislation passed in much the same way many corporate legislative deals are made (between lobbyists sitting around a table off a conference committee meeting in the waning hours of the legislative session). But the legislation itself, and the fact that MAPA's lobbyist was "on the inside," came about only through years of grassroots mobilization and education. Still, this tension between coalition work and the "insider" political negotiations necessary to pass a bill is an uneasy one. Focusing too much attention on the inside tactical maneuverings necessary to pass a bill can subvert the equally important work of building progressive coalitions and creating new ways of exercising power.

The law itself significantly strengthened accountability for business subsidies and is still one of the strongest, most comprehensive corporate accountability laws in the country. In 2000, the law was further strengthened, despite a spirited attempt by opponents to gut it. As it now stands, Minnesota law requires that all businesses receiving a public subsidy of more than $25,000 define how the subsidy meets a "public purpose" and serves the public interest other than simply increasing the tax base. It requires businesses to set wage and job goals or, in the absence of job creation as a goal, to establish "other tangible, measurable, and specific" goals. All subsidies over $100,000 must have a public hearing and all subsidies over $25,000 must be approved by an elected public body. Finally, the new law has strong and detailed reporting requirements and enforcement provisions, including repayment of the subsidy if the public purpose goals are not met.[22]

New Organizing Opportunities

Pushing for Community Corporate Accountability Standards

The 1999 law also requires that each local and state government entity that
provides business subsidies develop "public subsidy criteria," which must
include a wage policy. This requirement opens up new organizing opportunities in virtually every city in Minnesota. In a press release announcing the
bill's passage, Senator John Hottinger highlighted this opportunity for public involvement, saying, "Citizens will no longer be excluded from the critical decisions about how their money is spent."[23] Yet, in practice, the results
have been more mixed. Cities such as Minneapolis, St. Paul, Mankato, and
Duluth passed strong corporate subsidy criteria and accountability measures
because there were existing, organized groups advocating for more accountability. Cities that had no organized groups often passed boilerplate criteria
developed by a Minneapolis law firm that skirts the law's intent by meeting
the minimum legal requirements.

In cities where advocates pushed for significant subsidy criteria, new
opportunities for organizing have opened. Mankato, for example, passed
criteria that included requiring businesses to commit 2 percent of their subsidy to improving housing for employees. St. Paul and Minneapolis also
passed subsidy criteria that pushed beyond what the legislature mandated.
Duluth passed the strongest public subsidy criteria in the state. Included in
their criteria are specific questions that must be answered as part of a report to the city council defining the public purpose served by the subsidy,
the potential environmental and economic impacts of the subsidy, and full
disclosure of any conflicts of interest. This report is public and must be
completed at least two weeks before the city council can pass any subsidy
of $25,000 or more.

Using Corporate Accountability to Leverage a Better Deal for Workers

Duluth's public subsidy criteria also proposed "labor peace" language requiring "project labor agreements" for all construction over $100,000 done
by businesses receiving public subsidies and "card-check and neutrality language" for all business subsidy agreements of $25,000 or more. Project la-
bor agreements guarantee labor peace and that public money is not used for
substandard contractors. Card-check and neutrality agreements also preserve
labor peace and protect the city's proprietary interest by requiring the employer to recognize its employees' wishes to form a union if a majority of its

employees indicate that is their desire. This alternative recognition process avoids the long delays often experienced during traditional union elections directed by the National Labor Relations Board (NLRB) and the often hostile antiunion campaigns that many employers wage against employees who want to organize a union. Unfortunately, these labor peace criteria were vetoed by the mayor and did not go into effect. Under strong pressure from the mayor, the Duluth Building Trades quietly withdrew their support of project labor criteria, fearing that the mayor's opposition might result in fewer union construction projects.

Minneapolis led the way on these issues passing labor peace provisions as part of its 1997 living wage policy, and then, in 1999, passing an ordinance requiring card-check and neutrality provisions for all new hotels that receive public subsidies greater than $100,000.[24] Unions and community groups are building off of these earlier efforts. In early 2003, Teamsters Local 120 launched a non-NLRB organizing drive to organize nearly 400 parking lot attendants that work in municipal parking ramps. Throughout the spring, organizers mobilized workers and other community groups to demand card-check recognition from Municipal Parking Inc., the contractor who runs the city ramps. As part of its earlier living wage requirements, the Minneapolis city council had passed labor peace provisions. These provisions require all city contractors to engage in "responsible labor practices" defined as agreeing to card-check recognition. City ramp contracts go out for bid in the fall of 2003, and organizers are working to ensure that labor peace provisions are included as part of the contract specifications.

SEIU has employed similar tactics to leverage a historic card-check agreement with the Swedish corporation Securitas, one of the world's largest employers of private security guards, including about 2,000 private security guards in the Twin Cities. In 2001, Service Employees International Union (SEIU)'s Building Services Division launched a campaign to organize Minneapolis security guards as part of a nationwide strategy to organize Securitas's 250,000 U.S. security guards.

Key to the union's strategy was the Minneapolis Housing Authority (MHA), which subcontracts with Securitas along with two smaller firms to provide security services for its public housing units. But once SEIU began talking with workers, Securitas supervisors lashed back and threatened prounion workers. In the wake of 9/11, one supervisor remarked to a prounion Somali guard that he "had gotten a call from the FBI which said I should kill all Muslims."[25] SEIU filed unfair labor charges and mobilized employees along with the religious, labor, and Somali communities to express outrage and demand that the Minneapolis Housing Authority require their security contractors to agree to card check recognition. Then "Securitas went ballistic," according to SEIU organizer Julia Grantham, and fired and suspended several prounion employees.[26] The union along with the Minneapolis Central Labor Council (CLC) and community supporters went back to MHA to ask them to delay renewing Securitas's $2.5 million contract until the company agreed to card check and neutrality. Unfortunately, the board simply required Securitas to hold a "cultural sensitivity training" and remove the offending supervisor.

Although disappointed, SEIU with strong community support had successfully delayed the contract and demonstrated to Securitas that the union would not go away. When Securitas held an antiunion meeting under the guise of "sensitivity training," SEIU again filed lawsuits and mobilized a series of highly visible street actions and rallies.[27] One of the key turning points was a series of rallies organized by the Minneapolis CLC in front of American Express and other key Securitas buildings. After these highly visible events, Securitas quickly signaled interest in talking. After a year's negotiation, SEIU won card-check recognition for all Securitas security guards in five urban markets, including the Twin Cities. This potentially covers 100,000 workers nationwide.

On the other side of the river in St. Paul similar efforts are under way. Four years earlier, SEIU Local 284, which represents many Twin Cities bus drivers, launched a drive to organize 1,700 drivers, school bus aides, and wash rack employees working for Ryder Student Transportation Services. After a vicious antiunion campaign, Ryder employees rejected the union by a mere 59 votes.[28] The union filed unfair labor practice charges, and in March 2001, the NLRB ordered a new election. In the interim, Ryder sold the company to First Student Transportation. When a new election was held in April 2001, First Student also waged a very aggressive antiunion campaign, and once again workers rejected the union.

SEIU organizers and bus employees began looking at alternative election procedures, including card check and neutrality (or proprietary interest agreements).[29] They shifted their attention away from the NLRB to St. Paul's school board. The school district subcontracts the transportation of two-thirds of the district's 43,000 students with First Student Transportation and three other companies. "As long as the law allows disruptive employer tactics during traditional organizing drives, employees weren't going to win and continuous bus services for school kids was at risk," said Jon Youngdahl, SEIU's state council director, "so we had to convince the school board that it was in their interest (and the district's interest) to establish criteria that ensured a more peaceful and streamlined process."[30] SEIU, the Twin Cities Religion-Labor Network, MAPA, and others began educating and lobbying St. Paul school board members, held rallies, and dropped literature in key precincts throughout the city. In May 2003, just before bus contracts were put out on bid, the board passed what Shelly Hagglund, an SEIU organizer, called "truly a victory for workers"—a "proprietary interest agreement" that reinforces the district's 1999 "right to organize" policy and ensures that bus companies transporting district students must recognize the union and begin bargaining as soon as a third party verifies a majority of workers have signed union authorization cards.[31] In exchange, the union agrees not to take any economic action against the company that might disrupt the transportation of students.

The St. Paul fight is not over, and the companies have pledged to fight the provision in the courts. Yet, all of these new efforts build off earlier corporate accountability efforts and offer new models for insisting that private firms that do the public's work be accountable to basic community standards.

Raising State Revenue by Going After Tax Expenditures

During the 2003 Minnesota legislature, activists also began looking for innovative ways to secure new revenues for social spending by scrutinizing corporate tax breaks. Like many states, Minnesota faced huge budget deficits in 2003—more than $4.2 billion to be precise. Newly elected Governor Pawlenty vowed to balance the budget without raising taxes. In response, MAPA's Beth Fraser and I drafted a proposal to shift money going to tax expenditures (special tax breaks and loopholes) to other social spending priorities.[32] Every two years, Minnesota requires the Department of Revenue to publish a "tax expenditure budget," which lists all preferential tax breaks. There are over $8.5 billion worth of these tax expenditures in Minnesota; we targeted about $1.6 billion that we felt gave preferential treatment to corporations and wealthier Minnesotans. The proposal drew on ideas that first arose as part of the Corporate Subsidy Reform Commission in 1998. Our premise was simple: sunset certain preferential tax breaks so they could be debated in the context of other budget priorities.

Quite unexpectedly, this proposal gained widespread attention. Eventually, parts of it were adopted by various groups, including the state AFL-CIO, which incorporated about $900 million in its tax proposal, and the Coalition for the Homeless, which advocated capping the home mortgage deduction at $20,000 (approximately a $400,000 mortgage) and using the additional revenue to pay for low-income housing. The Senate included about $160 million in its tax bill, but failed to win the governor's or the House Republican leadership's support. There is much work to be done building coalitions and legislative support around this concept, but it shows promise as part of a longer-term strategy to hold corporate tax breaks as accountable to public scrutiny as other forms of spending.

New Groups—New Coalitions—New Directions

New organizing efforts continue to open up. In Duluth, the Living Wage Coalition has been replaced by a very active Community Religion Labor Network, which focuses on wage inequality and workers' right to organize. The Duluth Public Policy Alliance (DPPA) formed at the end of the living wage campaign as a citizen coalition committed to monitoring and demanding accountability for economic development projects in Duluth. It now claims a membership of more than 300 people. The Northland Sustainable Business Alliance (NSBA) emerged from earlier development and living wage debates as a progressive alternative to the Duluth Chamber of Commerce. Its focus is on promoting sustainable economic development and seeks "to secure the economic, environmental, and community health of the region by supporting independent local businesses."[33] The NSBA now represents 87 businesses and nonprofits.

Statewide, Joel Kramer, former publisher of the *Star Tribune*, launched a new nonpartisan think tank—Growth & Justice—in early 2003. Growth & Justice aims "to create economic growth in Minnesota that is widely shared and sustainable."[34] Its recent "Wage Project" takes as its problem "the inability of lower-income workers to support their families," and explicitly adopts as its standard the Jobs Now Coalition's "basic needs wage"—a wage significantly above minimum and most previous living wage measures.[35] Growth & Justice is gathering a multipartisan group of people from labor, environment, business, and economic development in communities across the state to explore a variety of ways of raising wages for low-income workers, including mandated wages and changes in tax policy.

MAPA is also building on its earlier corporate accountability coalition work. During the 2003 legislative session, MAPA brought together a coalition of over sixty labor, nonprofit, religious, and human service groups to counter the Minnesota Business Partnership and Taxpayer League during Minnesota's $4.2 billion budget battle. "There was a fear that we would all go to the legislature and cannibalize each other. We needed a common message and understanding that we were all in it together," recalls Beth Fraser, the MAPA lobbyist who facilitated the group.[36] During the session, this coalition—loosely called "The Budget Group"—worked closely with other groups, and by the end of the session these combined efforts morphed into an effort called "Minnesotans are Watching," which sent in over 600 volunteers to monitor conference committees in the waning days of the session. Although ultimately unsuccessful in achieving their immediate goal, this cross-constituency legislative effort was unprecedented in the state. This coalition is continuing to work together to set a long-term proworker, prohuman service agenda.

According to Fraser, the 2003 budget fight also strengthened two other MAPA coalition efforts—passing comprehensive, publicly funded campaign finance reform (the Fair and Clean Elections, or FACE bill) and a new Livable Communities initiative. FACE directly builds on previous corporate accountability efforts to show "how big business dominates the legislative process and often gets what it wants because it has a lot of cash to throw around."[37] In the 2003 session, MAPA researched campaign contributions and linked them to specific issues (like Minnesota's new "conceal and carry" law) to suggest how corporate and special interest money influences the legislative process. The Livable Communities project taps into what Bernie Hesse, a United Food and Commercial Workers (UFCW) organizer and key activist in the new project, describes as a growing awareness among many people that increased sprawl is connected to more low paying jobs. "They are no longer just resigned to the inevitability of low paying jobs in these malls; they are asking 'How do we make these jobs better?'" says Hesse.[38] He believes that the language of corporate accountability can help frame the issue of sprawl in ways that can leverage better deals for workers.

Lessons Learned

Despite all these efforts and with new efforts under way, it is important to note realistically that very few workers have seen wage increases or successfully organized as a direct result of living wage and corporate accountability initiatives. This is not an indictment of past efforts, but a caution that we are engaged in a long-term strategy. We have built a foundation, not achieved our goals. Below are some of the lessons learned along the way.

Change the Terms of the Debate

In recent years, the political left has not done a very good job of shaping public debate in ways that further a progressive agenda. In contrast, the political right has successfully claimed terms like "family values," "competition," "accountability," and "big government" and has used these terms to rhetorically mainstream its agenda. Living wage and corporate accountability campaigns take the rhetoric often used against progressives and turn it toward our own ends. For Alexa Bradley this meant, "The focus was turned from these people over here receiving public assistance to corporations over there that are receiving public assistance. It took businesses' own words and turned their spotlight back on them."[39] This can be a risky enterprise. MAPA was sometimes criticized for using the term "corporate welfare" as a negative term, since it played into negative social stereotypes of individuals on welfare. In a different way, the term "living wage" has achieved enormous cultural currency, yet defining a living wage as somewhere around the federal poverty line ignores that such a wage, although significantly higher than the federal minimum wage, is nowhere near a true "living wage."

Never Stop Organizing

One of the strengths of corporate accountability campaigns is their ability to unmask the hidden ways corporate power operates through tax policy, government regulations, and special-interest laws. They offer a way for progressives to be proactive and have others react to *our* proposals. In Duluth, the Living Wage Coalition won a strong ordinance, despite fierce opposition from the chamber of commerce and most elected officials, because it had built enough community support and political pressure that it did not have to engage in negotiating a weaker compromise ordinance. MAPA agreed to take out the living wage provision in the 1999 law and lost a critical issue necessary for mobilizing, yet was then able to pass a very good law. The bottom line is that where the most active grassroots organizing occurred is where the best legislation passed and where new efforts and coalitions continue to grow.

Building Ongoing Relationships and Broad-Based Grassroots Community Coalitions

Duluth was able to pass its ordinance because of the strength of its coalition, and building strong coalitions is a long-term enterprise. AFSCME and the Senior Federation had a long-term relationship working on shared issues like the county's attempt to close its two nursing homes and other health care issues. Because of this history, both organizations felt comfortable donating staff time to the campaign. Conversely, the 1995 St. Paul referendum lost, in part, because there was never a broad, unified coalition behind it. Issues such as hiring halls and residency requirements split off or dampened the support from what should have been key allies. ACORN, the principle backer of the ordinance, also did not have ongoing long-term relationships with key labor groups.

MAPA, on the other hand, has institutional relationships with a number of key unions such as AFSCME, the Steelworkers, and the International Union of Electrical Workers (IUE) within the MAPA coalition itself. They have also developed a close working relationship with other unions and the state AFL-CIO while working together on legislative issues such as the Dislocated Workers Program. Consequently, it was easier for labor to trust MAPA's corporate accountability proposal. One of the key negotiators was even AFSCME's seasoned lobbyist Steve Hunter (now secretary-treasurer of the state AFL-CIO). Whether his involvement was principally due to his serving on the MAPA board or because of AFSCME's support of the bill only underscores the importance of building long-term coalition relationships.

Sustaining Broad-Based Community Coalitions

Strong, ongoing community coalitions are necessary to enforce the laws that are passed, but sustaining such diverse coalitions is easier said then done. Looking back, Alexa Bradley sees constant vigilance as the key for long-term success, since "No law alone can make the difference. It's people who are organized who make it happen. If you don't have a committed activist base to maintain vigilance, the best law on the books won't do anything."[40] Yet, without an immediate, galvanizing issue to organize around, diverse coalitions tend to drift apart. In Duluth, the coalition's shift in focus from living wages to other corporate accountability measures, such as card check and neutrality and disclosure reports from subsidized businesses, began to lessen the coalition's solidarity. Groups such as the Duluth Building Trades had less enthusiasm for any requirement that might limit new construction projects, and although it never opposed coalition efforts, it was notably absent during the campaign. Those of us in the coalition who wanted to shift the focus to other corporate accountability measures never made the compelling case to other coalition members as to how such measures might open new ways of securing living wage jobs or building power for workers.

Changing the Electoral and Economic Development Culture

For Buddy Robinson of the Senior Federation, what is most significant is the fact that the Duluth Coalition for a Living Wage even formed. Participating in the coalition solidified his organization's ties with labor groups and built an informal coalition that has significantly transformed Duluth's political landscape. After the passage of the living wage ordinance, a loose alliance composed largely of coalition groups elected a coalition member to the city council, and then went on to win a majority of city council seats in the next election. This political shift has changed the way economic development is done in the city and made development a key electoral issue. Ironically, however, it may be the coalition's electoral success that has also made it harder to build and sustain the Living Wage Coalition itself, since the sense of "crisis" has passed. Nevertheless, living wage jobs have become a benchmark for evaluating economic development in ways that they were not before. And although no worker has actually seen a raise directly because of Duluth's ordinance, the city is also no longer pursuing low-wage businesses and many nonlabor groups now understand the need for further accountability measures, including labor peace agreements. These are all directly related to living wage and corporate accountability efforts over the past six years.

Looking Forward

Living wage and corporate accountability opponents often charge that such laws aren't really effective in achieving what they aim to achieve. If our goal is limited to raising the wages of specific types of low-wage workers, then our critics may be right. But living wage and corporate accountability laws are best used as ways of building coalitions and furthering a progressive agenda, not as ends in themselves. They can shape a public debate over corporate power and the economic inequities that go along with such concentrated power. Corporate accountability and living wage campaigns can help build broad-based political coalitions to secure more economically just legislation and exercise the power of government to leverage a better deal for workers. Finally, they can help change the political and economic landscape so certain types of practices become increasingly more difficult. One of the key lessons from the Minnesota experience is to always think of new ways to keep the issue alive. If we see such activities as tactics in a larger struggle, then we are at a point in the struggle where we must take a complex and strategic look at where we want to go next.

Notes

1. Minnesota Budget Project, "Making a Living? The State of Working Minnesota" (2000); Michael P. Ettlinger, Tyson Slocum, and Robert Lynch, *Tax Strategies for a Strong Minnesota* (Washington, DC: Institute on Taxation and Economic Policy, 1998); *Tax Facts*, newsletter of the Property Tax Study Project (November/December 1999).

2. Dave Mann, unpublished memo on MAPA's history. All quotations from this section are from Mann's memo.

3. Interview with Alexa Bradley, coexecutive director of MAPA from 1994 to 1999, St. Paul, 2001.

4. Greg LeRoy, *No More Candy Store: States and Cities Making Job Subsidies Accountable* (Washington, DC: Federation for Industrial Retention and Renewal and the Grassroots Policy Institute, 1989, updated in 1994). LeRoy wrote the book with Richard Healey, Dan Doherty, and Roger Kerson.

5. The term "corporate welfare" first appeared in newspaper stories in early 1993, but the term may have actually been coined by Senator William Proxmire. It broke into widespread usage when Robert Reich gave his famous speech to the Democratic Leadership Council on November 22, 1994. In this speech, Reich paraphrased President

Clinton's campaign slogan and pledged to make "ending corporate welfare as we know it" a goal. In Minnesota, the term was first introduced by the Minnesota Alliance for Progressive Action (MAPA) in an April 1994 op-ed piece in the *Star Tribune* titled "Minnesota Would Do Well to Consider Corporate Welfare Reform."

6. Bradley interview.

7. Interview with Buddy Robinson, executive director of the Northeast Minnesota Senior Federation since 1979, Duluth, 2001.

8. Tax increment financing (TIF) originated in the mid 1970s as an innovative way to redevelop polluted or blighted properties, known as "brownfields." When a property is developed using TIF, the property is given an initial property value assessment of x dollars. Once the property is developed, it is worth significantly more, or y dollars. The "increment" is the difference between the two (y value – x value), and it is the property tax on this increment that is used to pay off the costs of development. It is like individual homeowners being able to use their property taxes to pay off their mortgage. Since TIF redirects property tax revenue to private businesses instead of to general fund expenditures such as fire and police protection, sewers, and parks, unless a city cuts these services or reduces costs in other ways, the net result of a city's high reliance on TIF is to shift the tax burden from business property to individual property taxpayers. Twenty percent of Duluth's property value was under TIF in 1995. Robinson interview.

9. See Minnesota Statutes for 1996, chapter 224, sections 48 and 54 for the full Corporate Welfare Law. These sections were repealed in 1999 when the Corporate Subsidy Reform Law was passed.

10. Bradley interview.

11. Ibid.

12. Minnesota Alliance for Progressive Action, *Corporate Welfare Activist Handbook: A Comprehensive Handbook on Corporate Welfare in Minnesota*, 3d ed. (1999), 2–3.

13. LeRoy, Greg and Tyson Slocum, "Economic Development in Minnesota: High Subsidies, Low Wages, Absent Standards." Issued by Good Jobs First, 1998. See also Greg LeRoy and Tyson Slocum, "Another Way Sprawl Happens: Economic Development Subsidies in a Twin Cities Suburb," issued by Good Jobs First, 2000.

14. Based on the federal poverty level of $14,996 per year for a family of four, which, assuming a full-time worker, translates into a $7.21-per-hour wage.

15. Anthony Lonetree, "St. Paul Voters Kill Proposal to Tie Aid to Pay; Results Reflect Citizens' Renewed Faith in City, Coleman Says," *Star Tribune*, November 8, 1995, 1B.

16. Ibid.

17. Bernie Hesse quoted in Stephanie Luce, "Building Political Power and Community Coalition: The Role of Central Labor Councils in the Living Wage Movement," April 2000 draft of unpublished manuscript, 10.

18. Personal communications with Twin Cities living wage proponents. See also "Council Broadens Living Wage Rule, but Many Projects Remain Exempt as City Officials Tackle a Wide Range of Issues," *Star Tribune*, December 19, 1998, 1B; "Minneapolis Weighs Policy on Living Wage," *Star Tribune*, October 21, 2000, 1B.

19. The original ordinance applied the living wage requirement (set at $7.25, the federal poverty line for a family of four) to all businesses receiving $25,000 or more in public subsidies, all workers employed under city service contracts, and all non-union city employees.

20. Corporate Subsidy Reform Commission, "1997 Corporate Subsidy Reform Commission Report," Representative Karen Clark and Senator John Hottinger co-chairs (St. Paul, February 6, 1998).

21. Interview with Beth Fraser, current MAPA lobbyist and lead lobbyist on the 1999 legislation, St. Paul, 2001.

22. See Minnesota Statute 116.J.993–95.

23. MAPA press release, May 19, 1999.

24. See Minneapolis Code of Ordinances Title 16, Chapter 422.190.

25. Interview with Julia Grantham, SEIU organizer on the Securitas campaign, June 16, 2003, St. Paul.

26. Grantham interview.

27. At the cultural sensitivity training (held only for employees, not for supervisors) a Justice Department agent asked the employees who were involved with the union to raise their hands. When some did, he began questioning them. Later, when SEIU contacted the agent he denied it, but then proceeded to tell SEIU that he had "already turned them in to Homeland Security because he felt SEIU was 'fanning the flames of hate.'" Grantham interview.

28. Michael Kuchta, "School Bus Drivers Get New Union Election," workdayminnesota.org, March 5, 2001; "School Bus Drivers Vote to Not Join Union," workdayminnesota.org, April 20, 2001.

29. Interview with Todd Anderson, Minnesota Director of Field Mobilization, AFL-CIO, June 16, 2003, St. Paul; interview with Jon Youngdahl, Director, SEIU State Council, June 16, 2003, St. Paul.

30. Youngdahl interview.

31. Michael Kuchta, "School Board Puts Muscle Behind 'Right to Organize' Policy," workdayminnesota.org, May 15, 2003.

32. Erik Peterson, "Raising Revenues by Closing Loopholes and Preferential Tax Breaks," March 2003. See the online journal at www.growthandjustice.org for a copy of the article.

33. "Business Alliance Rolls Out New Website," NSBA Press release. June 3, 2003.

34. I serve on the board of directors of Growth & Justice. See "About Growth & Justice," handout to project participants, June 2003. See also their Web site: www.growthandjustice.org. The basic needs wage adopted by Growth & Justice is published by the JOBS NOW Coalition which defines a "minimum family budget" or "real living wage" in 1999 as $13.94 for a single parent with one child or $9.31 an hour for a single person. See "The Cost of Living in Minnesota," (2001).

35. Growth & Justice Wage Project narrative. June 2003, p 1.

36. Interview with Beth Fraser, current MAPA lobbyist, June 4, 2003, St. Paul.

37. Ibid.

38. Interview with Bernie Hesse, UFCW organizer and key activist on the Livable Wage project, June 6, 2003, St. Paul.

39. Bradley interview.

40. Ibid.

7

Anatomy of Vermont's Livable Wage Campaign

Ellen Kahler

In this primarily rural state of Vermont, where the total population is just over 610,000, 44 percent of all jobs have a median wage that pays less than $12.55 per hour ($26,094/yr), the livable wage for a single person.[1] Since 1997, the Peace & Justice Center (PJC) has used the widening gap between the need for and supply of family-supporting jobs as a tool to organize around an increasingly aggressive legislative agenda and to build an adaptive state-wide economic justice movement. While the specifics may be particular to Vermont, the main issues and the strategies used have wide application for livable wage activists wanting to move to the next stage after their successful city ordinance campaigns and for labor's efforts to redefine the meaning and practice of economic development. What follows is an analysis of the PJC's livable wage journey, who became involved, what has been won so far, and what lies ahead.

A Change in Direction

Founded in 1979, the PJC has its roots in antinuclear, Central American solidarity, and environmental activism. The center's staff provides critical support and technical assistance for numerous grassroots organizing efforts. Funding comes from its base of 1,400 members and small grants for specific projects. Beginning in 1993, the organization decided to shift its main focus from traditional peace and international human rights work to local racial and economic justice issues. We set out to reshape our identity—from being

considered "lefty," reactive activists (who nonetheless were perceived as being a voice of reason and conscience) who could easily be ignored by the
state's power elites to legitimately weighing in on economic development
public policy discussions with the ability to have an impact on legislation.
We knew that to affect the underlying power structure and maldistribution of
wealth, we needed to build a long-term movement of workers and we needed
to win over the hearts and minds of the middle class.

After coming across the Minnesota Job Gap Study and its foundational
methodology developed by Trudi Renwick and Barbara Bergmann[2], we saw
an opportunity to design a body of research that would raise people's awareness about how many Vermonters are working full-time and still not making
ends meet. By gaining widespread recognition and acceptance of the problem first, we could then move with greater authority into public policy recommendations, legislation, and grassroots mobilization.

1997: The Starting Point

Welfare reform had just passed in Congress and thousands of families would
soon be facing public assistance cutoffs. Anecdotally, we also knew that many
low-income Vermonters make the conscious choice not to accept public assistance even though they are eligible for it and that many Vermonters work
two or three jobs just to make ends meet. Thus, we strategically decided to
focus on the "working poor" and how they were faring in the "boom" economy
of the mid- to late 1990s.

After raising initial funds from Vermont's U.S. Department of Agriculture
—Rural Development office and the Vermont Community Foundation, hiring
a uniquely qualified policy analyst named Doug Hoffer, and forming a Research Advisory Committee of economists and nonprofit, government, and
business representatives to lend credibility to our work, we released *Phase 1:
Basic Needs and a Livable Wage* in January 1997. The report established
what it costs to live for five family sizes in both rural and urban areas of
Vermont and quantified how many families are not earning a livable wage
despite working full-time. Table 7.1 summarizes these original and more
recent calculations.

We made a strategic decision not to include activists, clergy, or labor unions
on the Research Advisory Committee because we knew it would be hard to
gain that all-important initial credibility. We wanted to establish a distinction
between the research and the organizing that would come later. Unlike other
advocacy-oriented research, ours contained no provocative rhetoric and no
policy recommendations, and it was short and accessible to any audience.
Our aim—at this stage—was simply to highlight the problem.

Table 7.1

Livable Wage Comparisons over Time (dollars per hour)

Family unit	1995 LW figures	1998 LW figures	1999 LW figures*	2000 LW figures*	2001 LW figures*	2002 LW figures*	2003 LW figures*
Single person	8.10	8.68	10.47	9.80	10.82	11.58	12.55
1 parent, 1 child	12.80	13.47	12.35	16.06	17.96	17.95	21.43
1 parent, 2 children	15.18	15.50	15.89	19.07	21.11	21.50	27.62
2 parents, 2 children, 1 wage	14.85	15.47	19.08	20.36	21.28	22.75	27.53
2 parents, 2 children, 2 wages	19.64 or 9.82 ea.	20.63 or 10.32 ea.	20.12 or 10.06 ea.	25.47 or 12.74 ea.	26.71 or 13.36 ea.	28.06 or 14.03 ea.	33.90 or 16.95 ea.

Note: All figures are the average of urban and rural livable wage calculations and include basic need expenses and all applicable federal and state taxes. Partial employer paid health insurance is assumed in the methodology. For exactly what is included in these budgets, see www.vtlivablewage.org/jobgapstudy.html.

*These living wage figures were published by the VT Joint Fiscal Office using our basic needs methodology with three additional budget items and a more generous food allowance. We include them here to highlight the importance of producing livable wage figures annually.

In May 1997, we released *Phase 2: The Jobs Gap*. This second phase found that: there is a critical shortage of full-time, livable wage jobs; under-employment is a serious problem (affecting at least 26,896 workers); the Vermont economy has, and is expected to continue to produce, a significant percentage of low-skill, low-wage jobs; and competition for low-skill livable wage jobs is an urgent problem and has direct implications for public assistance recipients subject to new workfare rules.

> Typically, economic development policy is framed in terms of whether it helps or hurts businesses, when struggling people is a more appropriate focus. They want to work; they want to be self-sufficient; and there is little opportunity for them to succeed.
> The Job Gap Study makes that point persuasively: Vermonters eager to work full time ought to be able to survive. (Editorial, *Burlington Free Press,* October 13, 1999)

The magic of this research was that the data confirmed what many people had always known—that thousands of Vermonters who are "playing by the rules," working full-time (sometimes with two or three part-time jobs) still cannot make ends meet. Those who read the Job Gap Study invariably got excited about it and passed it on to friends and colleagues, who then shared it with others. Interestingly, our fact-centered focus also helped secure positive media attention, including supportive editorials and news articles, and statewide radio talk shows after each phase of research. While the mainstream media had rarely covered these issues before, they eagerly drew from our reports. Because the language we used was not provocative and the facts presented were so compelling and their sources so transparent, they could not write us off as reactionary idealists.

> It would be easy for mainstream Vermont to dismiss the Job Gap Study because its sponsor is Burlington's Peace & Justice Center, better known for supporting indigenous people in Chiapas, or opposing the American bombing of Iraq. But the report and its sober economic message have gained acceptance in economic development circles, due partly to the study's conservative approach, its reliance on state and federal economic data, and its lack of political ideology. Even influential men in suits like the report. (Brian Pfeiffer, *Rutland Herald/Times Argus,* March 8, 1998)

Within a few months there was a noticeable buzz around the state. The reaction to our research was extremely positive—even business interests could not argue with our methodology or findings. And because we strategically decided not to release recommendations or to align ourselves with any political party, the educational process we were conducting had not yet become politicized. In essence, we had begun to build a statewide consensus on the problem. We acknowledged that the issue was complex and structural and that we did not have all the answers.

Getting Business on Board

We also made clear that the vibrancy of our small-business sector had to be part of the equation. According to the Vermont Department of Employment and Training, 89.4 percent have less than 20 employees (37 percent of all workers); another 9 percent have between 20 and 99 employees (31.2 percent of all workers), and 1.4 percent have 100 or more employees (31.7 percent of all workers).[3] In fact, only 24 businesses out of a total of 22,184 have 500 or more employees. Most of these firms will never be unionized because of their size (Vermont's unionization rate is 11 percent). Small business is the backbone of Vermont's economy, with many businesses just barely surviving. Because of this reality, we wanted to be engaged in a dialogue that combined the interconnected goals of raising wages and increasing small-business prosperity.

We knew it would not be politically feasible to mandate that all businesses pay a livable wage, so we decided to develop the means of encouraging business owners to create livable jobs voluntarily. Dozens of Job Gap Study presentations were made to local chambers of commerce, regional development corporations, human resource professionals, community and economic developers, state officials, and legislators so that we could more fully explain our methodology and they could have their questions answered. We also approached Vermont Businesses for Social Responsibility (VBSR) about creating a Livable Jobs Toolkit for small employers to teach them how to improve their compensation, benefits, and workplace practices.[4] Released in March 2000, the toolkit highlights the many hidden business costs caused by low wages and offers business owners practical ways to chart higher-wage success. By defying the conventional labor-versus-business framework, we disarmed a lot of would-be critics.

> Using data from the Vermont Job Gap Study, the Addison County Economic Development Corporation secured a federal loan that offers credit for manufacturers that create high-wage jobs. We had always been rejected for the loan, because, until now, we couldn't provide an estimate of the number of Vermonters working in jobs that don't pay livable wages. It's a problem that we all knew existed, but we didn't know how to quantify or qualify it. The study does an excellent job in defining the level and extent of the problem. (Jamie Stewart, Executive Director, Addison County

Economic Development Corporation, cited in *Rutland Herald/Times Argus*, March 8, 1998)

Grassroots Activism Begins

Vermont's healthy activist community became excited about the Job Gap Study as well. Central Vermonters for a Livable Wage (CVLW) formed and began a door-to-door canvassing operation designed to engage residents in a discussion about the need for livable wage jobs. Indeed, livable wages proved to be an issue that spoke to many Vermonters' own personal experience with the economy. In 1997, the group gathered the necessary signatures to put a livable wage resolution on three town meeting day agendas—all passed.

While door knocking in the city of Barre, members of CVLW learned that the school board was planning to privatize the janitorial staff. It was the classic scenario: fire the janitors making $10 per hour, sign a contract to clean the schools with a private company that would hire the same janitors at the minimum wage ($5.25 per hour). The savings would have amounted to less than one cent off the property tax rate, while the custodial staff would experience a $9,880 annual pay cut. The group met with some of the janitors and constructed a campaign that won widespread community support, turned out dozens of supporters at school board meetings, and eventually ended privatization plans. As a result of their success, many of the janitors joined CVLW and became active in subsequent campaigns. This successful community support strategy became the backbone of CVLW's approach to building community-labor coalitions during future campaigns.

1998: Building Consensus

After laying the groundwork in the previous two phases, we released *Phase 3: The Cost of Underemployment—The Income Gap* in March 1998. The report gave an opportunity to reach people in the middle—those Vermonters who may not have been as responsive to the issues we focused on in phases 1 and 2. This new research calculated the amount of taxpayer dollars being used to subsidize low-wage employers in the state. Our researchers found that Vermont taxpayers subsidize low-wage employers to the tune of $88 million per year in 1998 dollars (by comparison, Vermont's state budget was $2.6 billion at the time).[5] This subsidy is a combination of avoided wages that are covered by public assistance (food stamps, fuel assistance, Medicaid, etc.—all paid for with taxpayer dollars) and lost income- and consumption-based revenue (from lower income and sales taxes). The report proved to be a critical piece of research because it debunked the argument that business is "owed" something by society simply because jobs have been created and it revealed that many employers are receiving significant subsidies without realizing or acknowledging this fact.

In the spring of 1998, after our first three phases of research had been distributed throughout the state and had become quite widely accepted, we began a process of developing public policy recommendations. We convened ten focus groups with various constituencies (nonprofit organizations, labor unions, activists, state officials, and business leaders). We asked the same broad question of each group: "Now that you have seen the research and the extent of the problem in Vermont, what should be done about it?"

The ideas and suggestions were compiled into a draft report and taken before a large working session that we organized at the Vermont statehouse. Present at this conference were legislators, business owners, nonprofit advocates, labor representatives, activists, and state bureaucrats. Participants were split into small groups and asked to discuss each of the policy recommendations and "vote out" the best three. Every small group was composed of at least one person from each of the major stakeholder groups present. For many participants it was an eye-opening experience; activists, business owners and state officials had never before sat across the table from one another discussing economic development and public policy. While there was ideological disagreement about *how* to produce more livable wage jobs among the different constituencies—which was to be expected—many found more common ground and agreement than they had previously thought possible.

After further fine-tuning, we published *Phase 4: Policy Recommendations* in October. In all, twenty-four recommendations were grouped into four categories (Strategic Planning; Data Collection and Cost-Benefit Analysis; Wages; and Basic Needs) and included suggestions on both the wage and basic needs side of the livable wage equation. While we had succeeded in building consensus on the nature and extent of the problem, we now faced the politically more challenging waters of *how* to make needed change happen.

For instance, one of the most challenging decisions in developing the recommendations concerned what to say about the minimum wage. A traditional lightning rod issue, the activist community wanted us to call for an $8.50 per hour minimum wage. Many on our research advisory committee, however, did not want us to make a rate-specific recommendation, fearing a specific minimum wage would become *the issue* in public debates and the media, eclipsing our broader livable wage agenda. In the end, we decided to avoid making a targeted minimum wage recommendation, although we did call for an increase in general. While this decision angered our traditional allies, it had the desired affect of keeping the attention focused on livable wages. It should be noted that since phase 4 was released, we have continually sought and won significant increases in the minimum wage (including 50 cents in both 1999 and 2000, and 75 cents in 2003). The lesson here is to stay focused on the real goal (livable wages), while quietly going about the business of working on traditional legislative hot-button issues (minimum wage) in a more sophisticated way.

Many of the ideas and recommendations that we published in phase 4 have in fact been enacted into law or are under serious consideration at this time. We attribute this success to the fact that we spent over two years building a statewide consensus on the extent of the problem while at the same time disarming many would-be opponents with our objective facts and figures and our rational, common-sense approach.

These legislative victories could not have come to pass however, had it not been for the growing livable wage activism around the state. Members of the Burlington Livable Wage Coalition canvassed some 2,000 homes and built local support for a municipal employee livable wage resolution to raise their wages from $5.25 to $7.25 per hour (pegged at the federal poverty measure for a family of four at that time). While this was still shy of a livable wage for a single person in Vermont, it was a significant step nonetheless. The group also worked with the American Federation of State, County, and Municipal Employees (AFSCME) to successfully persuade the Burlington City School Board to raise wages for custodial staff and cafeteria workers to $7.50 per hour.[6]

CVLW moved on to work with the Vermont AFL-CIO and built community support for nurses who were on strike at Copley Hospital in Morrisville. They also worked with the Teamsters to turn out support for United Parcel Service strikers. In November, CVLW succeeded in getting the Montpelier city council to pass a municipal employee livable wage resolution—similar to the Burlington ordinance. The Barre city council followed suit in February 1999.

In order to more fully institutionalize their community-labor organizing model, CVLW decided to create the Vermont Workers' Center (VWC). Since its inception, the VWC has mobilized support for workers struggling to form unions, assisted workers in winning contracts, and stood in solidarity with Vermonters on strike. By developing a culture of workers supporting each other's struggles and educating around the need for collective action in the workplace, the VWC is helping to breathe new life into Vermont's labor movement and plant the seeds for community-wide solidarity.

Two additional local livable wage coalitions also formed in 1998. Members of the Bethany United Church of Christ in the small, rural town of Randolph formed a group, and human service workers in Addison County decided a local coalition was needed as well. Both groups hosted numerous livable wage workshops and started examining what local issues they wanted to tackle.

1999: Legislative Efforts Take Hold

To formalize the growing livable wage activism around the state, local livable wage coalitions, unions, nonprofit advocacy groups, and faith-based groups began to meet in late 1998, and launched the Vermont Livable Wage Campaign (VLWC) (which became a core focus project of the PJC)). The group established a legislative agenda to increase the minimum wage (then $5.25 per hour). In January 1999, the president of the Vermont senate introduced a bill to raise Vermont's minimum wage fifty cents an hour for each of the next four years. After a month of testimony, it became apparent that the senate was likely to approve only a one-year increase. We suggested that they move forward on this first step and, in addition, appropriate funds for a legislative summer study on livable wages. That bill passed in both the Senate and House in May 1999, allocating $60,000 for the summer study and raising the minimum wage to $5.75 per hour.

A summer study committee of five senators and five House members hired a research team composed of Doug Hoffer (author of the Vermont Job Gap Study), Deborah Brighton (author of the basic-needs-budget tax calculations and an advisory committee member for Job Gap Study), Elaine McCrate (an economist at the University of Vermont who assisted in developing the methodology for phase 2 and served on the Job Gap Study advisory committee), and Tom Kavet (one of the state's chief economists), to conduct additional research on the issue of a "livable income" (wages plus employer benefits plus public benefits). The fact that these legislators chose to work with the authors of the Job Gap Study is an acknowledgment of how much our research had become accepted and respected.

The state-commissioned study replicated much of the original Job Gap Study, with a number of important additional components. Legislators on the summer study committee ultimately approved basic needs budgets and livable wage figures higher than the Job Gap Study numbers (due to additional line items in the budget). The researchers utilized a complex economic forecasting model (the REMI model) and determined that the state could raise the minimum wage to $7 an hour with little or no impact on the state's economy. Researchers also conducted a vigorous literature search of the pros and cons of raising the minimum wage. Besides specific recommendations on actions to immediately raise wages for the working poor, the research team identified cutting-edge areas where additional data and research were needed. As part of its process, the legislative committee held a public hearing attended by over 200 people. This testimony, along with the research team's report, resulted in a draft bill on livable income prepared for the start of the 2000 legislative session.[7]

While the campaign made impressive gains at the state level, attempts to start four additional local livable wage coalitions in 1999 met with limited success—due mostly to the lack of organizing experience of those involved. Meanwhile, the four active coalitions continued to win local victories, and the Vermont Conference of the United Church of Christ passed a denomination-wide resolution endorsing the VLWC and committed all congregations to some form of involvement in this important justice work. We also organized a skill-building conference for livable wage activists to help increase the capacity of our growing movement, with workshops on working with the media, lobbying, forming a new group, coalition building, countering the opposition, and working with unions.

That same year also saw the release of *Phase 5: Basic Needs and a Livable Wage, 1998 Update* (August 1999), which provided updates to both phases 1 and 2 of the Job Gap Study. At that time, additional funding for our expanded organizing came from the Vermont Community Foundation and the Charles Stewart Mott Foundation.

2000: Further Gains and Big Victories

With draft legislation in hand, the VLWC directed its energies over the first five months of 2000 to securing passage of H.837, An Act Relating to Assuring a Livable Income for All Working Vermonters. The bill contained numerous provisions, including another fifty-cent increase in the minimum wage to $6.25 per hour, a 7 percentage point increase (from 25 percent to 32 percent) in the state's earned income tax credit (EITC) program (a $3.5 million appropriation), a directive to the joint fiscal office to update the basic-needs budgets (using the methodology from the summer study) for the next four years, and numerous requests for additional research. Most of the additional research was focused on finding ways to assist small businesses in becoming more viable—especially by improving the affordability of health insurance for employers.

Not surprisingly, once the livable wage issue became part of regular discussions in Montpelier, traditional opponents tried to derail our efforts using tired, knee-jerk arguments about the negative impact of mandating wage rates. Groups such as the Vermont Chamber of Commerce, Associated Industries of Vermont, the Vermont Retailers Association, the National Federation of Independent Businesses, and the Ethan Allen Institute tried their best to dissuade legislators from traveling down a "slippery slope" that would eventually lead to an $18-per-hour minimum wage. But legislators had been well prepared for these classic arguments and scare tactics (through the testimony they had heard from us in committee and by our talking-points), and ultimately our efforts served to diminish some of their influence in the statehouse on this issue.

Our legislative allies had constructed a bill that was both proworker and pro–small business—something very new for most legislators. As part of our strategy, we found small business owners willing to testify in favor of the legislation. After months of testimony, deletions, additions, and political haggling, the Senate and House passed a compromise bill that became one of the most comprehensive pieces of legislation on livable wages ever passed in the United States.[8]

To help secure its adoption, the VLWC used all the standard grassroots organizing tactics available. There were hundreds of phone calls to local legislators, press conferences, letters to the editor in local papers, radio talk shows, a full-page newspaper ad, testimony by low-wage workers, e-mail action alerts, public hearings, and high-level meetings with party leadership. Having a shared legislative focus also had the effect of building new and strengthening existing relationships among nonprofit advocates, labor unions, the faith community, and traditional activist groups.

While the battle went on in the state legislature, the VWC continued its impressive support of workers seeking livable wages and fair contracts at several worksites. As one of its longest community-support projects, the VWC assisted nursing home workers at Berlin Health & Rehabilitation Center to obtain a first contract. The year before, the VWC had worked with these workers to form the first unionized private nursing home in the state. In response, management at this multinational chain waged one of the fiercest antiunion campaigns Vermont had seen in decades, and community support was absolutely critical to securing the contract.

The year 2000 also saw internal organizational changes. To assist with administrative and fund-raising needs, the steering committee of the VWC elected to become a project of the PJC. In addition, the VLWC became more formalized by developing its own steering committee composed of representatives from member organizations. This committee approves an annual legislative agenda, decides on other statewide campaigns, and provides a forum for networking. To date, there are twenty-two member organizations, including labor unions (AFL-CIO, United Electrical Workers [UE], Vermont State Employees' Association, and Vermont–National Education Association [VT–NEA]), faith-based groups (Vermont Ecumenical Council, United Church of Christ), nonprofit advocacy groups (Vermont Low Income Council, Vermont Legal Aid, Governor's Commission on Women, Vermont Campaign to End Childhood Hunger, Vermont Coalition for Disability Rights, Vermont Coalition of Clinics for the Uninsured, to name a few), and local livable wage coalitions.

In addition to its legislative agenda, the VLWC assisted the Vermont State Employees' Association (VSEA) in its effort to win wage gains for 210 support staff at the four Vermont state colleges. Starting wages for support staff ranged from $6.25 to $9.86 per hour, with half of staff positions starting at less than $8 per hour. Many workers had been in their current positions for more than fifteen years and were still earning only $10 per hour. Heading into contract negotiations, the VLWC worked with the VSEA to design a community support campaign to pressure the board of trustees and the chancellor of the state college system. Job Gap Study researcher Doug Hoffer constructed basic-needs budgets to reflect the state colleges compensation package. This effort provided a powerful tool for union negotiators and has led to significant wage and benefit gains for these workers.

With the release of the *Livable Jobs Toolkit*, VBSR hired a trainer and conducted nine workshops around the state for business owners to learn how to use the Toolkit. The VT–NEA used the Vermont Job Gap Study in numerous contract negotiations with local school boards on behalf of K–12 school support staff. The campaign also maintained an active workshop and presentation schedule during 2000. We created a *Training for Trainers* for our Livable Wage Workshop so that a greater number could be offered at the community level. We also hired two part-time staffers to build more activism within the faith community (formally known as Vermont Faith Communities for a Just Economy). And we were pleasantly surprised by how many Democratic and Progressive Party candidates cited livable wages as a major issue in their campaign literature and during local debates.

2001 and 2002: More Community Organizing But No Legislative Wins

The VLWC's 2001 and 2002 legislative strategy was geared toward securing a cost of living adjusted (COLA) minimum wage. A bill was drafted for both the Senate and House that called for another fifty-cent increase (to $6.75 per hour) and then, beginning in 2003, an annual adjustment at the rate of inflation, not to exceed 5 percent per year. While we had the opportunity to educate legislators on the importance of a COLA minimum wage and we continued to build grassroots legislative involvement, the House defeated our attempts to bring the bill to the floor for a vote.

But the VLWC did succeed in getting seventeen additional town meeting day resolutions in support of livable wages adopted in March 2001. Building on the five that were passed in previous years, we estimate that more than 15,000 Vermonters have discussed and voted to support a livable wage resolution which calls on the governor, legislature, and business community to do more to create livable wage jobs.

The VLWC also began assisting the VT-NEA in a number of school districts where contract negotiations had stalled over pay increases for school support staff. Many of these campaigns have since won significant increases in hourly pay rates.

> It is fair to say that the research, the concepts, and the language of "livable wage" are now present at every negotiating table in Vermont where school support staff contracts are bargained (approximately 125 schools are presently unionized). The idea that an employer should pay a sufficient wage to keep their employee off of public assistance, and the facts which underpin and support this idea, have helped to transform collective bargaining for this large group of workers. (Ellen David Friedman, organizer for VT-NEA, in a letter of support for our work.)

2003 and Beyond: The Next Phase

A major change in the administration (Vermont now has a Republican governor for the first time in eleven years) and an interesting dynamic in the general assembly (the Democrats hold a 19–11 majority in the Senate while the Republicans hold a slim majority in the House) meant that securing an increase in the minimum wage seemed unlikely in 2003, especially during the recession. But to everyone's surprise, legislators and even the governor were supportive of another fifty-cent increase and were even willing to entertain the possibility of a COLA minimum wage. In fact, the governor focused one of his weekly press conferences specifically on the minimum wage and stated that he believed low-income working Vermonters deserved a raise. While it is believed that the motives behind his "enlightened" words were pure politics, it did, nonetheless, put the issue front and center as one of the major pieces of legislation that would come out of the 2003 session.

After the usual testimony, floor debate, and conference committee negotiations, the minimum wage was increased fifty cents (to $6.75/hr) in January 2004 and another twenty-five cents automatically in January 2005. Also secured was a provision to direct the Joint Fiscal Office to calculate the livable wage figures annually through 2006 (an extra two years). It would appear that the livable wage, in concept, has been so thoroughly integrated into the minds of a critical mass of public policy officials that the minimum wage is no longer the hot button issue it once was. Since it is not possible to legislate livable wages, the minimum wage is now seen as something concrete and tangible that can be done to help the lowest paid workers and have positive wage compression effects on the next tier.

With the 2003 minimum wage victory in hand, the VLWC decided to reevaluate its legislative priorities. The campaign continues to turn out important community support for K–12 support staff contract fights when needed, and released phase eight of the Job Gap Study, which delves much more deeply into 2000 census data on employment, income, and demographic characteristics of workers in Vermont.

Following up on its successful organizing efforts with the Berlin Health & Rehab workers, the VWC launched a Justice for Health Care Workers campaign statewide and lent crucial support for the nurses at the Fletcher Allen Hospital in Burlington who successfully negotiated their first contract after a bitter struggle. Additionally, they have assisted the unionizing efforts of newspaper workers at the *Brattleboro Reformer* and workers at two food coops (led by the UE). Their newest innovative strategy is a citywide organizing project to unionize all retail and restaurant workers in the city of Montpelier, thus creating a citywide wage standard. While each place of employment would have its own unique contract with its workers, by covering all of these workers at once, the payroll playing field would be leveled among service sector employers, significantly increasing the earnings of these traditionally low-wage workers, and giving these workers real power to negotiate their wages in the future. Whether they can bring this strategy to fruition remains to be seen at this stage.

Both the VLWC and the VWC are tring to promote greater discussion about the need for an alternative economic development vision for the state and organized a successful "People's Roundtable for a Fair and Healthy Economy" in March 2003 that drew 200 people.[9] In addition, Doug Hoffer made the rounds to various central labor councils to convince them that they needed to be more engaged in the broader economic development discussions and legislative efforts taking place, especially on tax subsidies to corporations.

Finally, exciting discussions have taken place within Vermont's faith community about economic justice. While the faith community has always been a helpful partner in various VLWC and VWC struggles, and for a couple years the PJC ran a Vermont Faith Communities for a Just Economy project, a bold new initiative holds open the possibility of greater and more cohesive leadership from this important moral force. Calling themselves Vermont Interfaith Action (an IAF organizing model inspired group), dozens of volunteers have conducted one-on-one sessions with parishioners to find out what social justice issues are of most interest to them. It appears that livable wages and affordable housing are at the top of the list. The plan is to collect information from these interviews and then develop a series of action steps to try to influence public policy in these areas in years to come.

Conclusion: What Has Changed in Vermont?

The ultimate goal of all our work is clear and simple: promote a variety of ways to increase the number of livable jobs in Vermont—ones that include good wages and benefits and safe work environments—so that families and communities can thrive. Along the way we are educating and mobilizing Vermonters around the need to be actively engaged in economic development discussions and decision making.

To date, livable wage efforts in Vermont have been constructed along parallel tracks—simultaneously employing an "inside" strategy and an "outside" strategy. While both strategies are grounded in Job Gap Study research, the inside strategy seeks to engage state and elected officials and the economic development community in discussion and public policy change around a progressive-minded economic justice agenda. Because power is never conceded willingly, the outside strategy employs traditional activism and grassroots organizing to create a climate and mandate for systemic change.

After seven years of research, education, public policy advocacy, and grassroots activism, Vermont has embraced livable wages as one of the standards by which to measure the state of Vermont's economy. We have helped to build a statewide consensus on a unified goal—livable wage job creation—and we continue to try many different organizing approaches to get there. Moving beyond traditional ordinance-based campaigns, we have focused on particular groups of workers to educate and mobilize—namely, K–12 and state college support staff, health care workers, municipal employees, child care workers, and state employees. The minimum wage has been raised three times and thousands of low-wage workers have received a raise—either from the wage compression effects of the minimum wage or through direct contract negotiations with their union (using Job Gap Study numbers).

In addition, we have begun to stimulate a broader discussion about an alternative economic development vision that will continue to build over the next few years. These discussions will likely include such topics as attaching conditions to the expenditure of public dollars (livable wage conditions to state contracts, worker retention policies, labor peace agreements, policy enforcement, affordable housing development, etc.) and developing new means of holding corporations accountable to the communities in which they reside and to the workers they employ. And largely through the efforts of the Vermont Workers' Center and creative new organizing drives by several unions, union leadership is being challenged to make important internal changes. While manufacturing union strength continues to erode, union density is increasing among health care, municipal, college and other employees and holds open the possibility of needed change within union culture and thus, the ability to seize new opportunities to organize workers in nontraditional sectors.

The other significant challenge, however, is to find ways to improve the wages and benefits of employees who work for locally grown small businesses. Because many of these firms may never be unionized, we need to find creative ways to help them change their assumptions about pay and benefit levels. Although such initiatives have significant limitations, publicizing model employers and their stories will be an important next step.

The Vermont experience shows how the livable wage agenda can be broadened and fully integrated into a more holistic alternative economic development agenda—an agenda that changes Vermont workers' expectations about what constitutes "just" compensation, one that builds workers' power and control over their lives, one that unionizes all those workers who can and want to be unionized, one that builds alliances between traditional activists, labor unions, faith communities and the community at large, and one that fosters transformative social power.

Notes

To learn more about current VLWC and VWC activities or to obtain copies of the Vermont Job Gap Study go to www.vtlivablewage.org or www.pjcvt.org. The VLWC can be reached at 21 Church St. Burlington, VT 05401 802–863–2345 x8, livablewage@pjcvt.org. The VWC can be reached at PO Box 883 Montpelier, VT 05601 802–229–0009, info@www.workscenter.org

1. www.leg.state.vt.us/jfo/topics.htm. This figure does not include tipped employees such as waitresses/waiters and bartenders.
2. See "A Budget-Based Definition of Poverty," *Journal of Human Resources* 28, no. 1 (winter 1993): 6.
3. Vermont Department of Employment & Training, ES202 Program, October 2002.
4.The Livable Jobs Toolkit can be downloaded free of charge at www.vbsr.org
5. The phase 7 update of these numbers revealed that this subsidy to low-wage employers increased to $173 million per year.
6. These hourly wage figures have been increased in subsequent years.
7. The Act 21 Summer Study on Livable Income can be downloaded at www.leg. state.vt.us/jfo.htm
8. To read Act 119 (formerly H.837), go to www.leg.state.vt.us/docs/2000/acts/ ACT119.htm
9. The summit was organized by a wide array of unions, the VWC and VLWC and others, with the VT SEA playing a leadership role.

8

Smart Growth for Cities

It's a *Union* Thing

Greg LeRoy

In 1996, Teamsters Local 264 in Buffalo faced a struggle unlike any it had ever seen. Dutch grocery giant Royal Ahold had acquired Tops, a regional grocery chain in the Buffalo area. Now Ahold proposed to construct a sprawling megawarehouse on the metro fringe and import a new system called "cross-docking," a hyperefficient, just-in-time grocery warehousing system from Europe.

"Cross-docking" means literally moving goods from one truck across the warehouse dock to another truck. In its most extreme version, it even bundles beer, soft drink, milk and dairy, bakery, and snack deliveries into one truck from the warehouse to the store, instead of separate product deliveries. It can harm jobs, product freshness, and consumer choice.

To counter Ahold's plans, Local 264 had to quickly analyze cross-docking's impact and then organize a coalition to counter it. Finding that the system would harm independent inner-city grocers and their customers, the union organized Buffalo churches, civil rights advocates, and the Coalition for Economic Justice/Jobs with Justice. Seeing that the megawarehouse would favor more big-box stores on the fringe, the union also organized environmentalists and land preservationists.[1]

The campaign won an agreement, a company code of conduct that blocked most of Ahold's cross-docking plans, preserved most separate product deliveries to the stores, and thereby reduced the harm to workers and communities. Local 264's coalition was a blueprint for the kinds of alliances unions are beginning to join against urban sprawl.

"Developing coalitions is *work*. You need a comprehensive campaign.

It's very time-consuming," said Local 264 President Tom Dziedzic. But "I don't know any unions that have opposition to environmental issues or church issues. Their issues were very aligned with ours." He noted that the Teamsters even coalesced with Friends of the Earth to pressure Ahold in Europe, which was "very high impact."[2]

Dziedzic notes with satisfaction that Ahold/Tops had opened a store on the East Side of Buffalo, in the heart of an underserved African American community that supported the Teamsters' fight five years ago. "That market will do well, and the prices will be competitive with other communities in the region," predicted Dziedzic.[3]

Sprawl: Bad News for Union Members

In at least ten different ways—detailed below—suburban sprawl is bad for union members. Simply put, unions are urban institutions. Urban density is good for union density. Some threats to union members are obvious, such as Wal-Mart versus United Food and Commercial Workers (UFCW), runaway shops versus manufacturing unions, and "edge city" hotels evading the Hotel Employees and Restaurant Employees union (HERE). But the damage is far more sweeping than that.

Unions risk losing their voice in the "smart growth" debate as environmentalists, transit advocates, and elected officials have so far dominated the debate. Almost one thousand ballot initiatives and smart-growth laws have been enacted since the mid-1990s, and the rate of activity is increasing. These measures will change the shape of America's metro areas, and unions may benefit from those changes. But like the "urban renewal" scandal that devastated so many neighborhoods in the 1960s, smart growth could also become a disaster for working families. Unions need to assert their self-interest while the smart-growth movement is still malleable.

What Is Sprawl?

"Sprawl" is a contested concept. Most commonly, it refers to development patterns that have low density and a lack of mixed-use projects (for example, no apartments above stores); a lack of transportation options (forcing everyone to drive to work); strict separation of residential from nonresidential property; and job growth in newer suburbs with job decline in core areas (including both the core city and older suburbs).

Those trends result in increased dependence on automobiles and longer average commuting times, deteriorating air quality, and rapid consumption of open space in outlying areas. They also cause disinvestment of central city infrastructure and services, and they strain city budgets at the core (caused by a declining tax base) and in the suburbs (caused by overly rapid growth at the edge).

The decentralization of entry-level jobs in manufacturing, wholesale, and retail means work is farther from concentrations of low-skilled, unemployed workers. Since the suburbs lack affordable housing and public transit fails to reach many suburban jobs, sprawl effectively cuts off central city residents from regional labor markets. That means greater concentrations of poverty in core areas.

The numbers are shocking. Every day, America loses 3,000 acres of productive farmland to sprawling development—the equivalent of the area of Delaware every year. And according to a recent Brookings Institution study, between 1982 and 1997, the U.S. population grew by 17 percent, but the urbanized land area increased 47 percent.[4] In areas with stagnant population growth, such as Cleveland and Rochester, the disparities are much worse. Between 1970 and 2000, urbanized land use in Detroit grew by 67 percent while population only rose 6 percent. Such growth patterns cause terrific strains on the tax base and extremely inefficient use of infrastructure.

Most Americans do not yet use the word sprawl to express their anxiety about long commutes, skyrocketing children's asthma rates, or the lack of affordable housing close to jobs, but when polled about its component parts, people today rate sprawl as their number one public concern after homeland security, even higher than crime.[5]

What Causes Sprawl?

Urban experts cite numerous factors that combine to fuel sprawl: some people's preference for large-lot/low-density housing; white flight from urban areas with minority residents; lack of regional planning or the lack of a coordinating agency with real power; cities competing for economic development instead of cooperating; "redlining," or the practice of geographic and racial discrimination against older areas by banks, other lenders, and insurance companies; crime and perceptions of crime; declining quality of central city schools; contaminated land or "brownfields" in core areas; restrictive suburban zoning that effectively excludes multiunit dwellings and mixed-use development; federal capital gains tax rules that are used to encourage people to buy ever-larger homes; the historically low price of gasoline; and large federal highway spending coupled with comparatively little funding for public transportation.

That's a daunting list, to be sure. But it means there are many solutions and therefore many ways unions can be part of those solutions. (For a primer on sprawl and the many injustices and strains it causes, see the book *American Metropolitics: The New Suburban Reality*, by Myron Orfield [Brookings, 2002]).

What Is Smart Growth?

Like "sprawl," the phrase "smart growth" is also up for grabs. The term was coined in 1997 by Maryland governor Parris Glendening as he won a law explicitly intended to curb sprawl. The Maryland law says, in essence, that people can build anywhere they like, but if they build outside designated "Priority Funding Areas" (areas that already have infrastructure or are planned to get it), the state will not subsidize it.

The main kinds of smart growth policies include:

- State land-use laws that encourage development (and redevelopment) in areas that already have infrastructure, encourage adherence to long-term planning goals, or encourage cities to cooperate through regional strategies. Twelve states have adopted some version.
- Regional tax-base sharing among cities to deter job piracy and other tax-base competition and encourage regional cooperation. A version exists in the Twin Cities metro area.
- Metropolitan or "Unigov" systems to merge counties with cities and thereby deter regional infighting, such as Indianapolis/Marion County and Nashville/Davidson County.
- New criteria for state investment funds to give preference to projects that revitalize blighted areas, promote public transit, or involve mixed-use structures. California State Treasurer Phil Angelides is actively pushing such preferences through various funds in that state.
- Open-space preservation, including bond referenda to pay for the public purchase of open space (dozens have been passed by voters since the mid-1990s), incentives to encourage private donations of land, and state land preservation programs.
- "Urban growth boundaries" or "greenbelts" around metro areas to set geographic limits on new development and encourage more intensive use of core areas and suburbs inside; Portland and other Oregon cities have long had them, under a state law.

More local kinds of smart growth actions include:

- "In-fill" development projects on vacant or underutilized parcels of land in areas that already have infrastructure. Think urban *Rogaine*.

- Reclamation and reuse of "brownfields," or contaminated land sites left behind by previous industrial users.
- Affordable housing programs in the suburbs so that lower-income workers can have greater access to jobs. Montgomery County, Maryland, has an exemplary program that requires home developers to build 12 percent to 15 percent of their units for low- and moderate-income renters; in exchange, they receive a density increase. The system has resulted in a stable, mixed-income community.
- "Transit-oriented development" (TOD), in which cities use subway and commuter rail stations as hubs for mixed-use developments within a half-mile radius, including retail, housing, and day care. TOD makes it possible for residents to walk (or connect by a short bus ride) to their commute in the morning and run errands on foot on their way home in the evening.

Chicago Fed: Building Leadership Consensus

Retired Chicago Federation of Labor (CFL) president Don Turner is passionate about sprawl and its antiunion impact. "This is *the* urban issue for the next twenty years," he said. "Either labor gets involved in how smart growth unfolds, or it happens *to* us, and we all know what that means."[6]

Based on his beliefs, Turner, in his last term as CFL president, agreed to serve on the board of Chicago Metropolis 2020, a bipartisan business-civic association promoting smart growth. But some members of Turner's executive board did not initially see labor's self-interest. To help build consensus among his leadership, Turner prevailed upon 2020 to have a curriculum and conference developed on how Chicago-area unions are affected by sprawl and how smart growth could benefit them.

The resulting curriculum, "Smart Growth, Good Jobs," was created by Good Jobs First and delivered in a day-long session to 107 local union leaders in April 2000. Shortly after the conference, the CFL executive board voted unanimously to authorize Turner to represent labor's interests in smart growth. "Our leadership understands now that smart growth could be a very good thing for labor," Turner said. "The building trades, the public employees, transit, health care, hotel and restaurant—they get it."[7]

Spreading the word, Turner's CFL, along with the Central Labor Councils (CLCs) in Cleveland and Contra Costa County, submitted a resolution that was passed by the national AFL-CIO convention in December 2001. The resolution condemns the many ways in which sprawl harms working families and urges labor leaders to weigh in on the smart growth debate.

The Many Ways Sprawl Harms Unions

In at least nine economic sectors—each one affecting specific unions—and in political geography, sprawl is antilabor.

Grocery Retailing

High-profile campaigns against Wal-Mart and other "big box" retailers are a strong example of the potential for coalition work between unions and smart-growth advocates. These retailers threaten rural lands and small merchants. Typically accessible only by auto, they increase congestion and pirate sales from stores that are accessible by public transit, reducing shopping opportunities for people without cars.

Labor activists usually oppose such retailers because they undermine unionized jobs. Most major grocery chains are at least partly unionized, making food retailing a bright spot in the notoriously low-wage retail sector. Among grocery workers, unionized workers (about one in four) earn 28 percent more, and usually much better benefits.[8] Most of these unionized jobs are in urban chains that are now threatened by the big-box giants that penetrate metro areas from the exurbs first.

It is not just Wal-Mart's lower wages and benefits that provoke labor's opposition. It is the company's aggressive antiunionism. In February 2000, ten Wal-Mart meat cutters in Texas voted to join the UFCW. Two weeks after the National Labor Relations Board (NLRB) certified the election, Wal-Mart announced it was closing the meat departments in 180 of its stores and switching to outsourced, prepackaged meats. (For more, go to www.walmartwatch.com and www.walmartyrs.com.)

Wholesale/Warehousing

While it has only a third as many jobs as retailing, wholesaling is better organized. As explained in the Teamster story, the new threat to jobs and open lands is "cross-docking." Cross-docking favors suburban stores (which are able to purchase large shipments with the lowest shipping costs) at the expense of inner-city stores and their shoppers (who get higher shipping costs when the customer base of the existing warehouse system is "creamed").

Transit

When most of a region's growth occurs at the fringe, transit jobs are undermined because commuters no longer have a choice: They must use a car.

Transit ridership declines, forcing cities to cut service, defer maintenance and improvements, reduce crew sizes, and consider privatization.

Besides direct harm to transit workers, sprawl-induced service cutbacks hurt other low-wage workers. For example, after the Chicago Transit Authority eliminated late-night bus service, unionized hospital workers getting off second shift after midnight found themselves waiting until 4 or 5 a.m. for a bus home. In a few cities, transit unions have joined forces with community groups, such as Chicago's Campaign for Better Transit, cofounded by two locals of the Amalgamated Transit Union.

Education and Other Public Services

Schools usually get the largest share of local property tax revenues. When core communities are disinvested and their tax bases are eroded, schools suffer in many ways: Class sizes grow; amenities are eliminated; teacher salaries lag regional averages (making it hard to attract talented teachers); and capital improvements and maintenance are deferred.

Families that are able to leave (disproportionately white) move to higher-tax-base suburbs with healthier schools. The loss of such families makes the student body less diverse. It also harms home values, which in turn means either less property tax revenue or higher tax *rates* for families that stay. The resulting degradation of schools leaves core-area graduates less attractive to employers and becomes one more "push" for companies to migrate outward.

For teachers, the tax-base erosion caused by sprawl means lower pay, tougher working conditions, and increasing pressure for privatization schemes such as vouchers that undermine public education.

The tax-base issue affects other local public employees, too. A declining tax base creates a systemic web of problems for urban governments: It lowers the municipal credit rating and raises borrowing costs. It also forces city councils to raise tax rates, which can become one more "push" driving businesses and homeowners away, further eroding revenues.

Those problems undermine every kind of public job: police, fire, sanitation, maintenance, human services, and parks and recreation. Agencies are forced to reduce services and defer maintenance. When emergency-response times are long, when library hours are cut, when parks are ill-kempt, or when potholes aren't repaired, citizens lose faith in their public institutions. That encourages some politicians to propose antiunion quick fixes, such as privatization.

Health Care

Inner-city hospitals are the most likely to close; they are also the most likely to have been unionized. Sprawl causes a hyperconcentration of poverty in core areas, and that means a high share of families lacking insurance coverage. In turn, that squeezes hospitals financially because Medicaid reimbursement rates have been cut. On top of that, managed care shortens hospital stays, which creates overcapacity in some hospitals. In the ensuing shakeout, the financially weakest facilities forced to close have been mostly in core areas. Combined with a trend toward more outsourcing of support services, the effect has been to drive more health care dollars—and good jobs—away from urban cores. Of course, hospital closures also mean the loss of access to health care, yet another push for families who can to leave the neighborhood.

Hospitality

Hotels and restaurants are home to some of the nation's fastest-growing job titles, but they are notoriously low-wage except when unionized, which is only in some urban cores, airport areas, gaming centers, and amusement parks. With the proliferation of sprawling "edge cities," including hotel and convention centers, unionization rates, wages, and benefits in the hospitality sector have suffered. For example, Figure 8.1 (p. 136) shows the only union hotels in the metro-Chicago area are in the older urban communities in and close to Chicago. HERE's strategy for organizing new hotels located in core areas, such as those next to convention centers, has been a smart success for the union, but the big picture is that hospitality employment is thinning out, making it harder to organize.

Building Services and Operations

The cleaning jobs and physical maintenance and operations work in office buildings are unionized in many urban cores. However, the growth of "edge cities" and suburban office parks has led to the geographic dispersion of office space. That means these jobs are less accessible to inner-city residents who need them most and they are less likely to be unionized. Service Employees International Union's (SEIU) Justice for Janitors campaign has made major strides in rebuilding metro density rates by winning new contracts in some suburban markets, but the dispersion of office space is a broadly anti-union trend.

Manufacturing

Manufacturers migrate to suburbs and exurbs for the same "push" reasons as other businesses (such as crime, taxes, and services), and for reasons specific to manufacturing, such as new production processes that require "large footprint" single-story plants, lack of available urban space due to development or contamination, and a desire to hire younger or first-generation factory workers with lower health care and pension costs. Manufacturers also often seek to avoid unions. As Figure 8.2 shows (p. 137), in Chicago, for example, union density in manufacturing declined as work moved from older urban areas of Cook and Will counties to the exurbs.

Besides migrations within regions, some manufacturing sectors are undergoing massive geographic realignments, such as the new auto belt in rural Kentucky, Tennessee, southern Indiana and Ohio, Alabama, and the Carolinas, with more than 300 plants built since the mid-1980s. Most of these factories are foreign owned, and very few are unionized. They are also overwhelmingly located in areas not served by public transit. Many have been found to have workforces in which people of color are underrepresented, and a few foreign-owned auto assembly "transplants" have been charged with discriminatory employment practices, such as designating recruitment territories that exclude urban areas with minority populations.[9]

To be sure, manufacturing unions have also lost members because of job flight offshore and advances in automation. But unions should seek smart-growth support for industrial retention strategies, such as early warning systems, planned manufacturing districts (to shield factories from displacement due to gentrification), employee ownership (especially attractive for aging family-company owners), and "cluster" or "sectoral" strategies designed to build and reinforce loyalty between a group of companies and community institutions. A cluster strategy promotes regional linkages by helping all firms in a given sector get better at noncompetitive activities such as training, quality control, or export promotion. Table 8.1 (p. 139) summarizes the links between unions in specific industries and sprawl.

Working Families Legislative Concerns

Finally, the way sprawl affects politics is also harmful to union members. After presenting the regional data on the nine economic sectors, the Chicago curriculum finished its argument by presenting maps of the voting records of the region's state representatives, state senators, and members of the U.S. Congress. We shaded the maps based on the AFL-CIO's nonpartisan COPE ratings. These percentages measure the portion of times that each member voted the way advocated by labor on specific key legislative issues.

The maps are striking. As Figure 8.3 illustrates (p. 138), legislators representing Chicago, its mature inner-ring suburbs, and its blue-collar south and southwest suburbs voted far more favorably for working families (reflected in a higher union COPE percentage) than those in outer-ring suburbs and the

Figure 8.1   **Hotels and Hotel Jobs in the Chicago Region**

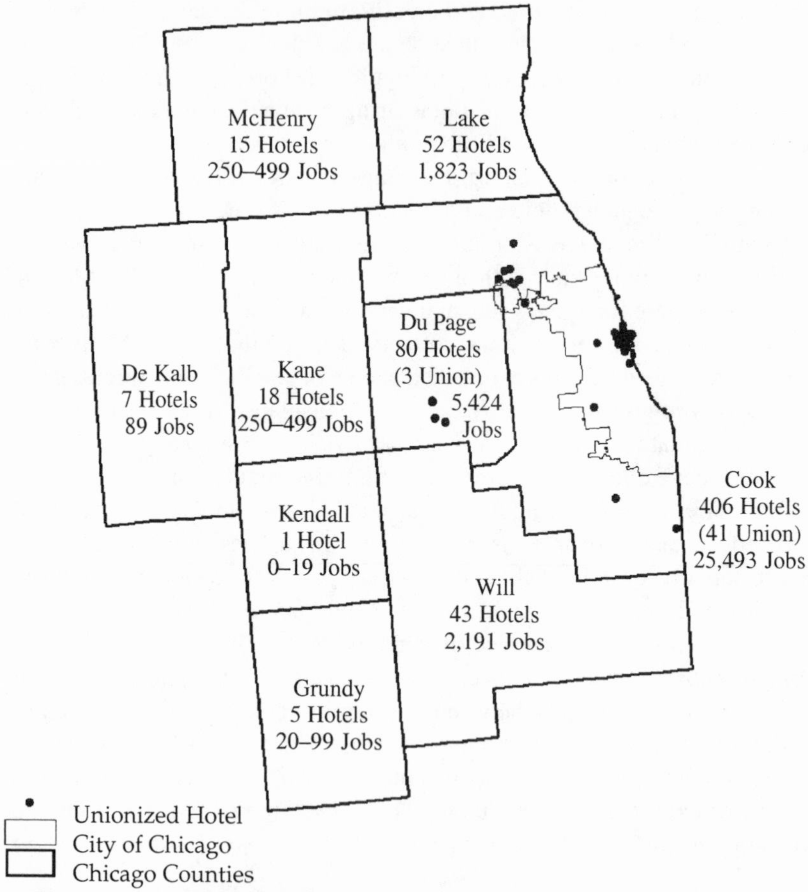

McHenry
15 Hotels
250–499 Jobs

Lake
52 Hotels
1,823 Jobs

De Kalb
7 Hotels
89 Jobs

Kane
18 Hotels
250–499 Jobs

Du Page
80 Hotels
(3 Union)
• 5,424
•• Jobs

Kendall
1 Hotel
0–19 Jobs

Will
43 Hotels
2,191 Jobs

Grundy
5 Hotels
20–99 Jobs

Cook
406 Hotels
(41 Union)
25,493 Jobs

• Unionized Hotel
City of Chicago
Chicago Counties
44 Unionized Hotels in Region
(Job ranges given where data are suppressed.)

north and northwest; high-tech DuPage County was especially adverse. The same pattern would be apparent, no doubt, in almost every urban region of the United States.

The growing political power of the suburbs has been fueled by sprawl. With population decline or stagnation in core areas and population growth in the outer-ring suburbs, sprawl areas gained the most new political power in the legislative redistricting after the 1990 census, and again after the 2000 census. National analyses of the 1994 election (when so many legislative bodies changed their political majorities) point to "swing" districts mostly located on urban fringes.

Figure 8.2   **Union Density in Manufacturing by County**

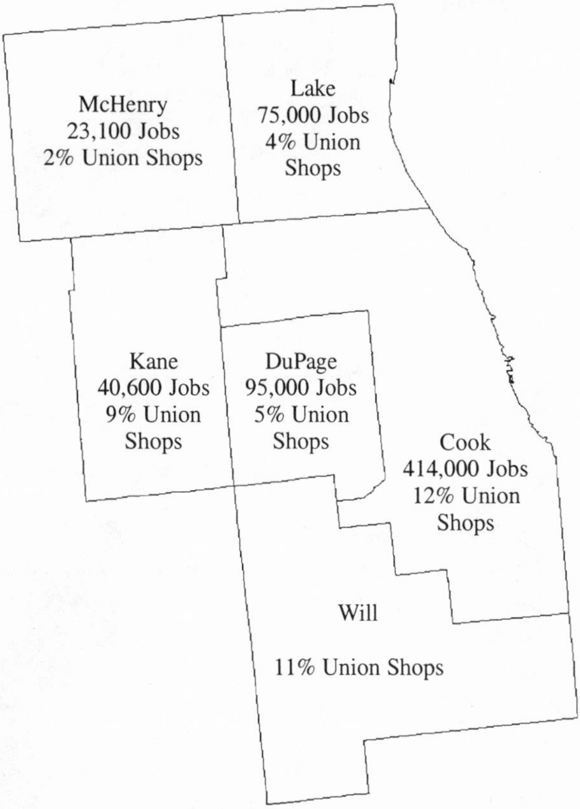

McHenry
23,100 Jobs
2% Union Shops

Lake
75,000 Jobs
4% Union
Shops

Kane
40,600 Jobs
9% Union
Shops

DuPage
95,000 Jobs
5% Union
Shops

Cook
414,000 Jobs
12% Union
Shops

Will

11% Union Shops

Source: International Association of Machinists Analysis.

The Building Trades Exception, and an Exceptional
Trades Council

One group of unions has occasionally self-identified against smart growth: the building trades. To be blunt, many members of the trades suspect that smart growth is "no growth" in sheep's clothing. In some places, they have actively supported sprawling highway construction or even opposed smart-growth ballot initiatives.

While this is a complex issue, it is important to remember that the trades have close ties to developers and contractors, and the building industry is rarely presented any persuasive arguments for smart growth. The least-unionized seg-ment of the industry, single-family construction, has also been the most politi-

Figure 8.3 **AFL-CIO Working Families COPE Ratings of Illinois State Senators**

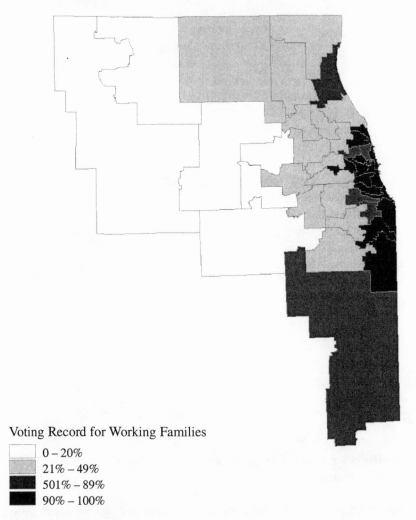

Voting Record for Working Families

☐	0 – 20%
▨	21% – 49%
■	501% – 89%
■	90% – 100%

cally aggressive against smart growth through the National Association of Home Builders. At the other end of the spectrum, a small but growing number of developers has gained expertise at high-quality, mixed-use construction, doing urban infill and transit-accessible projects. One real estate investment trust (REIT) that specializes in upscale apartments, Post Properties, even claims smart growth as its market niche. Some architects and planners use the term "new urbanism" to describe projects that embrace "traditional neighborhood design" elements such as narrower residential streets, front porches set close

Table 8.1

How Sprawl Harms Union Members

Types of jobs	How sprawl harms them	Unions usually affected
Grocery retailing	Wal-Mart and some other big-box retailers pay less and are antiunion, taking market share from unionized grocers	UFCW, Teamsters
Grocery warehousing	"Cross-docking," a hyperefficient warehousing system, eliminates delivery jobs, harms inner-city food stores	UFCW, Teamsters
Transit	Job growth off the transit grid reduces ridership, costs jobs, creates pressure for concessions and privatization	ATU, UTU, TWU, Teamsters, SEIU, AFSCME, TCU
Teachers and school support jobs	Tax-base erosion caused by sprawl means larger classes, deferred maintenance, lower salaries, pressure for concessions and vouchers	NEA, AFT, AFSCME, SEIU, CWA
City and county employees	Tax-base erosion means service cutbacks, deferred maintenance of infrastructure, pressure for concessions and privatization	AFSCME, SEIU, CWA, Building Trades, Teamsters
Health care	Hyperconcentration of uninsured families at the core contributes to hospital closures, and they are more likely unionized	SEIU, AFSCME, AFT, ANA, Teamsters, CNA
Hotel and restaurant	"Edge cities" pull hospitality dollars away from core, driving wages and benefits down	HERE
Building services	"Edge cities" and suburban office parks disperse janitorial and maintenance work away from affordable housing, unions	SEIU, Operating Engineers, Boilermakers
Manufacturing	Corporate relocations to exurban or even rural sites, seeking fewer unions and lower wages, reduce job opportunities for city residents	Auto Workers, Steelworkers, PACE, Machinists, UNITE, IBEW, Teamsters, BCT, Carpenters, GCIU, IUE/CWA

enough to the curb to invite neighborly interaction, and other pedestrian-friendly elements. A study comparing home resale values in traditional developments versus "new urbanist" developments found that those in the new urbanist areas sold for $20,000 more, an 11 percent premium.[10] Developers are now the second-largest occupational group in the Congress for the New Urbanism.

But there is precious little data about *job creation* resulting from policies such as reclaiming brownfields, repairing infrastructure, creating higher-density mixed-use projects, or expanding mass transit.[11] As a result, most of the building industry continues to lobby for what it knows best—sprawling-style development—and the trades often follow suit. Good Jobs First began to fill this gap with a study released in late 2003. We found that more compact building styles (i.e., townhomes versus single-family homes) and "fix it first" road-building budgets (i.e., lane rehabilitation versus cutting new freeways) create more jobs per dollar spent. We also found that metro areas with growth-management policies have more construction jobs (mostly due to rehab work) and higher rates of construction union density.[12]

In a few areas, building trades councils have joined forces with smart-growth advocates. The Contra Costa County Building Trades Council in northern California made a deliberate decision in 1992 to reach out to environmentalists, such as the Sierra Club, the Greenbelt Alliance, and Citizens for a Better Environment. The effort began with a small private meeting at which members of each group shared their stereotypes of each other. To their amazement, they discovered many shared concerns.

Building on that ice-breaking meeting, the county's labor-environment alliance has worked together on several campaigns and won three ballot initiatives, including two that created an urban limit line to preserve a third of the county as open space.

Council CEO John Feere, whose office features an Alaskan bear he killed with an arrow and ate, sees a clear relationship between different kinds of development and union self-interests. He points out that the market consists of commercial work (including multifamily), industrial, and single-family (most common on the fringes). By far the worst story is single-family, with shoddy construction, cash pay, piecework, and no pensions.

"It's not just reaching out to environmentalists," Feere said. "You have to reach out to minorities, women, the disadvantaged. You can't be isolated and be successful. They have this stereotype of the cigar-chomping, Lincoln Town Car guy. You have to explain your apprenticeship programs and what people need to survive. We want to recruit more diverse members. People are very sympathetic once you explain what the unions are about. But if you don't talk to them, they'll never know about you."[13]

As a mindful coalition partner, Feere said that his council now looks at the whole story when a new project is proposed. "Just because a project is going to be built union, but if it is bad for the infrastructure, bad for the schools, bad for the air, then just offering us tokenism, no, we won't just roll over and support it," he said. "To some degree, everyone is an environmentalist. A project has to benefit the community."[14]

The county's Central Labor Council president, John Dalrymple, sees many positive side effects of the labor-environmental work on growth. The Sierra Club is supporting a local living wage campaign. A labor-community coalition issued a statement explicitly tying the growth boundary to social equity. The CLC and Trades Council cosponsored an all-day leadership training on growth, and a town meeting in high-growth Antioch enabled rank-and-file union members to become experts able to debate growth policies publicly. "There was a lot of work to get where we are, but things have really matured," he concludes.

It's Not No Growth—It's *What Kind* of Growth

Opponents sometimes claim that smart growth is actually a Trojan horse for no growth. But supporters respond that the population is growing, the economy is expanding, and smart growth isn't going to stop those trends. The real argument is whether growth should continue the same way it has: Should our consumption of land continue to outpace population growth by three times? Or eleven times as it has in the Detroit area?

Representative Earl Blumenauer (D-OR) founded the Livable Communities Task Force in the U.S. House of Representatives in 1996. He has an active relationship with organized labor, and believes that smart-growth opponents present "false choices" to working families.

Livable communities using smart-growth policies give families more housing and commuting choices, with more jobs likely to be union, according to Blumenauer, citing Portland's $1 billion light rail link to the airport built with all-union labor. More Portland students walk to school than in perhaps any other major city, he says, and Portland has only one Wal-Mart because neighborhood-scale retailers thrive.

Blumenauer points out that Portland's housing prices, often cited by smart-growth critics, are actually lower than other large West Coast metro areas. And families with one less car can afford 25 percent more housing, he estimates, which translates into more construction work.

Blumenauer sees smart growth as "a different kind of environmentalism" that promises to unite union members with environmentalists, unlike divisive past issues such as the spotted owl or salmon concerns. Smart growth "allows people to pick their shade of green," he says. "A blue-green alliance can build new bridges."[15]

Housing: A Critical Issue Unions Are Addressing

By many measures, the supply of affordable housing in America is tight and getting tighter. And because many high-growth suburbs use restrictive zoning rules to keep out rental housing, the affordable housing that remains is increasingly distant from new jobs. Since 1965, the AFL-CIO Housing Investment Trust (HIT) has pooled the pension funds of building trades unions to build housing, including tens of thousands of multifamily units, many of them with below-market rents made possible by the federal low-income housing tax credit program and other public subsidies. HIT-financed projects are built 100 percent union. HIT now has more than 409 participating funds and manages more than $2.6 billion in investments. It recently announced a new partnership to build 5,000 to 7,000 new rental units, with 30 percent targeted to low- and moderate-income families. HIT, along with a growing number of other investors, continues to promote promising new opportunities in urban areas that have been overlooked. In-fill projects—building on vacant or underutilized land that already has infrastructure—can help revitalize communities, promote other reinvestment, and restore the tax base.

"There is a critical shortage of housing that is affordable to working families in urban areas across America," stated Steve Coyle, CEO of HIT. "The development of in-fill housing is key to alleviating this shortage and creating livable communities where Americans work. Our experience has also shown that well-conceived in-fill projects are sound investments. Over the last decade, the trust has invested over $1 billion in in-fill development projects, 90 percent of which included units affordable to low- and moderate-income persons."[16]

Labor's Environmental Allies

As detailed in the stories above from New York and California, unions have occasionally found environmental allies. The 740,000-member Sierra Club stands out for its deliberate efforts to find common ground with labor. Sierra Club president Carl Pope campaigned with AFL-CIO president John Sweeney during the 2000 elections, and many of the club's chapters have positive histories with unions and labor federations.

Tim Frank is the founding chair of the Sierra Club's Challenge to Sprawl. He is explicitly seeking out labor ties for his state chapters. "We consider unions to be absolutely critical to the smart growth movement," says Frank. "They want a healthy tax base for schools and public services, they want more transit, they want more affordable housing, they want to rebuild the cities, and so do we. Bringing America's cities back to life is the only way to take the pressure off of farmland and forests."[17]

On the national level, the club filed an amicus brief with the U.S. District Court for the District of Columbia in defense of Project Labor Agreements (PLAs) after they were attacked by the Bush administration. "Project Labor Agreements promote workforce development, save taxpayer dollars, and preserve skills that are critical to higher-density construction," says Frank. "Besides, it's our experience that a polluting contractor is more likely to be anti-union, too."[18]

How Smart Growth Can Be Union Made

Now for the raw political calculus. For several reasons detailed below, unions have a unique opportunity to greatly strengthen the smart-growth movement. In exchange for their support, unions should be able to shape the new policies to secure their members' jobs and promote future organizing. But time is of the essence. If labor stays on the outside, all bets are off.

First, unions can bring woefully underrepresented constituencies to a smart-growth movement that is not very diverse. Most antisprawl coalitions are dominated by white, college-educated, suburban environmentalists, along with assorted regional planners, transit advocates, architectural and farmland preservationists, civic associations, public interest litigators, and politicians. Indeed, calling it a smart-growth "movement" is a stretch. These are usually loose networks composed of groups that work on many other issues and may view each other competitively. Anyone seen a march against sprawl yet?

It's a weakness of these coalitions that they have failed to organize many people of color or pink- and blue-collar allies. It is also labor's strength: Unions can bring much-needed diversity to smart-growth alliances. And given labor's new organizing priorities—focusing on women, people of color, immigrants, and younger workers, that is, the people who need unions the most—this strength will only grow over time.

Second, unions are focused on urban-justice issues, which are also woefully underrepresented in the smart-growth debate. That is, suburban environmentalists are especially concerned about preserving open space by containing growth at the fringe. But union members are more concerned about fair and affordable housing, immigrant rights, transit services, living wages, access to health care, saving the schools, rebuilding infrastructure, and restoring decent public services.

As labor actively sheds its past reputation for being aloof, unions and central labor councils are coalescing on these issues as never before, encouraged by the AFL-CIO's Union Cities program. It is all about organizing: By helping solve problems of greatest concern to their target populations, unions gain community allies who are critical to winning new-member campaigns.

A few urban-justice groups have begun to engage the smart-growth debate, including some fair housing and low-income housing advocates, and some church-based efforts like community groups affiliated with the Gamaliel Foundation. But most community organizations working on issues such as predatory lending and enforcement of the Community Reinvestment Act against redlining don't identify their work as having regional benefits, even though they should—it is a legacy of the Saul Alinsky "turf" style of organizing.

The fact that unions can bring new constituencies and urban-justice strength to the smart-growth movement is no small matter. For if the movement against sprawl remains a predominantly white suburban formation dealing with growth limits and open spaces, it is doomed to failure—it will not save the cities and take the pressure off the suburban fringes. Because of their strengths, unions can make smart growth a compelling issue to a far broader audience. And because unions represent people who work and live all over their metro areas, they do not have the "turf" definitions that constrain their identities, unlike many community groups. Indeed, if you mesh the urban-reinvestment agenda of smart growth with labor's organizing priorities, the fight against sprawl looks like a coalition blueprint for Union Cities.

Third, unions understand organizing and mobilization. Like other issues dominated by college-educated whites, the sprawl debate sometimes suffers from the "paralysis of analysis." But unions make things happen: They take on strikes, they build up to organizing-election dates, they break ground on construction projects, and they mobilize to elect pro–working family politicians. This "can do" culture will inspire others to make decisions and move.

Finally, union members stand *for* specific things. No movement can win big if it is only *against* something and lacks positive alternatives. In so many things they do—both in campaigns and in programs—unions defend tangible self-interests that serve the smart-growth cause. When the UFCW helps fight a new Wal-Mart, when the Amalgamated Transit Union (ATU) pushes for transit improvements, when HIT builds a new affordable apartment complex, when the American Federation of Teachers and the National Education Association fight for fair school-funding formulas, when HERE helps promote downtown hospitality, when an industrial union helps save a city factory—those are contributions that deserve recognition as smart growth.

Indeed, a 2003 survey of labor federation leaders (mostly central labor council presidents), found that they all see problems with sprawling development and have all lobbied for urban reinvestment policies that are central to smart growth. For example, 88 percent have lobbied for more funding to repair and rehabilitate existing schools, 66 percent have lobbied to preserve or expand mass transit operating budgets, 82 percent have helped fight a "big box" retail project such as a Wal-Mart, and 66 percent have lobbied to increase funding for the rebuilding of aging infrastructure.[19]

But it's much more than pouring old wine into new bottles. Unions need to learn the issues, consciously analyze their regional situations and potential allies, and start to deliberately weigh in, with a long-term agenda of influencing smart-growth policies.

Unions must engage in coalitions to shape those policies, to make sure that good jobs are integral to the outcomes. Together, we can win Union Cities with quality, accessible health care, a choice for people in how to get to work and reasonable commuting times, a mix of affordable housing, an adequate tax base for good schools and public services free from the threat of privatization, healthy central business districts supporting hospitality and office building work, neighborhood retailers free from the siege of big-box invasions, revitalized neighborhoods that benefit rather than displace residents, and reclaimed brownfields making efficient use of existing infrastructure.

That is why it is time for us to make smart growth a *union* thing!

Notes

1. Gordon McClelland, *Royal Ahold and Cross-Docking: A Study of the True Cost of Supermarket Industry Restructuring*, (Ithaca, NY: Cornell University, School of Industrial and Labor Relations, 1995.)

2. Tom Dziedzic, interview, summer 2001.

3. Ibid.

4. William Fulton, Rolf Pendall, Mai Nguyen, and Alicia Harrison, *Who Sprawls Most? How Growth Patterns Differ Across the U.S.* (Washington, DC: Brookings Institution, 2001.)

5. "Sprawl Now Tops Crime as Top Concern," Pew Center for Civic Journalism, February 15, 2000.

6. Don Turner, interview, summer 2001.

7. Ibid.

8. Robert C. Johansson, Jay S. Coggins, and Ben H. Senauer, "Union Density Effects in the Supermarket Industry," working paper 99–05, Retail Food Industry Center, University of Minnesota, August 1999. The period studied was 1984 to 1993.

9. For example, see summaries of research by University of Michigan professors Robert Cole and Donald Deskins in "Japanese Rapped on Black Jobs: Transplant Hiring Called Below Par," *Automotive News*, August 29, 1988.

10. Mark J. Eppli and Charles C. Tu, *Valuing the New Urbanism: The Impact of the New Urbanism on Prices of Single-Family Homes* (Washington, DC: Urban Land Institute, 1999.)

11. A Good Jobs First study due out in late 2003 will seek to address the issue of how smart growth policies affect construction jobs.\

12. Philip Mattera with Greg LeRoy, *The Jobs Are Back in Town* (Washington, DC: Good Jobs First, 2003).

13. John Feere, interview, summer 2001.

14. Ibid.

15. Earl Blumenauer, interview, summer 2001.

16. Steve Coyle, interview, summer 2001.

17. Tim Frank, interview, summer 2001.

18. Ibid.

19. Greg LeRoy, *Labor Leaders as Smart Growth Advocates* (Washington, DC: Good Jobs First, 2003).

Web Sites

AFL-CIO Housing Investment Trust (www.aflcio-hit.com): union pension assets building affordable housing nationwide

American Farmland Trust (www.farmland.org): for the preservation of farms, rural culture, and wildlife habitats

Chicago Metropolis 2020 (www.chicagometropolis2020.org): a business-civic association organizing for transit choice and more affordable housing

Congress for the New Urbanism (www.cnu.org): architects, developers, and planners promoting the restoration of cities and towns

Funders' Network for Smart Growth and Livable Communities (www. fundersnetwork. org): foundations that support work against sprawl

Gamaliel Foundation (www.gamaliel.org): the nation's second-largest community organizing network; builds church-based urban-suburban coalitions against sprawl

Good Jobs First (www.goodjobsfirst.org): see especially "Talking to Union Leaders About Smart Growth" (written for people new to labor) and "Another Way Sprawl Happens"

National Neighborhood Coalition (www.neighborhoodcoalition.org/smart %20growth. htm): focused on urban justice; practical resources for low-income neighborhoods and communities of color

National Trust for Historic Preservation (www.nationaltrust.org): for protecting Main Street and downtowns against big-box retail

Sierra Club's Challenge to Sprawl (www.sierraclub.org/sprawl): an environmental group that understands mobilization

Smart Growth America (www.smartgrowthamerica.org): a national advocacy network of diverse groups

Sprawl Resource Guide (www.plannersweb.com/sprawl/sprawl11.html): a primer on key sprawl issues and pointers to other useful Web sites

Sprawl Watch Clearinghouse (www.sprawlwatch.org): the leading information center on smart-growth research and legislative developments

Surface Transportation Policy Project (www.transact.org): promoting transit choice through a more balanced transportation policy

9

Building Political Action Coalitions in Connecticut

Louise Simmons

During the past twenty-five years, labor and community groups in Connecticut have built a solid tradition of partnership in politics and struggles for social justice. Although the forms and ease with which the respective parties work together vary, these partnerships have produced many strong relationships and accomplished much. Yet, today's tough political climate—with ever deepening social problems, a public fiscal crisis, and renewed assaults on workers, the poor, and the programs that serve them—compels the state's progressive forces to build on this legacy to expand and deepen collaboration and joint strategy development. Reviewing how past and current coalitions have operated offers some indications as to just how complex this work of forging and maintaining relationships really is: there are enormous obstacles, but still great potential.

LEAP: Establishing the Coalition Tradition

One of the longest-lasting and most successful political coalitions of labor and community groups in the United States has been the Legislative Education Action Program (LEAP) in Connecticut. Over its twenty years of existence LEAP helped create the local environment that has been so conducive to forming durable coalitions. LEAP's history offers useful insights into some of the issues faced by coalitions that bring labor and other forces together.

LEAP formed in Connecticut during the early 1980s as the Reagan era dawned and conservative political action committees were targeting progressive state legislators. Unions and citizen action groups decided it was time to put together a coalition that would unite forces behind progressive candidates, defend those in office, and back initiatives in the legislature. LEAP member organizations would participate in candidate screening by jointly developing questionnaires, having a committee interview candidates, and then determining whether or not to endorse candidates. Endorsements sometimes carried monetary contributions, but most important often meant volunteers and trained campaign staff. LEAP staff might coordinate voter identification and voter turn-out operations on election day. LEAP also convened issue-oriented work groups to lobby the legislature and helped coalesce legislators during the legislative sessions to pass priority legislation.

Over its two decades of work, LEAP's accomplishments were impressive. The candidates it backed by and large were elected. One report estimated that more than 80 percent of LEAP-endorsed candidates for the state legislature won office (Shorey 1998). It also was instrumental in shaping policy at the legislature. LEAP helped convene movements to enact a state income tax, to defeat "English only" legislation, and to advocate corporate responsibility legislation. It was involved in movements to defend reproductive rights, patients' rights under managed care, and gay rights, and it marshaled support for progressive candidates for higher offices in Connecticut. Close to thirty different organizations—unions, women's organizations, human service advocates, citizen action groups, civil rights groups, and others participated (Reynolds 1997, 1998, 1999; Simmons 1994, 1998; Caplan and Rapoport 1993; Brecher and Costello 1990).

LEAP was the prototype for several other similar coalitions in other New England states: the Dirigo Alliance in Maine, the Commonwealth Coalition in Massachusetts, and others in the northeast, and even served as an example for coalitions in the midwest and southwest such as Missouri Pro-Vote. Ironically, having inspired many continuing political coalitions around the country, LEAP has run its course. By the beginning of the twenty-first century, LEAP decided to reexamine its mission and modus operandi. Ultimately it disbanded, but its legacy is evident in the current array of coalitions and social justice organizations in Connecticut.

One of LEAP's most lasting accomplishments, through its work and that of its affiliates, has been the creation of an important space in the public policy agenda of Connecticut into which activists can assert progressive and social justice issues. Depending upon the particular configuration of legislative forces, policy issues have been raised and victories have been won in the legislative arena. Thanks to LEAP, issues such as the fairness of the state's tax structure, campaign finance reform, and corporate accountability are squarely on the public agenda. The groups that were part of LEAP can generally amass wider support for their issues than if they had to struggle on their own by drawing on the enduring relationships that developed within the coalition. Moreover, for activist unions, now there are public officials, especially several whose early political careers were facilitated by the LEAP network, who routinely get involved in labor issues. They are willing to sponsor prolabor legislation, support strikes and organizing drives, or even become involved in civil disobedience activity with unions on picket lines or at demonstrations. Several union activists now serve in the legislature and take leadership on progressive issues: Representative Chris Donovan is an organizer for the Congress of Community Colleges, which is affiliated with the Service Employees International Union (SEIU), and is a past cochairperson of the legislature's Labor Committee. Another SEIU organizer for a public employee local has also been elected from West Hartford, Representative David McCluskey. Other SEIU members are considering candidacies. Senator Tom Colapietro and Representative Zeke Zalaski are United Auto Workers (UAW) members who have been active in their union's political action program. The most recently elected union member in the legislature is Peter Tercyak, a rank-and-file leader of the New England Health Care Employees, District 1199-SEIU.

The LEAP coalition also developed methods of screening and endorsing candidates with respect to positions on progressive issues that are now common for many groups, including some who were not routinely involved in political matters. The former LEAP-affiliated unions and other organizations continue to assert their priorities within the electoral and legislative arenas and often still draw support from each other on their key issues such as tax structures, privatization, health care, education, community college issues, incentives for economic development, and many more. While some of the organizations would be involved in these activities whether or not they had ever been part of LEAP, other groups learned the "whys and hows" through this coalition.

The Challenges LEAP Encountered

LEAP's success generated a complex set of problems. One issue reflects the problem experienced in a variety of progressive organizations in which whites constitute the majority of participants. Many activists from the organizations in LEAP became so accustomed to working together, and such a tight-knit group developed, that it was sometimes difficult for emerging political activists from communities of color to find a comfort level in joining the coalition (Reynolds 1999). Participation by activists from the African American and

Puerto Rican/Latino communities was sporadic. They often bypassed LEAP and took their issues directly into Democratic Party politics. Moreover, LEAP focused more on statewide issues and brought together groups that operate on a statewide basis. Much political activism within communities of color finds expression at the local or municipal level and also has significant involvement of leaders from the faith community. Municipal politics was not a consistent focus of LEAP, nor were partnerships with the faith community.

Although the issue of inconsistent participation by people of color received considerable attention from LEAP's leadership who launched several initiatives to address the problem, it remained a major shortcoming. However, many of the unions that participated most consistently have substantial numbers of members who are African American and Latino. The problem reflected itself at the board of directors level and in terms of LEAP's perception in the larger community.

Turnover of leaders and key activists was another issue. Many activists who helped found LEAP and shape its direction moved on into other endeavors, sometimes related closely to LEAP's work but sometimes in distinctly different areas. As LEAP accumulated electoral victories and demonstrated its viability, building regional networks and LEAP-prototypes in other states commanded the attention of founding organizer Marc Caplan. Others who helped build the group won statewide office—Miles Rapoport became the secretary of state in Connecticut in 1994 and Bill Curry served as state comptroller in the mid-1990s—and their attention necessarily turned to those duties. (Both also sought higher office: Curry ran unsuccessfully for governor twice and served on the White House staff for several years for President Clinton. Rapoport ran unsuccessfully for Congress, then built a new organization, Democracy Works, which focuses on building democratic processes and civic participation, and now is executive director of Demos.) New talented leaders and staff emerged within LEAP, but many of these individuals also eventually moved on. Working for LEAP was immensely demanding, and sometimes LEAP staff moved into jobs that are easier to mesh with family responsibilities.

Maintaining LEAP's resource base presented a huge challenge and ultimately proved a major factor in the coalition's dissolution. Funding sources look to support specific projects on such issues as campaign finance reform, or research such as who receives state economic development assistance. By contrast, finding financing for the day-to-day coalition operations proved increasingly difficult over time. As the last LEAP board president and former state teacher union president George Springer put it, when LEAP was at the cutting edge in its early years, grants were a great deal easier to obtain. Twenty years later, support for overhead and operational costs was harder to find.

LEAP was no longer asking for seed money to launch a new and innovative project, but needing long-term support. Other coalitions developed in the northeast and across the country, all of which also sought the same foundation funding as LEAP. Unions and other constituent organizations did provide some financial backing for LEAP. However, despite their generosity, and because all of these organizations dealt with their own priorities and scarcities, it was impossible to generate the requisite funds from affiliates alone. Foundation support became critical to LEAP's ability to maintain itself and this support required a great deal of attention to sustain. Thus, as LEAP staff devoted time to other organizational priorities, foundation support became more difficult to obtain.

LEAP's ability to reshape the public agenda also led to the perception that unions overwhelmingly influenced LEAP's deliberations and policy priorities. By virtue of the number of unions in the coalition, labor did exert a significant presence, yet since the point of the coalition was to bring together a broad coalition, nonlabor organizations were accorded the same respect and consideration as unions. However, this also meant that those nonlabor organizations affiliated with LEAP did have to feel comfortable working closely with labor. Conversely, groups that were not comfortable in coalitions that embraced labor had difficulty within LEAP. Moreover, it was at times difficult to hold some politicians (even a few who were elected with LEAP's backing) accountable and to get them to vote favorably on those economic issues that were important to labor. Labor's presence and labor's agenda in the LEAP coalition put it squarely at odds with corporate political power and it was often a major target of the business lobby.

Conservative or personally ambitious politicians also perceived LEAP as a threat. So, to counter the power of the coalition, political leaders from the governor to legislative leaders tried to encourage individual constituent parts of LEAP to essentially "cut deals" on their own. One previous House speaker was instrumental in the dissolution of the legislative progressive caucus that LEAP helped to coalesce. This individual did not want to see a division among Democrats between the progressive caucus and the moderate caucus that formed in response to the progressive presence in the legislature. Since liberals and progressives were in key leadership positions, a progressive caucus was deemed unnecessary and divisive from his perspective. More recently, within the Connecticut General Assembly power has concentrated more and more within the legislative leadership offices. With the absence of an organized progressive caucus and the demise of LEAP, groups have found it considerably more difficult to advance a progressive agenda or even individual pieces of legislation in Connecticut.

The LEAP coalition encountered additional challenges in maintaining participation by affiliates and coping with the changing technology surrounding elections. LEAP's founders envisioned that affiliated organizations would involve their rank-and-file members in campaigns for LEAP-endorsed candidates. And LEAP did nothing short of a remarkable job in campaign training. By 1998, more than 800 individuals from unions and other affiliates had participated in training for candidates, campaign management, and volunteers (Shorey 1998). However, not all LEAP organizations could accomplish rank-and-file participation on a consistent basis. Some affiliates never developed a sufficiently developed political action apparatus to effectively mobilize members. Moreover, other affiliates functioned as advocates on behalf of various constituencies rather than as organizations based on membership. Such groups did not have as solid a base to mobilize as unions do.

Within the span of LEAP's history, the novelty of the coalition's endorsement and its operation also wore off, creating an interesting dilemma. As impressive as it may sound to have a large number of organizations come together, develop candidate-screening methods, and jointly interview and endorse candidates, the process proved a time-consuming and inefficient use of many activists' time. Thus, with a large number of endorsements, the value of a LEAP endorsement meant less and less over time, especially given an increasing use of outside consultants. As former Connecticut SEIU State Council Director Jill Hurst characterized it, LEAP was trying to be too many things to too many groups and ended up spreading itself too thin. A great laundry list of issues was generated, but a progressive base was not being built.

Even if every LEAP affiliate had produced a highly developed political action operation, LEAP would still have had to compete with a sophisticated money-driven "election business" that, as former LEAP staff member John Murphy describes it, has changed the nature of campaigns and reliance on volunteer operations. During its early years, volunteers from LEAP organizations would staff phone banks, research voter lists, and perform the other "grunt work" of elections. However, an entire industry of consultants can now perform these tasks for a fee. While upstart progressive candidates with limited funds found the volunteer-based effort of LEAP campaigns an important resource base, seasoned incumbents who could more easily raise campaign contributions—progressives among them—had the option of "buying" phone banks and coded voter lists. This may seem antithetical to progressive politics, yet it is a shortcut that is attractive to some candidates. Moreover, these developments allowed candidates who didn't want to be tied to LEAP's agenda to more easily bypass the group.

LEAP's Legacy

Despite all of these complicated issues, LEAP created a network of organizations and individuals that remain important sources of energy for progressive politics in Connecticut. Particularly for the labor movement in the state, LEAP helped broaden support for issues through both its formal agenda and the relationships that developed among participating organizations. Thus, for example, although LEAP no longer exists, labor activists and women's rights activists can easily coalesce when issues of sexual harassment in the workplace arise in union-organizing drives, or labor can call upon a number of community organizations to press for corporate responsibility legislation. Since LEAP trained many individuals on the mechanics of running campaigns and provided a model of how to involve organizations' members in political activity, many organizations in Connecticut now routinely mobilize constituencies on political issues. These lessons and models live on and are replicated by other, newer networks.

One additional project that LEAP undertook is still being used by some unions: the use of geographic information systems (GIS) technology to develop accurate membership and voter lists. Traditionally associated with urban geography and urban planning, GIS used in this manner provides a new election technology, enabling organizations to map their membership, track voter registration among members, and evaluate where a critical mass of several different organizations' members reside and can be mobilized. Since many of the voter lists maintained by election consultants are highly inaccurate, this project has been extremely useful to the organizations involved.

Coalition Building Deepens

While LEAP brought groups together, its endorsements and election campaigning always drew on a laundry-list of progressive issues that represented a kind of sum of each constituent group's major concerns. LEAP never generated a long-term process for groups to build a new holistic progressive agenda that transcended each group's traditional work. Yet, the continued search for such an agenda can be seen among the new generation of coalitions that developed in LEAP's wake.

Public-Sector Unions and Living Wages

For public-sector unions, what can't be won solely at the bargaining table often necessitates effective political solutions. SEIU in Connecticut—which includes the New England Health Care Employees–District 1199, Local 32BJ (formerly Local 531, a local that represents custodians and janitors), the Congress of Connecticut Community Colleges, and other public-sector locals—has taken on major fights and won several huge victories. In the 1999 session, the legislature passed a "standard wage" bill affecting state contracts with service vendors such as for maintenance and food service. Unionized workers in these industries found that their wages could always be undercut by nonunion companies in the state's competitive bidding process. Such low-paid competition made it virtually impossible for workers to enjoy any significant increase in their wages and living standards. Similar to prevailing wage laws, the new wage law helps protect union wage levels by setting standards for the private firms with whom the state of Connecticut contracts. The victory came as the culmination of a several year effort by SEIU and the Hotel Employees and Restaurant Employees (HERE) union. During the 1999 legislative session, the unions designated every Wednesday as a lobby day and brought dozens of rank-and-file members to the state capitol each week to press their issues. Careful targeting of specific legislators and turning former opponents into supporters won the bill's passage. SEIU has held similar weekly lobby days in the subsequent legislative sessions to pursue further its legislative agenda. In their signature purple jackets, berets, and shirts, SIEU members can't be missed in the halls of the legislature as they create an impressive "purple haze."

The purple haze descended over city hall in Hartford, when many of the same unions and additional community allies came together around a municipal living wage ordinance for companies doing business with the city. The ordinance passed in the fall of 1999 after months of lobbying, rallying, and negotiations with city officials.

Citizens for Economic Opportunity

A unique coalition has highlighted the issue of corporate responsibility in public discourse and concrete legislative proposals. Citizens for Economic Opportunity (CEO) involves a number of unions, the Connecticut state AFL-CIO, and community allies. CEO's ambitious agenda has included: a multiyear campaign to enact standards for corporations receiving state economic development assistance; public education and organizing around the job loss and community impacts caused by insurance industry restructuring; and a campaign over the conversion of Connecticut Blue Cross from a nonprofit to the for-profit Anthem Blue Cross. CEO also successfully raised the issue of corporate accountability and community standards in Hartford both during the debate over the stadium proposal for the aborted move of the New England Patriots to Hartford and also in other redevelopment projects.

After several years of arduous work at the Connecticut legislature, in the 2002 session, one portion of CEO's corporate responsibility legislation became law. This statute established stronger "clawback" provisions for firms receiving state economic development assistance. If such firms fail to live up to job creation promises that were conditions of the assistance, they must repay the state a portion of the aid. CEO continues to advocate for stronger corporate reporting requirements, more public access to such data, and living wage provisions for firms that receive economic development assistance. It also has been part of several local campaigns to halt Wal-Mart development.

CEO receives substantial support from such key LEAP players as Region 9A of the United Auto Workers, the Connecticut AFL-CIO, several other unions, and the Connecticut Citizen Action Group. In recent years, the state's chapter of the National Organization for Women has become involved. CEO can mobilize the rank and file and staff of a number of unions and citizen organizations in its legislative agenda. In one of its most successful efforts, CEO was instrumental in initiating a health-care access foundation that came forth as a result of a $31 million settlement from litigation over the conversion of Blue Cross to the for-profit Anthem Blue Cross.

The Connecticut Center for a New Economy

Building on the work of the Stamford Organizing Project (analyzed by Janice Fine in this volume), and also taking inspiration from the Los Angeles Alliance for a New Economy, the Connecticut Center for a New Economy (CCNE) formed in the spring of 2000. CCNE works to address the growing income disparities in Connecticut through organizing and policy initiatives that raise wages and increase activism among the working poor in urban communities. In the process of pushing policies such as living wage ordinances and other measures that involve community benefits, CCNE also seeks to create a climate that encourages and supports the unionization of low-wage workers. CCNE pursues its agenda through supporting specific union struggles, partnering with faith-based organizations and congregations, community organizing, policy advocacy, and action research.

As originally envisioned, CCNE planned to have a presence in New Haven and Hartford, and in Stamford through supporting the Stamford Organizing Project. However, with changes to the Stamford project and weaker organizational capacity in Hartford, CCNE's main endeavor since 2002 has focused on New Haven's relationship with its largest employer: Yale University. Yale has acquired the reputation of having the worst labor relations in the country for an academic institution (Greenhouse 2003): There have been eight strikes at Yale since 1968. Job actions and strikes in 2003 are the latest chapters in this contentious history. Yale is by far the single most powerful institution in New Haven; it is the largest employer in the city, it controls huge amounts of land, and, despite enjoying tax-exempt status with respect to much of its property, it still pays a considerable amount of property taxes on its for-profits subsidiaries. Taking advantage of the exceptional expertise among its faculty, students, and staff, the university and its affiliated teaching hospital have become exceptionally entrepreneurial, particularly in biotechnical areas. Yet New Haven's residents remain among the poorest in Connecticut and most do not share in Yale's prosperity.

CCNE has been the vehicle through which the federation of unions at Yale (HERE Locals 34 and 35, District 1199–SEIU and the Graduate Employees and Students Organization, or GESO) have developed strong community support and incorporated community issues into their organizing. CCNE staff and union organizers work in a coordinated fashion and have mounted a number of campaigns outside the traditional boundaries of union contract fights. This has included framing demands for more job training for New Haven residents and expanding housing programs for Yale employees to include the city's Latino neighborhoods. It has also involved some unusually creative strategies and campaigns. CCNE backed the candidacy of activist New Haven minister Dr. David Lee for an alumni seat on the Yale Corporation Board of Directors. Lee is an alumnus of the Yale Divinity School, a board member of CCNE, and the pastor of a large African American congregation in New Haven. His campaign stressed the themes of fostering better relations between Yale and the community and also the Yale workforce. Although he did not win, the campaign provoked a great deal of debate and controversy, as the Yale administration clearly did not want him on the corporation board.

The Yale campaign has also taken up the major issues of the debt encumbered by indigent or uninsured patients of Yale-New Haven Hospital. The hospital has acquired the reputation as one of the most aggressive in Connecticut in going after indigent patients to collect their unpaid hospital bills. Wage garnishment and liens and foreclosures on real estate were not uncommon methods of debt collection employed by the institution. Yet charitable funds earmarked for the bills of poor patients were underutilized. CCNE was able to work with the Connecticut Attorney General and legislators to address these issues and its Hospital Debt Justice Project has pursued law suits and legislation to: (1) provide greater access to funds for the medically indigent that have been underutilized by the hospital; (2) grant relief to those whose wages and homes have been attacked by the hospital; and (3) change the laws to limit the ability of hospitals to aggressively pursue medical debt through such methods as high interest rates and foreclosing on homes.

Through these projects, CCNE's agenda continues to expand and evolve, encompassing more of the complex issues that affect the working poor.

One Connecticut: The Campaign to Fight Poverty and Build Economic Security

As LEAP was on the wane, another megacoalition was forming that included many organizations from the LEAP network. Several dozen human service and advocacy organizations began to work together in the 2000–01 electoral and legislative seasons to share information, maximize resources, and define common priorities. As yearly public budget cutbacks become the norm and welfare reform and retrenchment of other public benefits continue to tear apart the social safety net, advocates in different arenas realized that only a coordinated effort would prevent them from being pitted against each other in legislative battles. By 2003, the coalition claimed over 100 member organizations. One-Connecticut (One-CT) acts as a clearinghouse for information and as a lobbying network for five defined priority areas of work: housing, health care, economic security, education, and effective democracy. It draws on the expertise of one of its members, Connecticut Voices for Children, an advocacy organization that conducts superb research and analysis on the state's budget and tax policies.

In 2003, as the state experienced an unprecedented budget crisis, the governor and Republicans proposed deep cuts in public services and massive state layoffs. One-CT worked in partnership with the State Employees Bargaining Agent Coalition (SEBAC) and the Connecticut Conference of Municipalities (CCM) (particularly with the urban mayors who are active in CCM) to craft alternative budget proposals to save public services and benefits, keep the state workforce in tact, and raise taxes on the state's wealthiest citizens. SEBAC consists of eighteen different state employee unions who negotiate jointly on matters of pensions and benefits with the state and who lobby on matters of mutual concern. SEBAC itself faces all of the attendant issues of coalition maintenance. Yet it maintains a generally high degree of unity in its dealings with often hostile or difficult state officials.

The partnership between One-CT, SEBAC, and CCM was a critically important step for maximizing the resources and power needed take on Governor John Rowland (R) and the legislative leadership of both parties who were all to willing to slash services and lay off public employees rather than consider raising taxes on Connecticut's super-wealthy residents. The 2003 experience proved to be one of the most grueling state budget battles in recent history, and there were few victories for progressive and popular forces. However, the degree to which these parties were able to coalesce provides important foundations for future activities when economic conditions are less dire. The collaboration between One-CT and SEBAC has been an especially important development: Sometimes deep splits can develop between nonprofit organizations and public-sector unions as issues of wages, subcontracting, and other divisive matters surface. These tensions have arisen in Connecticut in recent years and the maintenance of this particular partnership may also prove important in progressive politics in Connecticut in the future.

Other Critical Coalition Partners

Several other important partners are a part of the coalition picture in Connecticut. The Connecticut Citizens Action Group (CCAG) is involved in most coalition activity within Connecticut. It has been a significant force within CEO, as well as previously in LEAP and on other specific issue campaigns. And as LEAP began to scale back some of its activities, CCAG expanded its role and strengthened its capacity. Besides its work in CEO, it coordinates a health-care reform coalition, "Health Care for All," and takes a lead role in campaign finance reform battles. It is part of the regional network in New England and New York, Northeast Action, and is setting the pace for many citizen action organizations.

Another partner in the most recent round of coalitions has been Democracy Works. As discussed earlier, this organization was founded by Miles Rapoport to foster democratic participation and works on such issues as campaign finance reform, voter registration, and other related matters. It has provided critical in-kind support for One-CT and is involved in a variety of efforts to expand voting rights, streamline political procedures, and open up state and local government to more citizen input and participation.

Partnerships with the faith community also are becoming increasingly significant in terms of contributions of labor's agenda and other progressive issues. For example, a previous director of the Capitol Region Conference of Churches in the Hartford area has been a key activist within CEO and consistently appeared before the legislature to testify and lobby for the coalition's legislative initiatives. In recent years, local clergy in Hartford, along with several elected officials, participated in sit-ins and civil disobedience actions at picket lines of striking nursing home workers who were District 1199–SEIU members, or at the state capitol building. CCNE in New Haven calls upon an entire network of local congregations, the Elm City Congregations Organization (ECCO), for support and a number of pastors have participated in civil disobedience and strike support activities in the Yale campaigns. Several local affiliates of the Gamaliel Foundation are also developing in the state. As labor's essential message of social and economic justice is coming through more and more effectively to the public, the ties with local clergy and congregations are also strengthening as they see commonalities with labor.

Lessons Learned: Building Solidarity into Reality

Experiences in LEAP and other political battles in Connecticut offer several insights as to what it means to build and sustain political coalitions that effectively champion labor and the community's issues. While not all of this message may apply elsewhere, the issues that manifested within LEAP and other Connecticut community-labor alliances illustrate some of the inherent problems of coalition building, particularly those that are longer lasting. Initiating and growing a coalition provides one set of challenges, but sustaining coalitions for twenty years presents quite another set.

A coalition like LEAP that works over a long period of time is built upon a strong network of organizations whose activists trust each other based on their work together over periods of years. The unions that were in LEAP have all faced survival struggles whether they are machinists at United Technologies, health care workers in the public and private sectors, janitors, teachers, or others. The leaders of these unions respect the serious struggles that their counterparts face in their respective industries and recognize that each union must develop the most effective strategy possible to defend its members' interests. But some leaders also recognize that the labor movement has to stand for more than the sum total of its parts, and so the LEAPs, the CEOs, the CCNEs and other coalition efforts receive substantial attention. And because all of these unions need allies in the broader community, they know that in order to have allies, there must be reciprocal support for the priorities of these community forces.

Coalition partners in these formations have to recognize that there simply are times when there will be disagreements and everyone will have to live with those differences. Organizations within LEAP sometimes endorsed opposing candidates in primaries and even in general elections. A case in point: In 1994 when LEAP activist Bill Curry ran for governor as a Democrat, he faced two opponents, the Republican John Rowland and Eunice Groark. Groark ran under the banner of A Connecticut Party, the party formed by Lowell Weicker in his successful third-party bid in 1988. Several women's organizations that are members of LEAP endorsed Groark and worked hard on her behalf. Curry lost to Rowland by less than 4 percent of the vote. There were other differences over endorsements among the coalition partners over the years, but somehow organizations found a way to stay in LEAP for twenty years and work on issues or campaigns over which there was consensus.

Sometimes the ill feelings lingered over these differences and the problems were not necessarily publicly aired or resolved, yet the groups found ways to stay in the coalition.

Since so often the issue priorities of political coalitions take several years to win in the legislative arena, an additional lesson from this work, certainly not a novel one, is the need for patience and perseverance. To redefine the terms of political debate often proves a difficult process and victories may indeed take several years to accomplish. A setback on an issue one year does not necessarily constitute a permanent defeat. In fact, in some battles in Connecticut, such as the standard wage bill, there was an expectation by officials in the legislature that several years of effort would be required.

Perhaps one of the most important lessons from LEAP's work is something that is at the heart of every political action program, the need for rank-and-file mobilization. There are new ways in which this issue is being thought about now within the labor movement, and unions or other organizations may also need to reconsider their own mobilization strategies. According to the AFL-CIO's northeast region deputy director, Merrilee Milstein, the AFL-CIO has been emphasizing a "member-to-member mobilization" approach, that is, the need for unions to activate their base through outreach by members to other members. This approach has been adopted by SEIU in Connecticut and involves the recruitment of rank-and-file political organizers, "member political organizers," or MPOs as SEIU calls them, who pledge four hours a month to political action and recruit other workers to become MPOs. SEIU aims to have several hundred MPOs active in fall election campaigns. What Milstein emphasizes is that union endorsements do not carry much meaning if the base is not organized. But, even more important, if unions do not talk to their members and do not explain the issues, they lose strength in the political arena. As the AFL-CIO retooled its electoral apparatus, it learned through experiences during the Labor 96 and Labor 98 mobilizations what members want most of their unions: They want their unions to inform them about the issues and tell them where candidates stand on these issues. They do not just want their union to send them a letter telling them to vote for Candidate X. They want to base their voting decisions on information about issues, and they generally trust the information their unions provide them. Moreover, the most effective way to reach workers is in person, at the job (Rosenthal 1998).

The lessons through the 2000 and 2002 elections drove home even more essential points: No matter how much labor mobilizes its own base and no matter how unified its vote, labor simply cannot prevail electorally without allies. Now, with the Republicans and rightwing forces more and more skilled at electoral strategies and voter mobilization, and with their vast amounts of financial resources, progressive coalitions are all the more important to counter the message and strength of the right. Therefore, the AFL-CIO is embarking upon several additional strategies: It seeks to work with allies in nonpartisan coalitions to expand the electorate and register people to vote, particularly in communities of color and working class communities. It also is encouraging unions to do political work on issues on a year-round basis in workplaces, not simply at election time. Finally, according to Milstein, the AFL-CIO is experimenting with door-to-door canvassing in several areas to offer "associate membership" to people who are not union members, but who could gain specific benefits from affiliation with the labor movement, and in turn, be activated politically on critical issues and campaigns. In several communities, including Seattle and Cleveland, projects are under way to develop this model of mobilization.

Conclusion

When LEAP was being organized over twenty years ago, many of the issues that labor and popular forces confront today were just beginning or could not have been imagined. The ferocious and concerted attack on the role of government as a means of alleviating poverty or guaranteeing a minimum standard of living, the victim-blaming ideologies inherent in the scaling back of the welfare state, the unrelenting attack on the labor movement or affirmative action, the disregard for the natural environment, the repressive moralism around gender identity and roles, and the frightening militarism as the strategy for foreign policy—these developments and more compel progressives to seek common ground and common solutions. Coalition building thus becomes a strategy for survival. Often the goals of political coalitions are more limited in scope than these huge questions of social policy or international relations, but the lessons in crafting partnerships are nonetheless worthwhile. Sometimes we have an opportunity to elect candidates from the ranks of our movements or to win legislation that addresses real needs or builds our power. LEAP's history and the ongoing work in Connecticut give us some useful insights for the next generation of political coalitions of community and labor. There is much ahead to do.

References

Brecher, Jeremy, and Tim Costello. 1990. *Building Bridges*. New York: Monthly Review Press.
Caplan, Marc, and Miles Rapoport. 1993. "Rebuilding Politics from the Ground Up." *Social Policy* 24, no. 2 (Winter 1993): 40–50.

Greenhouse, Steven. 2003. "Yale's Labor Troubles Deepen as Thousands Go on Strike." *New York Times*, March 4, p. B-1.

Reynolds, David. 1997. *Democracy Unbound*. Boston: Monthly Review Press.

———. 1998. "Building the Rainbow." *WorkingUSA* 2, no. 1 (May/June 1998): 9–20.

———. 1999. "Coalition Politics: Insurgent Union Political Action Builds Ties Between Labor and the Community." *Labor Studies Journal* 24, no. 3 (Fall 1999): 54–75.

Rosenthal, Steve. 1998. "Building to Win, Building to Last: The AFL-CIO's Political Program." In *Not Your Father's Labor Movement*, ed. Jo-Ann Mort. New York: Verso Press, pp. 99–111.

Shorey, Peggy. 1998. "Electoral Coalition Strategy: Building Progressive Power. A Progress Report on Coalition Strategy from the Coalitions' Inception to the Present." Report for Northeast Action, March.

Simmons, Louise. 1994. *Organizing in Hard Times: Labor and Neighborhoods in Hartford*. Philadelphia: Temple University Press.

———. 1998. "Community-Labor Coalitions: A Well-Spring from Connecticut." *Shelterforce: The Journal of Affordable Housing Strategies*, no. 101 (September/October 1998): 16–18, 42.

III

Institution Building

10

Contemporary Community Unionism

Some Lessons from Baltimore and Stamford

Janice Fine

Although in the past few years the spirit of the American labor movement has been revived by a new leadership team committed to major institutional change and devoted to organizing, the actual results have been discouraging. It is estimated that unions now represent less than 8 percent of private-sector workers, or fewer than one in twelve workers.[1] Despite enormous focus and effort, in the face of explosive job growth on one hand and attrition of union jobs on the other, the labor movement has barely been able to maintain mid-1990s levels of density.

What these numbers tell us is that despite much more emphasis on organizing, it is still not proving to be enough—labor is struggling to break through. A mismatch between labor laws and the new economy and virulent union busting on the part of the vast majority of employers with sanctions coming too little too late, are two major reasons that organizing is so difficult. In response, many union drives avoid the National Labor Relations Board (NLRB) election process altogether by gearing up campaigns that demand card-check recognition in which an employer agrees to recognize the union after a majority of workers sign authorization cards to join. In fact, in 2001 only 18 percent of new organizing was accomplished via conventional NLRB election strategies.[2] Avoiding the NLRB election trap is a smart strategy and it is proving to be successful in certain cases—but it begs the question of how unions build enough power to compel employers to agree.

In this new era of high worker mobility, organizing needs something more than a worksite as a base. In labor markets that are overwhelmingly non-union (as most are today) and in which a larger and larger percentage of the workforce moves between jobs, firm-by-firm organizing is inadequate. A 1998 report by the Economic Policy Institute and the Women's Research and Education Institute estimates that in 1995, 29.4 percent of all jobs were in nonstandard work arrangements (NSWAs), which include independent contracting, working for a temporary help agency, contract or "on-call" work, day labor, self-employment, and regular part-time employment.[3] Just as they did in the early years of craft and industrial unionism, unions have concluded that they have to focus more on geographic or industrial strategies in order to take wages out of competition across a city, region, or industry.

Given that unions can no longer court workers and build unions exclusively at worksites, they must concentrate more on reaching workers and building relationships through their ethnic communities, their neighborhoods, and their churches. Often, to do this effectively, they need community organizations to partner with. Indeed, in a real sense, the community itself has become the new "unit" for labor-organizing campaigns. Taking wages out of competition across a city or industry has evolved, at least in some significant measure, into a community-organizing project.

There are examples all over the country of what this "community unionism" might look like. During the period of labor's quiescence new forms of worker organization began to appear at the local level. Some are connected to unions and others are not. Some of these worker-organizing projects, such as immigrant worker centers, were begun by community organizations to fill the void left by traditional unions in terms of organization and representation of low-wage immigrant workers. Others, like the Industrial Areas Foundation (IAF) groups and ACORN (Associated Communities Organized for Reform Now), got involved because as urban redevelopment strategies matured in central cities across the United States, they came to understand just how ineffectual these policies had been in expanding employment opportunities for inner-city residents. Community organizations have long been caught in battles where all of their organizing cannot turn back the one trend that could save their communities: the loss of decent-paying jobs with benefits. Partnership with unions gives such groups the chance to take on wage fights and win.

The IAF and ACORN have taken the lead in mounting living wage-campaigns across the country, and ACORN, historically a neighborhood-organizing group, has become integrally involved in union-organizing efforts with the Service Employees International Union (SEIU). Hundreds of community organizations are now involved in all sorts of employment-related activity, from organizing around living wage and local hiring policies to running job training programs and basic hiring halls and operating temporary employment agencies and cooperatives.

For a growing number of community organizations and unions scattered across the country, the line separating "community issues" from "labor issues" is breaking down—just as it always has in the lives of poor and working-class families. Unions and community organizations are sharing turf and creating new alliances that go well beyond isolated acts of "solidarity" to ongoing partnerships based upon mutual self-interest.

The theory of community unionism is being worked out every day, on the ground. The challenges faced by organizers in Baltimore, Maryland, an early exemplar, and Stamford, Connecticut, a more recent effort, point the way to the questions we need to ask about the future. Of course, the AFL-CIO is well aware of these efforts. However, the debate about them too often centers around how they contribute to increased numbers in the short run rather than how they transform the climate for organizing, and can be a valuable part of the strategy for reviving the labor movement.

In Baltimore's case, although the organization is a coalition between the American Federation of State, County, and Municipal Employees (AFSCME) and the faith-based Industrial Areas Foundation (IAF), it is the IAF group that is in the lead and whose culture is predominant. By contrast, labor is the dominant partner in the Stamford Organizing Project (SOP) in Connecticut although it forged a powerful partnership with several key members of the clergy and their congregations.

Climbing Jacob's Ladder to a Living Wage in Baltimore

In the fall of 1992, the Maryland Food Bank conducted a study of the people using its affiliated 140 soup kitchens and food pantries and found that 27 percent of them were people who worked every day, many of them in downtown Baltimore. For pastors like Reverend Doug Miles, the study confirmed what many of them had long suspected, and it reinforced their disillusionment with downtown redevelopment as an economic strategy: "We saw that workers were not benefiting from all of the new development in the area: wages were stagnating, jobs were part-time with no benefits."[4]

From the 1950s through the early 1990s, the city of Baltimore was the victim of a strategy of economic development and urban revitalization based upon the redevelopment of the downtown. The linchpin of the strategy was a menu of financial incentives and public subsidies to private developers calculated to entice them into investing in office and hotel development as well as convention centers, stadiums, and upscale commercial and residential projects.[5]

More than $2 billion was spent in Baltimore to subsidize the development of a downtown hospitality industry, but the fortunes of inner city residents got worse, not better, during this period. The percentage of residents living in poverty increased in the majority of Baltimore's neighborhoods, and housing conditions continued to be among the worst in the nation. Baltimoreans were faced with the contradiction of a thriving corporate center in the midst of increasingly depressed inner-city neighborhoods.

But Baltimore had something many other devastated communities did not—a group of pastors and laypersons organized under the IAF banner. BUILD (Baltimoreans United in Leadership Development) pastors and leaders began to look at ways to put money back into downtown neighborhoods. In the late 1980s, the organization's approach had been to demand subsidies for housing, education, and the like, but in the words of Arnie Graf, East Coast director of the IAF, "We came to realize that we could not subsidize our way out of the crisis. And why did we need so much subsidy? Why do people who are working every day need this subsidy in order to send their kids to school or to buy a home? We had to get to the root of it. We had to deal with people's work and wages."[6]

BUILD pastors and leaders began to explore the development of a new social compact between the city and business. As a part of this process, they discovered that the city itself was a major source of contracts for low-wage jobs. A new idea was born. If BUILD could not yet get the city to cut off subsidies to downtown developers, they could demand that the city mandate that municipal service contractors pay a living wage. The organization also favored this strategy because it felt that the first step toward organizing low-wage workers was to find ways to stabilize their conditions of employment. The living wage was a way to do that for one segment of Baltimore's low-wage labor force.

BUILD mounted a major campaign to pass the living wage ordinance. Early tactics included subsidy tours—hanging huge price tags on various downtown buildings with the amount of public subsidy those companies had received; pastors marching through downtown hotels decrying massive public subsidy and going floor by floor talking to chambermaids; persuading organizers of huge conventions to tell the hotels they would pay a dollar more a room if it would go into the salaries of workers. Taking advantage of political rivalries and the impending mayoral election, BUILD held several actions with more than 1,000 people targeted at the city leadership, and the mayor in particular.

Most important, BUILD set out to build a new organization of low-wage workers called Solidarity. From the outset, Solidarity's ambition has been to be a different kind of organization of workers. As lead organizer Jonathan

Lange describes it, "We are a little bit of church, a little bit of union, a little bit of social service, and a whole lot of politics!"

Solidarity filled a void that unions were not filling in Baltimore. In answer to the question "Why did you join Solidarity?" many workers said simply, "Because they asked me to." While some of them had experiences with unions in the past, and some had attended churches, for the most part they spoke of these relationships in the passive sense. They said things like "The union was a good thing, it got me decent wages and benefits," but many did not know the name of the union or key leaders of the union, and when asked if they had ever been requested to participate in a union event, most said "no."

In answer to the question, "What was different about Solidarity, from going to your church or being in a union," workers clearly viewed the organizations in entirely different ways. Many of them said that union membership was beneficial or that going to church on Sunday was important to them but that, before Solidarity, no one had ever asked them what they thought about anything or what they wanted out of life—or to join their organization. Jeanette Scott, a janitor at the World Trade Center, summed it up: "I was never political. Once I was in a union when I had an eight-hour a day job at Dover Poultry, but I did not have a whole lot of say. I was just in a union, you know. . . . But this was different, the organizer gave everybody a chance to tell a story if they had one to tell."

BUILD did not launch this effort alone. After initial negotiations with the SEIU broke down, BUILD partnered with the AFSCME, the largest public-sector union in the nation with a national membership of 1.3 million. Lange remembers the meeting where the organizations first went public with their announcement to work together to build a low-wage workers association: "My favorite part of the meeting was when Reverend Vernon Dobson concluded the meeting with these words: 'The church is going to protect these workers. I have a message for employers—people who are upset because they don't want to pay workers more money . . . who don't want workers to organize. You keep your hands off these people because they are children of God.' I thought lightning was going to come off of his fingers. I don't think those workers had ever been wrapped around by so much power before."

AFSCME viewed the living wage issue as a way to stem privatization. Bob Linehard, the AFSCME attorney who worked closely with BUILD and Solidarity, described the union's thinking: "Privatization is the maquiladora of the public sector, so we had been wrestling with how do we confront this low-wage competition in an environment that is hard to organize and where people are paid well below a living wage you could raise a family on."[8] AFSCME's view was that if the union could pass a local ordinance, it would have a chance to put limits on the extent to which contractors could compete on the basis of slashing wage and benefit levels. In addition, at the time Solidarity was getting started, the union was planning to expand its membership ranks by launching a major campaign for collective bargaining rights for state workers. The union felt that the alliance with BUILD would also help this effort. It won this campaign in 1996 and has since built the state membership to more than 30,000.

Able to draw power from BUILD's established base of forty-six churches and AFSCME, Solidarity hit the ground running and scored a major victory. On December 13, 1994, the living wage ordinance was signed into law. When the law took effect in July, wages went from $4.25 to $6.10 an hour. After July of 1998, the policy's wage level was tethered to 110 percent of what it takes to bring a family of four above the poverty line in the Baltimore standard metropolitan statistical area, assuming 2,000 hours of full-time work a year. In July of 2000 it rose to $8.03, 55 percent higher than the federal minimum wage of $5.15 an hour. By statute, the living wage was to be automatically adjusted each year. Beginning with the living wage, BUILD worked to call the city to a new social compact between government, corporations, and workers in which public policies, primarily at the municipal level, would reestablish a set of labor market protections for low-wage Baltimore workers.

In addition to the living wage, which touched off over a hundred successful efforts across the country, the organization's accomplishments included a right-to-organize ordinance denying city contracts to contractors charged with unfair labor practices; a right-of-first-refusal ordinance that gives workers the right to stay on the job when contracts change hands; and a statewide antidisplacement executive order (another first in the nation achievement), which ensured that state agencies could not eliminate full-time positions and replace them with $1.50-an-hour workfare slots. BUILD was one of the first groups in the country to develop powerful and effective grassroots strategies in response to the passage in 1996 of federal "welfare reform."

In 1998, evoking the Old Testament story of Joseph and the Pharaoh, the organization called on the gubernatorial candidates to create the Joseph Plan— a proposal to set aside 20 percent of the state surplus to be used for job creation and training that kicks in whenever the state experiences three consecutive months of economic downturn. Democrat governor Parris Glendenning, who won reelection in some significant measure due to the voter-education efforts of BUILD members, set up the Joseph Plan and appointed Lange, BUILD's lead organizer, to chair it.

The victories described above are all examples of Solidarity's successes in the political sphere. But the organization's founders had not set out to build a political organization alone. They viewed the living wage victory as a victory for a small part of their base—workers employed by city contractors—but more importantly, as a way to stabilize the workforce so that it could be organized into a union. It wanted to organize large numbers of low-wage workers into a new model union that, in its organizing strategies and structures, would be more suited to the realities of the service economy. The public policy campaigns were viewed as a means to the end of organizing a union, and not as ends in themselves.

Like many other regions of the country, the labor movement in Baltimore was able to achieve high density in the industrial sector, but was unable to keep pace with the exploding service sector. In 1999, out of a total of 2.4 million workers employed in Maryland, 367,000 belonged to unions, with the Baltimore region accounting for more than half of them. Between 1984 and 1999, while the Maryland economy grew by 516,000 jobs, union membership grew by only 16,000.[9]

Graf and Lange began the organizing of Solidarity with a strong critique of the unions they had been part of and worked with. They wanted to organize a new kind of union that could serve as one model of how to rebuild the labor movement through non-NLRB strategies of minority unionism. The current NLRB system is an all or nothing proposition. Either a majority of the workers voting in an election chose the union, in which case the union is recognized by the law, or the union has no legal status at all. Employers have huge incentives to manipulate and scare workers into voting the union down. By contrast, a minority union strategy seeks to build a lasting and growing organization of workers that can mobilize people inside and outside the workplace. Although outside the existing legal labor-relations system such organizations can exist irrespective of whether the union has won a single highly contested vote. Unlike the NLRB route in which the parent union's organizing energy and resources focus on the specific period of the election effort, a minority union strategy requires an ongoing commitment to support worker activism, often of a small group, in a context without a formal relationship with the employer and the corresponding dues check-off mechanisms to provide funds.

Graf and Lange believed that widespread worker recruitment to a union-like organization required the provision of some kind of positive selective incentive and set out to create a benefits plan that could offer a tangible incentive to join. In January of 1995, they began to offer a benefits package. For their $10 monthly dues, workers got a life insurance policy and discounts on hearing, dental, and eye exams and prescription drugs.[10] After two more years of investigation, Solidarity was also able to offer health benefits as well.

In the beginning, Solidarity hand-collected dues at the worksites it was organizing. However, Lange and others soon became convinced that in order to build a large and consistent membership base, they would need to achieve some form of dues deduction from member's paychecks. People would join and pay dues for a few months, but the organization struggled to get around to all the worksites every month to collect the month's dues. Only two employers voluntarily agreed to deduct dues. Solidarity was able to set up a sort of shop steward system, but only at a small percentage of the organized worksites. Add to this the high turnover in many of the contract jobs, and Solidarity faced a real problem. They expressed as much to AFSCME in October of 1996. Given the inhospitable nature of federal labor law and the general hostility of employers toward unions, Solidarity set a goal of avoiding NLRB elections and instead getting city contractors to agree to deduct dues from workers' paychecks.

With the help of AFSCME, Lange researched the legal options for creating a voluntary employees' beneficiary organization, or IRS 501C(9), and developed a strategy to use it as the vehicle for the dues check-off for "worker-sponsored benefits." On September 1, 1996, the Board of Estimates of the Baltimore City Council passed a resolution approving a system of mandatory payroll deduction (mandatory for the employer to do it, but voluntary for the individual worker to sign up for it). Locating the dues deduction policy firmly in the context of the living wage and social compact ideas, the preamble began: "Whereas, it is in the interest of all citizens of Baltimore City that working men and women have health and welfare benefits and insurance coverage and . . . many part-time employees of city contractors do not enjoy employer-sponsored benefits due to part-time status and lack of benefit plans. . . ."

Even with this creative solution to the problem of dues deduction in a minority union model, there were still major negatives to overcome. The resolution required city contractors to give the option of check-off to employees for worker-sponsored benefits but it did not require the employer to tell employees about it. In other words, if the worker presented the employer with the completed worker-sponsored benefit form, the employer was required to cooperate and facilitate the paycheck deduction, but it did not mean that the employer had to proactively inform the employee about the option—that was up to Solidarity.

The Solidarity organizing model was to build an initial membership by recruiting from service-sector workers at downtown contractors and other employers. By spending time in different service industries, Solidarity organizers could both recruit individual members and evaluate which industries would make promising targets for concentrated organizing. Under this model, Solidarity would train and place workers, and then bargain on their behalf by negotiating multiemployer agreements through master contracts. They did not want to organize through the NLRB election process for another reason: the expectations of members. Solidarity did not want to be viewed as a traditional union by workers who joined, because they did not want to have to fulfill the servicing function of a traditional union. They were convinced that having separate agreements at dozens of different employers would mean having to spend an enormous amount of time just negotiating and keeping on top of the contracts. In their view, it was better to be able to sign individual workers up through their employers, but not via an election and a contract.

From 1993 through 2000, as it solidified a benefits package and a system of dues deduction, Solidarity mounted a number of organizing efforts in several segments of the low-wage labor force including hotel housekeepers, downtown janitors, school bus drivers, food service workers, and child-care workers. Most of them were unsuccessful.

Although the stories of the individual drives are quite interesting and instructive, space limitations prevent me from reviewing them in this chapter. In general, I believe that what explains the failure to succeed at direct labor market intervention was a bias toward community organizing strategies over labor organizing—an understandable bias, but one that had a dramatic effect on the work of the organization.

Given the dire straits and general powerless of the working poor in Baltimore, Solidarity organizers felt great pressure to "put some early numbers up on the scoreboard" in terms of organizing victories in order to demonstrate to potential members, AFSCME, and other funders, that winning was indeed possible. This was much easier to do through issue organizing than union organizing. Given the fact that BUILD already had political power in the city, the shortest route to victory was to combine that power with innovative ideas and smart strategies to pass public policies. This early imperative started Solidarity down a path of choosing political fights over economic ones.

While it is clear that there were some built-in advantages for Solidarity to pursue public policy, it is equally true that there was a set of built-in disadvantages for Solidarity to pursue union organizing. First of all, they could anticipate strong employer opposition. Avoiding that opposition is what led to the second difficulty: embracing alternative minority union strategies. These were either too difficult to pull off or sustain for a long enough period of time, or they were untested and quite likely to run up against unsympathetic labor law. Both of these obstacles kept the organization from fully investing in minority union strategies and carrying them out all the way. Third, at the low end of the service sector where Solidarity was organizing, profit margins are thinner, and employers are smaller, more precarious, and less able to raise wages or improve benefits on their own.

As difficult as the above scenario is for union organizing, it is even more difficult to organize private-sector employers who are not receiving public subsidy. There are the same problems of high turnover, strong employer resistance, and unsympathetic labor law. These problems are coupled with the same difficulty posed by the structure of the secondary labor market—indirect relationships between owners and employers of record—only this time it is without the leverage provided by public subsidy. Because organizing under these circumstances is so much more difficult, it is essential to have an effective strategy and the resources to be able to apply pressure across a critical mass of employers in a sector. Solidarity attempted this organizing strategy with hotels and downtown office buildings, but gave up almost before it began.

One aspect of the IAF's organizational culture may have contributed to Solidarity's struggles with organizing a union—its institutional, as opposed to individual membership base. The IAF's model for building organization is through affiliating "units" like churches and other religious institutions, and in more recent years, schools and unions. These units are carefully recruited to join and pay dues and a tremendous amount of attention is paid to leadership development among the participating members of that church, school, or union, but it is the unit that joins and not the individual. The IAF clearly knows how to do this type of membership recruitment. But to build an individual member-based institution like a union requires enormous focus on recruitment, day in and day out. While IAF organizations stress the importance of one-on-one meetings and insist that their organizers do a sizeable number of them each week, what constitutes "a sizeable number" for a community organization versus a union, is dramatically different.

Unions and community organizations have different institutional imperatives. In order to win an election, a union needs to get a majority of workers at the workplace to join. In order to win on an issue, a community organization just needs to mobilize a dedicated minority. For a union to alter the labor market dynamics of a particular sector of the low-wage service economy, a significant number of individual workers and workplaces have to be organized. For a community organization that is pursuing a strategy of passing public policy to alter labor market dynamics—at least in many cases—far fewer recruits are necessary. If there is a trade-off to be made between quantity and quality, in a union organizing drive the choice is likely to be quantity, while in the IAF it is likely to be quality.

One major limiting factor in terms of being able to organize a union of low-wage workers of any scale in Baltimore, was the total lack of a union partner or partners to work with on the ground. Solidarity's relationship with AFSCME was always with the international union, and not the city workers' local. From the outset of the project, Lange and Graf ruled out a working partnership with the AFSCME local due to the corruption of its leadership, (and the local leadership also made clear it had no interest in collaborating.) Thus Solidarity was never able to partner with the local AFSCME affiliate and leverage the local's labor market power to organize workers. Nor were they able to tap into the power of any other local unions because during most of the time they were actively trying to build Solidarity as a local union, none of the "usual suspects" like SEIU, HERE (Hotel Employees and Restaurant Employees), or CWA (the Communication Workers of America) were organizing in Baltimore. In addition, the area central labor body was not playing an active, public role either in terms of supporting organizing drives or on broader economic justice issues.

The coming apart of the early partnership with SEIU and subsequent relationship with AFSCME led Solidarity to pursue a strategy of targeting the formerly public, contracted-out workforce that in turn led it to focus its efforts on public policy change. Whereas AFSCME's focus is on public-sector workers for whom public policy is key in terms of both collective bargaining rights and privatization, SEIU organizes much more widely among private-sector workers. Not only was AFSCME less able to offer advice in terms of organizing private-sector workers, it was also not interested in Solidarity organizing private-sector workers because they were not the union's targeted workforce. Also, AFSCME did not want to get into jurisdictional battles with other international unions. Had the SEIU relationship endured, Solidarity not only would have been free to organize among private-sector workers, but it may also have gained the level of resources necessary to do so and been able to avail itself of the strategic resources of the international union with the most experience in organizing low-wage service-sector workers.

When it came to organizing among the contracted-out formerly public sector workers, in the end the organization was really caught in a "Catch-22." As Lange explained, "If we bid wages up enough, the jobs would get 're-publicized' and so those jobs would then fall under the jurisdiction of the city workers' local union. If we tried to organize among the workers who had been contracted out, as we did in the case of the SES workers, once we built up a head of steam, the international told us to give the workers over to the local city workers' union. So once again we couldn't build up our own membership ranks. And if we organized private-sector service workers we were both violating our charter from AFSCME and getting the international into jurisdictional problems with other unions."[11]

Finally, serious union organizing drives among unorganized constituencies in difficult-to-organize sectors require large staffs. Solidarity never had more than four organizers.

For all of these reasons, Solidarity favored political over economic action. Given the low-ranking position of its members in the labor market—they were unskilled and for the most part, easily replaced—and the limitations of their partnership with AFSCME, this was arguably the right choice. In politics, despite the distortions of personal wealth, special interest money, and skewed structures of representatation, when it comes to the weighing of actual votes, each one counts equally. In economics, all jobs—and all workers—do not.

The organization succeeded not only in establishing itself as the major voice of low-wage African American workers in Baltimore, but also in using that voice to powerfully alter the terms of debate about the right to organize, and about poverty, jobs, the minimum wage, economic development, and welfare policy in the city. By making the connection between economic arrangements and democratic prospects in its social compact campaign—and the national living wage movement it spawned—Solidarity resurrected a fundamental debate about the role and purpose of the market economy in American life.

In addition to the new ideas it fostered in the public policy arena, Solidarity also pioneered several new ideas relating to union organizing and dues collection in low-wage settings. If those ideas have yet to bear fruit, they may be picked up some time in the future by an organization that has more capacity to see them through. Low-wage workers are still better off for the fact that these ideas were tried and can be tried again.

In spite of all of these achievements, however, the organization's reach—in terms of union organizing—has far exceeded its grasp. So far, its greatest successes have been in the political arena and not in the economic arena. Despite the success of the living wage campaign and the temp agency it created, most attempts to directly intervene in the labor market through economic organizing have not succeeded.

The AFL-CIO Goes to the Belly of the Beast—Stamford

Just as in Baltimore, where redevelopment gone bad provoked churches into action, the effects of a similar approach to redevelopment made Stamford an attractive target for an AFL-CIO multiunion organizing drive. While AFSCME played more of a supporting role to the community organization in Baltimore, labor played the leading role in Stamford.

The mayor of Stamford charges admission to his annual state of the city address—although it is still by invitation only. A $40 minimum will get you in the door, but he would prefer it if you would take a table. Who is on the guest list? The chamber of commerce and SACIA (the Business Council of

Southeastern Connecticut), the *Fortune* 500 business lobbies. The Stamford area has the third-highest concentration of *Fortune* 500 corporations in the country, surpassed only by New York City and Chicago. The "by invitation only" state of the city event is no aberration; Stamford has been catering to the corporate elite for close to forty years.

During the mid-1960s, Stamford's leadership made a conscious decision to reinvent itself—changing from a small town to a major commercial center, creating the space for corporate headquarters to move in by eventually razing ninety-nine acres of the downtown and displacing 1,100 predominantly African American families. "When my husband and I first moved here in 1965, urban renewal was in full swing," recalled Stamford City Council President Carmen Domonkos. "The downtown was leveled, or almost leveled, and what was not was slated for redevelopment and allowed to deteriorate. . . . There was huge displacement of everybody who lived downtown— mostly minorities and low-income people."[12]

As Bettina Drew writes in *Crossing the Expandable Landscape*, her book about urban redevelopment, "There was no real intention to concentrate housing in downtown Stamford after renewal. The idea was to establish businesses, cultural outlets, and restaurants to make the downtown generate more money."[13]

Thirty years later, the results are plain to see. Stamford's nighttime population of 107,000 quadruples during the day with wealthy business commuters. The luxury housing market is booming as more and more of these commuters are coming to stay. Meanwhile, life for Stamford's nursing home workers, home health aides, taxi drivers, janitors, and hotel workers has grown increasingly difficult. Wages are low, conditions of work leave much to be desired, and, if they can find a place to live in Stamford at all, rents are skyrocketing.

It was these service-sector workers that the AFL-CIO wanted to organize when it decided to target Stamford: "We felt there was a lot of potential in Stamford. It's the richest county in the U.S. and has some of the poorest people living in it. There was huge growth going on in the service sector and it was a perfect tale of two cities, so rich on the one hand and on the other so much poverty," said Merrilee Milstein, deputy regional director of the AFL-CIO for the Northeast Region.[14]

During the first years of the Sweeney administration, the AFL-CIO embarked upon an all-out offensive to encourage internationals to transfer a much higher percentage of their resources to organizing. They did this in a variety of ways, which for a period of time included devoting significant federation resources to match and support multiunion organizing efforts. The Stamford Organizing Project was one of four multiunion, "geographically

based organizing projects" that grew out of this aggressive period of experimentation. There had been more turnover at the helm of the AFL-CIO Organizing Department than in any other part of the building—three directors in
five years—and the "geo" projects had always been a bit of an orphan inside
the department. They were extremely controversial among international
unions from the start. Some internationals believed that the projects would
take them off their industrial strategies. In addition, some questioned the
federation's direct involvement in multiunion drives, period. Beyond these
issues, critics also raised questions about how the Stamford model could be
sustained and replicated.

Despite the compelling strategic logic of multiunion drives, they are notoriously tricky—locals almost never establish the level of trust necessary to
share information on their targets or coordinate strategy, both of which sometimes require subordination of individual agendas for the health of the overall effort. Internationals have often been unwilling to fund efforts they cannot
control by themselves, and, despite the efforts of the Sweeney administration, they are not at all certain they want the federation anywhere near their
organizing efforts.

But by most accounts, the unions worked well together here. Out of a tiny,
nondescript office in downtown Stamford, four different unions—Local 1199,
HERE, SEIU Local 531, and the United Auto Workers (UAW)—targeted at
least six different industries and organizing among at least that many ethnic
groups. You could feel the momentum right away when you walked through
the door. It had the air of a movement organization combined with the tight
organization of a political campaign. Rather than maintaining separate offices and only coming together around specific activities, organizers from all
four unions shared the same space, along with the AFL-CIO central staff,
encouraging a joint sense of purpose and camaraderie that has too often been
lacking in multiunion efforts. Taped to the walls, alongside the requisite
Fasanella posters and children's drawings, were elaborate campaign timelines,
lists of worksites, and picket signs. In the conference room, a ten-foot-long
scroll chronicled the story of the Stamford effort, with multicolored stars
bearing campaign benchmarks and victories affixed to it.

Julie Kushner, lead organizer for the UAW, talked about some of the reasons she thought the unions worked well together: "The sectors we represent
complement each other very well: 1199's nursing home workers are often
new immigrants and extremely poor, SEIU's janitors bring in a different sector of low-wage, immigrant workers, and the UAW brings in a combination
of low-wage workers from child care centers—primarily African American
and some Latino, immigrant taxi drivers, along with middle-class municipal
employees and newspaper reporters. What is also unique is that we have

found a group of unions very committed to changing the economic and social structure of Stamford through enlarging membership . . . people who
have a vision that goes beyond organizing workers to changing the status of
workers economically and socially by changing the power dynamics in the
city and region."[15]

Stamford was chosen because it had the highest concentration of unorganized workers in the state. The UAW and 1199 had both begun organizing
drives there, and, with the Senate majority leader, House Speaker, chairs of
the House Finance and Appropriations Committees, and attorney general all
hailing from lower Fairfield County, it also had the highest concentration of
political power in the state. The reason this much political power has become concentrated in lower Fairfield County is the presence of the *Fortune*
500 corporations and their vigorous campaign giving.

Starting out on virgin turf, the project knew that community support would
be crucial to the success of organizing campaigns. That is why, as the unions
stepped up their organizing activity in Stamford, aggressively targeting nursing
homes and taking on the mayor in a bitter contract fight for municipal workers, Jane McAlevey, the director of the project, worked with Local 1199,
HERE, SEIU Local 531, and the UAW to survey all of their new members to
find out what churches they belonged to in town. These new members then
went out in teams to their churches to speak with their ministers about the
union-organizing efforts. Several of those ministers became important allies,
coming out to worksites and rallies in support of organizing and contract
fights. Along the way, the union became more and more conscious of pressing community problems.

"The first time we all sat down with members and African American clergy,
we wound up talking about the cost of housing being so high as one of the
main reasons workers needed unions—they needed more money to pay the
rent," McAlevey remembers.[16] The unions and the clergy began to strategize
together about the need for ways to control skyrocketing rents and increase
the supply of affordable housing.

In April 1999, some newly organized nursing home workers were "invited" to a discussion with the Stamford Housing Authority about the future
of their housing complex. McAlevey recalled, "We did some digging and
realized that this was the next public housing development that the City wanted
to target for demolition and privatization. These were the workers at Courtland
Gardens, the Vencor-owned home where these women had just prevailed in
a massive anti-union campaign. They had just learned to fight the boss. They
were the first to say, 'Hey, we just beat a huge multinational company, surely
we can beat the housing authority and save our homes!'"[17] When the unions
considered the idea of becoming more involved in the housing campaign at

the next SOP staff meeting, it was a watershed event. They were no longer talking about the affordable housing crisis in the abstract, or even contemplating doing a campaign around it just to cement ties with community allies—they were talking about their own union members losing their homes.

For the next several weeks the project conducted exhaustive research. Union leaders and organizers door knocked throughout the housing complex and turned out 150 residents to the housing authority meeting. The headline in the *Stamford Advocate* the following day was "Healthcare Union Fights for Housing." By the end of the summer, they had stopped the city dead in its tracks and placed the affordable-housing crisis front and center on the public agenda—generating tremendous media attention to the fact that for four years running, Stamford had been ranked the most expensive city in the nation in which to rent a home.

Within a year, with the SOP providing research, staff, and strategic leadership, hundreds of Stamford workers and public housing residents mobilized to block the privatization and demolition of two public housing complexes, kicked off an inclusionary zoning policy debate, and generally placed the housing crisis at the top of local lawmakers' agendas.

At the state level, by bringing labor in, the project added considerable political muscle to the affordable-housing agenda—leading to the repeal of a pilot housing privatization law, generating a legislative deal to move $10 million in affordable-housing construction dollars, and, perhaps most significantly, offering to match the state spending on affordable-housing programs dollar for dollar up to $50 million in finance capital from AFL-CIO pension funds. At the local level, labor is sometimes accused by community groups of being all take and no give, so taking money from labor's coffers and making this kind of financial commitment to rebuilding communities was a tremendously important step—as important symbolically as it would have been practically, if the state had accepted the challenge.

Without question, the SOP's work on housing strengthened its standing in the eyes of community organizations. According to Reverend Winton Hill III, minister at Bethel Church AME, the SOP's coming to town made a dramatic difference: "The Stamford Project has given us the ability to concretize what our observations have been about how things really are for an awful lot of Stamford residents. They have enabled us to crunch the numbers, which we just did not have the resources to do, helped us to put on paper how many families were displaced, how many units destroyed, how many units at risk. The coalition with the union has helped us to move the agenda forward."[18]

According to Jeff Freiser, executive director of the Connecticut Housing Coalition, "Labor was an absolutely essential partner in providing political clout that by and large the affordable housing constituencies do not have.

Our colleagues in the labor movement worked with labor-friendly legislators to deliver their support. This is the first time that labor has made affordable housing a legislative priority. But it makes perfect sense—every morning, one out of every five persons who leave Connecticut's emergency homeless shelters are on their way to a job and have to return to the shelter at night because income does not meet the cost of housing."[19]

At a time when organized labor was feeling it was do or die in terms of organizing new members, it would have been easy for union leaders to dismiss the housing work as an altruistic distraction from the urgent task of rebuilding the labor movement. But union organizers in Stamford viewed the housing fight as integral to their work: "Our members were saying a 75-cent raise is great, a pension terrific, but we still can't afford to live in the city. We can't achieve the wage increases it would take to live in the city. A worker would have to make $22 an hour to afford an apartment here. The only two cities in the country more expensive for workers to afford the fair-market rent for a two-bedroom apartment are San Jose and San Francisco!" said Kate Andreas, 1199 lead organizer in Stamford.[20]

The UAW's Kushner adds, "We knew that there was not much history of community activism in Stamford and that relationships had to be built and trust had to be won. We knew that the basis of a partnership with the community was the clergy and that establishing trust meant we couldn't just go to them and say, 'How can you help us with our organizing drives?' We needed to say, how do we really work together to change this city and make it a better place for working people—so it is not just about asking the community to express solidarity with a drive, but it is about changing the community to make it a better place for working people to work and live."[21]

Kushner, Andreas, McAlevey, and the other organizers believed the housing work advanced their organizing in important ways. The unions were seen as real advocates for the poor and working class because they stepped out hard and acted boldly in the campaigns to block the demolition of housing. This built a good name for the unions fast among those they were seeking to organize. Local 1199 organizers pointed out that in a field where everyone works two jobs, where the workforce is tightly segregated by immigrant group, and where people live in tightly condensed areas, word about the union travels fast. People who partook of the antidemolition fight were impressed with the union, and organizers found that residents they first encountered during the housing fight were also working at facilities they are organizing. "When we knocked on their door, they knew us, invited us in, and signed the union card," says McAlevey.[22]

The housing work also created additional opportunities for members to become active in the union. Members met with legislative leaders and testified at hearings, at both the state and municipal levels. They led actions, marches, and protests. Organizers noticed that some members who were not necessarily leaders during organizing drives or contract fights became extremely involved through the housing campaign, reaching out to their ministers, playing important leadership roles, and becoming more active in other union activities as a result.

One final story helps to illustrate the use to which the housing work was put for organizing. The UAW was deep into its first contract fight with the mayor during the throes of the housing campaign. The union's goal was to break the existing unfavorable wages-and-benefits pattern for city workers. The mayor did not want to agree to it, and at a certain point, he broke off bargaining with the UAW and declared his intention to force them into arbitration. The union did not want to go to arbitration and wanted to get the mayor back to the table. To accomplish this, they needed to turn the heat up dramatically—the housing campaign helped them to do just that. They called a march on the mayor's house for affordable housing, a contract settlement, and an end to talking about the privatization of the city-owned nursing home. The rally was a success: city workers and public housing residents turned out in droves, and the mayor was sent a clear message about the SOP's growing base in the community. Other actions followed, which helped to keep the mayor on the defensive. Eventually he resumed negotiations, and the UAW achieved its goal of establishing a new pattern for city workers.

The locals believe that the SOP's community-oriented approach made a decisive difference to the outcome of organizing drives. Local 1199's successful campaign on the Atria Corporation's Courtland Gardens made it the first assisted-living facility ever to be organized in Connecticut and the first major win against Atria in the country. Atria, one of the biggest assisted-living chains in the nation, aggressively resisted the union, and, by organizers' accounts, the workers were scared to death. SOP's strong relationship with key clergy meant that ministers not only adopted a strong prounion position, but they reached out to workers who attended their churches to encourage them to remain strong in their commitment to bringing the union in (the SOP provided the information on workers' church affiliations that made this outreach possible). They talked with their parishioners directly, sent them letters, and stood outside facilities during the final days before the vote with a clear message: the union is the way up and out of poverty. When the CEO of Atria received a letter at his Kentucky headquarters signed by clergy and elected officials urging the company to maintain neutrality, he felt compelled to jump into his corporate jet and head to Stamford. The clergy and elected officials were so appalled by what he had to say that they became even more committed to standing with the workers.

The UAW believes that the SOP's strong support from elected officials and clergy tremendously bolstered their organizing campaign on Head Start. The agency relies heavily on state money, so it took notice when the Senate majority leader, the secretary of state, local board of education members, as well as clergy contacted them to urge neutrality. As a result, what might have been a nasty fight was toned down considerably.

The SOP changed the organizing climate in Stamford and more broadly transformed the city into contested ideological terrain where both the economic problems besetting poor and working-class people and proposed solutions to them were on the table and a matter of serious concern and debate. City Council President Carmen Domonkos witnessed a dramatic change: "No one was representing and speaking out on a consistent basis for working people—until the AFL-CIO came to town. They have turned it on its ear—this has made some people uncomfortable and some of us very happy!"[23]

Like BUILD in Baltimore, Stamford faced some challenges among its triumphs. In Stamford, unions filled a void that community organizations were not filling, and it was able to skirt a lot of tensions because there were no power-building community organizations with which turf and strategy had to be negotiated. The SOP, so much more resourced than any of the local churches, spoke out and organized on behalf of community issues, without really having to negotiate the terms of those issues or broader organizing strategies on an equal basis with any other group.

In addition, although at the national level the AFL-CIO was moving to greatly strengthen central labor councils (CLCs) and state federations, the SOP was never involved in any meaningful way with the local central labor body. The project decided that the returns would simply not justify the effort that would be required to turn the CLC into a more dynamic labor coalition.

Stamford Today

Between 1998 and 2001, the SOP operated in the form described above and succeeded in altering the relations of power in Stamford, winning major housing victories and organizing approximately 4,500 workers. But it was really always shadowed by questions of sustainability. In 2000, McAlevey moved on and was replaced at the helm by Shannon Jacovino, an organizer from Local 1199. From the time Jacovino started she was faced with dramatically contracting resources for the work. She remembered, "There was a new organizing director at the national AFL-CIO and a new program, so we were the only geo project that was still open when I got there. When they started the project, the intention was that it would at some point become self-sustaining. The AFL funded the project for two years beyond what it had intended to do and was always clear that the support would not last forever."[24]

In 2001, the AFL-CIO began drastically curtailing the resources it was putting into the project, ceasing to fund the community organizing and research positions, and in December of 2001, it reduced its funding to one staff position, agreeing to fund the project director for one final year. Jacovino reflected "The reality was that in terms of new worker organizing, in some respects the SOP member unions had gotten what they could get out of the project. Pretty much in terms of the city of Stamford, 1199 had organized all the nursing homes and at that point that was their focus and the janitors' organizing was also concluded. . . ."[25] According to the UAW's Kushner "With the Stamford project, we were successful in organizing city workers and childcare centers but after a while, we had so much organizing going on especially in higher education, we just couldn't afford to keep a full-time staff person there."[26]

In December of 2002 the SEIU state council in Connecticut made a decision to place Jacovino on the payroll. "SEIU said yes—the work we have done down here and the relationships we have built are important, we need to continue to have an anchor in Stamford. But the idea is also to keep the door open should the UAW and HERE want to come back here and do some real organizing in the area. This is all very fluid and SEIU likes the fact that we have been able to do work together and make the focus organizing."[27]

While the SOP, through SEIU's continued support, was able to maintain some presence, it was certainly nowhere near the level at which the project had operated during its heyday. This meant that the organization could no longer function as the major power-building organization for the poor and working class in Stamford that it had earlier been. Jacovino described the situation, "At this point, in terms of our relationship with clergy and housing groups we have depth that doesn't exist in a lot of places, but it is primarily around *our* struggles as opposed to the housing struggle. . . . I don't know whether we would have been able to establish ourselves without the housing fight, but there wasn't a will to say that this is a part of our work in any sort of long-term way."[28]

To try to ensure continuity, Jacovino tried to think of strategies for continuing both the ongoing multiunion and housing efforts. "In terms of the Fairfield County Central Labor Council, for a year and a half, we pushed hard. The deal was that all the locals were supposed to affiliate with the labor council and this would be a way to institutionalize it. When 1199 had a long strike in Fairfield, we got a lot of support from the labor council. But while our relationships with the council are much improved, nobody has made the decision to affiliate with them, although in my opinion that would have been the best thing to have happen." Jacovino worked to maintain support for the local housing work but also to engage the statewide housing organizations more deeply in the work in Stamford. The groups responded well. "They were happy to be brought into something that was already going. We still have a relationship with the tenants and when something happens, they want us there and when things happen with us, they will bring people to our events."[29]

In terms of more sustained community organizing, there is at present no community organization actively engaged in neighborhood or faith-based organizing efforts but Jacovino feels it would be great if there were. "There is no power-based community organization in Stamford and this is really a void. It is very hard to maintain relationships with all of the ministers and rabbis, especially since the Council of synagogues and churches disbanded, there is no one place we can go to talk to them."[30] Conversations with faith-based organizing groups about coming into Stamford are now in the beginning phases.

Many things have changed and many lessons have been learned since John Sweeney first took the helm at the AFL-CIO in 1995. In terms of major accomplishments, most labor leaders and observers would agree that the federation's signature achievement has been in the area of improving the effectiveness of labor's political operation, and not yet in organizing.

At the national level, the AFL-CIO's approach to supporting organizing has changed dramatically since the inception of the SOP. The geo projects turned out not to be a long-term strategy pursued by the organizing department. For a time it turned instead to trying to sign partnership agreements with international unions on targeted organizing projects in which the AFL-CIO actually lent staff and worked to shape the organizing strategy jointly with the international. This has also since been reconsidered. "Now there is a consensus," according to Milstein, "that the role of the AFL-CIO is much more in the 'Voice at Work' campaign to build a workers' movement to support workers' right to organize. We do still have some internationals we are trying to work with to develop strategies for organizing, but I would say that we have kind of dropped the rhetoric of saying 'a million new members a year.' What we are saying is that we have to build a workers' movement that supports workers' right to organize and that so far we haven't done that."[31]

Milstein feels that a lot of the lessons of the SOP, like working closely with community organizations and engaging in a sophisticated power analysis, have found their way into work that AFL-CIO staff are doing in many other cities. "Building power, as we did in Stamford, is becoming more a part of the overall strategy of the labor movement. More people are thinking that we need to build power rather than just we need a voice. . . . It's going beyond thinking about can you get a bill passed or get a contract at work to are you really able to make systemic change."[32]

Milstein and others acknowledge that the weakness of Stamford was that it was difficult to sustain and didn't change the central labor council. In the work that field mobilization staff are presently engaged in, rather than trying to do it all, they are more aggressively forging partnerships with community organizing groups who can work in tandem in a community. According to Milstein, "We are developing a really good model of getting faith-based, neighborhood-based, and workplace-based organizations to all work together. This work doesn't depend upon AFL-CIO organizing funds to make it happen and has the possibility of being deeper and more long term."[33]

During the time when Stamford was selected as a target city, there was a great deal of debate occurring at the national level about how and where the federation could best catalyze and support new union organizing on a large scale. The Union Cities program that focused on working with central labor councils to drastically improve support for organizing, politics, and the ability to mobilize the grass roots, was initiated during the same time period as the SOP and has continued to be refined. In its current iteration, the AFL-CIO is working intensively with a targeted group of central labor councils that are in places where there is relatively high union density that could be harnessed to support union organizing drives and electoral and public policy initiatives around the right to organize. The Stamford drive had a totally different logic: to choose a place for its political and symbolic importance that had a lot of potential and was essentially "virgin territory" for the labor movement, and to utterly transform it. From this vantage point, it had tremendous success. Although Stamford can arguably be viewed as a unique headquarters for multinational corporations that makes it an important battleground and linch pin for cities in southwestern Connecticut, it seems clear that if the decision had been made on the basis of where existing density could be used to leverage the power to organize very large numbers of new workers, Stamford would not have been selected.

Conclusion

Is it a paradox or the wave of the future? A community organization in Baltimore invents and wins the nation's first living wage law—igniting the most exciting new organizing around wages in decades. The AFL-CIO organizing project in Stamford, Connecticut, takes on the skyrocketing cost of housing—and leads the most successful community housing fight-back in contemporary Connecticut history. It may well be the wave of the future, but like most waves of the future, it is hard to tell what it will ultimately look like until it hits land.

In the face of twenty-first–century capitalism, labor needs to do more than simply doing better what it has almost always done. And what U.S. labor has almost always done, at least in contemporary times, is try to organize the workplace while ignoring what is going on in the larger community. As Piore has argued, the narrowness of the American labor movement in some sense has its origins in the initial separation between home and work life that was occasioned by the industrial revolution and reinforced in the New Deal and post–World War II periods. What resulted was a form of industrial unionism that embodied a conception of society that was characterized by a sharp distinction between work and other activities. This industrial system evolved into the archetypical 1950s' model of a single dominant wage earner with a wife and family at home in the suburbs. The isolation of workingmen's issues to the narrowest of workplace concerns meant that labor's legislative agenda was mainly procedural in character—focused on preserving the rights of unions to organize and to engage in collective bargaining, but the larger agenda of families was left out.[34]

Unions are used to organizing the majority of a workplace and calling it a victory. They have been doing this for so many years that it has made many unions act as if winning hearts and minds outside the workplace does not matter. Unions stopped making their case to the broader community—hence the prevalence of the "special interest" label. But this will not work anymore. What unions have to do now is move to transform the overarching political climate and power relations in a community.

Because of massive privatization of public services at the local, state, and federal levels, and increased corporate welfare, public policy has become a central battleground. To succeed legislatively, worker organizations must gain the support or perceived support of an electoral majority. It is not easy to do. They do it by casting worker issues in broader terms—by speaking explicitly about social, economic, and racial justice; by speaking on behalf of the working class as opposed to a particular group of workers; by nesting pay and benefits issues within broader frameworks like quality of care and education; and by forging deep partnerships with community organizations. As the federation debates how to build its density and change the organizing climate, these community-labor efforts provide clear examples of thinking outside the box. It is important to understand that the examples cited here are not exceptional cases—efforts like them are happening all across the country.

There is breathlessness, a "no time to lose-ness" about the labor movement today that can get in the way of the kind of open-mindedness and experimentation that is essential to forging a new paradigm. "We're dying," some labor officials say, with obvious justification. But since labor unions have more than 16 million dues-paying members and around $4.5 billion in assets, claims of labor's imminent demise have been wildly exaggerated.[35]

Of course, there is no one answer to the question of how to rebuild the labor movement—depending upon the local context, different strategies will make sense—but there is enough evidence to demonstrate that community unions, for all of their shortcomings, will prove indispensable.

To achieve the kind of expansion that labor desires, a new generation of workers will have to be wooed and won, and it will not be done solely on the basis of targeting and tactics—women and men must be won to the *mission* of labor. For the labor movement to have the opportunity for organizing on a massive scale again, it must be perceived as speaking on behalf of the whole. As Freeman has shown, the American labor movement has always grown in great spurts as opposed to slow accretion.[36] It grew the most in the 1930s, during the height of popular unrest over the economic crisis. What today's unions need in order to succeed is the moral legitimacy that community unions have demonstrated they have built in Baltimore, Stamford, and a growing number of other communities across the country.[37]

As labor historian James Green reminds us, labor history is full of important lessons for the present.[38] During each epoch of organizing on a mass scale, unions benefited enormously from shifts in the broader political climate. Unions also relied heavily upon community organizations and newspapers that could reach ethnic communities as essential pieces of infrastructure for organizing. It might well be that the greatest contribution community union efforts make will be in challenging the status quo, recapturing the moral high ground, and providing a gathering place and an entrée into collective action for low-wage workers. That is enough to justify a sizable investment on the part of the labor movement.

Notes

1. These numbers were taken from the following sources: AFL-CIO, Department of Public Affairs, press release, January 19, 2000; telephone conversation with Lane Windham, AFL-CIO, Department of Public Affairs, June 30, 2000; and Bureau of Labor Statistics, "Union Members in 1999."

2. This estimate is based on the data detailed above as well as that provided for *Work in Progress*, an AFL-CIO weekly publication that provides the total number of new members organized per week and for the year to date in each issue. Special thanks to Michael Eisenscher for helping me calculate these estimates.

3. A report by the Economic Policy Institute and the Women's Research and Education Institute estimates that, in 1995, 29.4 percent of all jobs were in nonstandard work arrangements, which includes independent contracting, working for a temporary help agency, contract or "on-call" work, day labor, self-employment, and regular part-time employment. See Arne Kalleberg and Edith Rasell et al., *Nonstandard Work, Substandard Jobs: Flexible Work Arrangements in the U.S.* (Washington, DC: Economic Policy Institute, 1997).

4. Reverend Doug Miles, interview, November 1996, Baltimore, Maryland.

5. Marc V. Levine, "Downtown Redevelopment as an Urban Growth Strategy: A Critical Reappraisal of the Baltimore Renaissance," *Journal of Urban Affairs* 9, no. 2 (1987): 103–23.

6. Arnie Graf, interview, November 1996, Columbia, Maryland.

7. Jonathan Lange, interview, November 1996, Baltimore, Maryland.

8. Bob Linehard, telephone interview, May 1998.

9. Corporate Affairs calculated that if Maryland union density remains at its current level of 15.1 percent, membership will increase from 367,000 members in 1999 to 412,000 in 2006, but if density declines at the rate it did between 1984 and 1999 (1.3 percent per year) it will be at about 377,000 members and 12.1 percent density. If union density of 18.3 percent in 1984 had been maintained, Maryland would have had 447,000 members in 1999 and 499,000 in 2006.

10. There was an option of a $5 per month membership that did not include benefits.

11. Lange, telephone interview, December 2003.

12. Carmen Domonkos, interview, November 2000, Stamford, Connecticut.

13. Bettina Drew, *Crossing the Expandable Landscape* (St. Paul, MN: Graywolf Press, 1998).

14. Merrilee Milstein, telephone interview, June 2000.

15. Julie Kushner, telephone interview, June 2000.

16. Jane McAlevey, interview, July 2000, Thetford, Vermont.

17. Ibid.

18. Reverend Winton Hill III, interview, June 2003, Stamford, Connecticut.

19. Jeff Freiser, telehone interview, June 2000.

20. Kate Andreas, interview, June 2000, Stamford, Connecticut.

21. Kushner, telephone interview, June 2000.

22. McAlevey, interview, July 2000, Thetford, Vermont.

23. Domonkos, interview, June 2000, Stamford, Connecticut.

24. Shannon Jacovino, telephone interview, June 2003.

25. Ibid.

26. Kushner, telephone interview, June 2003.

27. Ibid.

28. Jacovino, telephone interview, June 2003.

29. Ibid.

30. Ibid.

31. Milstein, telephone interview, June 2003.

32. Ibid.

33. Ibid.

34. Michael Piore, "Historical Perspectives and the Interpretation of Unemployment," *Journal of Economic Literature* 25 (December 1987): 1834–50.

35. AFL-CIO Organizing Department, 1999 CPS figures.

36. Richard B. Freeman, "Spurts in Union Growth: Defining Moments and Social Processes" Working Paper 6012, National Bureau of Economic Research, April 1997.

37. This phenomenon is young but already widespread. A national study of immigrant worker centers that I direct for the Economic Policy Institute has identified close to 130 organizations in more than 30 states.

38. James Green, *Taking History to Heart: The Power of the Past in Building Social Movements* (Amherst: University of Massachusetts Press, 2000).

11

Working Partnerships

A New Strategy for Advancing Economic Justice

Bob Brownstein

The leaders of the Silicon Valley Chamber of Commerce never knew what hit them.

On November 17, 1998, by an 8 to 3 vote, the San Jose City Council adopted the highest living wage policy in the nation. Businesses that provided contract services to the city would have to pay their workers a minimum of $9.50 an hour with health benefits or $10.75 without benefits. Moreover, here in the self-described "Capital of Silicon Valley," the living wage policy included two other significant elements of importance to labor. The first of these was a worker retention clause, protecting contract employees from displacement when new firms are selected by the city. The second, a labor peace provision, allowed the city to consider the potential consequences of unstable labor relations when it evaluated individual bidders for contracts.

To the chamber, it all seemed to be an inexplicable nightmare. They had relied on the kind of tried-and-true campaign of distortion that others had used so effectively in the past. Faxes and e-mails swarmed out of their head-quarters informing small-business owners that a living wage was, in fact, a separate San Jose super-minimum wage. The *San Jose Mercury-News* made wild charges that the living wage would poison the business climate, driving away the very firms that were pulling the region out of the recession of the early 1990s. All these claims were supposed to reduce the city council to quivering compliance, and they failed.

What had produced this unexpected reversal for the business establishment was an extraordinary development of the capabilities of the labor movement in Santa Clara County. At the heart of this movement stood a reinvigorated Central Labor Council (CLC), Working Partnerships USA (WPUSA), a policy and research institute that helped shape the public debate over the regional economy, and a growing coalition of community groups determined to reintroduce their values into government and business decision making.

Although labor has made only limited inroads into the high-tech workforce during the expansion of Silicon Valley industry, it has nonetheless organized substantial numbers of workers in other fields. More than 100,000 of the 937,600 workers in the county belong to unions, with significant densities achieved in the construction trades, the public sector, health care, certain retail sectors, and hotels. As regards labor's political involvement, during the 1960s and 1970s the region overturned a Republican "old guard" and elected Democrats to city, county, state, and federal legislative offices. Labor played a part in this transformation, but it was only one of numerous driving forces, including neighborhood organizations, women's groups (at one point activists proclaimed San Jose the feminist capital of the country), and environmentalists seeking to control urban sprawl.

The resurgence of labor in Silicon Valley would require, as it so often does, a combination of vision, leadership, and energy. These were provided in San Jose in the person of Amy Dean, who became the executive officer of the CLC in 1994. Dean recognized that for labor to advance in the new economy, it would be necessary to understand the unprecedented changes in corporate structures and strategies and in labor market institutions and practices that were taking place. She also knew that understanding without power could accomplish little, so union-organizing efforts and involvement in electoral campaigns became priorities. Finally, for labor to succeed, other constituencies in the valley needed to find common cause with labor's initiatives, so coalition building became a third critical emphasis. Labor's program had to expand to include a broad notion of social equity and a concern for the needs of all working families.

In retrospect, the focus on these three pillars—policy analysis and research, organizing and coalition building, and political action—constituted the critical decision that accounted both for the labor movement's substantive successes and for the continuing and potentially long-term solidity of its expanding role in Silicon Valley. As will be noted below, each of these pillars reinforces the others, creating a whole that is greater than the sum of its parts.

Gradually, Dean built a staff committed to this structural vision. Members of the CLC and WPUSA teams were characterized by skill and dedication. They reflected the ethnic diversity of the South Bay. Leaders of many of the critical programs were women.

Functionally, a division of labor was established to separate the activities of the CLC and WPUSA. The CLC assists affiliate union locals with organizing campaigns and manages labor's increasing role in regional politics. WPUSA, a nonprofit organization, is a vehicle to produce an understanding of economic issues that can be of value to policy makers and organizers alike. Created by a decision of the labor council, WPUSA has the capacity to perform research on changing labor market dynamics and their implications for working families. It can develop and evaluate policy alternatives. It also implements popular education programs that disseminate economic information both within labor and to other groups, thereby producing a foundation for coalition development.

Taking this conceptual model for the components of a stronger labor movement and translating it into institutions and action required years of effort and incremental accomplishment.

WPUSA, which was established in 1995 with a minimal staff, hit the ground running. In 1993, the state legislature had adopted AB 1823, which allowed counties to offer a property tax rebate to manufacturing firms considering expansion in the region. A year later, several rebates were issued with no systematic policies in place to ensure that the community received adequate benefits from these tax expenditures. This free-ride philosophy was about to be challenged.

In the summer of 1995, WPUSA analyzed the types of controls on tax subsidies employed successfully in other jurisdictions. The CLC organized a coalition calling for change. By September, a county task force (in which both WPUSA and the CLC had participated) proposed policies requiring that tax rebate recipients provide jobs with health insurance, and refund the rebate if they fail to generate the number of jobs promised. Guidelines for allocating rebates included a history of fair labor practices and adequate workplace health and safety policies. Over the opposition of the leader of the Santa Clara County Manufacturing Group, the board of supervisors unanimously approved the new requirements. The linkage in Silicon Valley between research, coalition building, and political action had been born.

In 1996, WPUSA issued its first research report, "Shock Absorbers in the Flexible Economy," which described the rapid expansion of contingent employment in Silicon Valley. The document also revealed the hardships for working families associated with temporary work—low pay, no health insurance, no pensions, and often unreasonable administrative practices.

By 1997, WPUSA had initiated its first program for popular education— the Labor/Community Leadership Institute (LCLI). Based on a cooperative agreement with San Jose State University, the LCLI offers an eight-week course that trains activists in economic issues, regional power analysis, and government structures and processes. Attendees come from unions, neighborhood groups, the clergy, and others. They have even included elected officials ranging from school board officials and city council members to the sheriff of San Benito County. Institute graduates praised the LCLI for both the quality of its curriculum and the unusual opportunity to network with members of other groups and develop new working relationships.

In 1997, WPUSA founded the Interfaith Council on Religion, Race, Economic and Social Justice, which brought together more than sixty community groups and congregations to generate positive social change based on the moral values of social compassion, economic justice, and personal responsibility. This collaborative network of religious, labor, civil rights, and community-based organizations explicitly frames responses to events and issues from a moral perspective. By doing so, it can shift the dialogue from a contention for power between labor and business to one demanding that corporate and government practices reflect a high moral ground. Members are often seen at the front of marches and rallies supporting fair treatment for janitors, cannery workers, and farm workers. Since its inception, the council has helped to inspire and organize a wide variety of community groups to advocate successfully for several projects, including an additional $25 million in Redevelopment Agency funds for very low-income housing, greater access to public benefits for immigrants, and adoption of the San Jose living wage policy.

During this period, the CLC also began improving its political capabilities. Increasing amounts of funds were raised for the Committee on Political Education (COPE), labor's political action arm. Volunteer recruitment operations became systematized, producing greater turnouts for precinct walks and phone banking. Importantly, the COPE endorsement process became more demanding. Where candidates might once have been asked if they would respect picket lines and support fair contracts, they now encountered probing questions on public policy issues. For example, candidates for county supervisor had to answer what they would do if the state lowered its subsidies for indigent medical care, a consortium of private hospitals proposed a low-cost contract to treat the poor, and the local press began crusading to close the county hospital. Evasive responses produced aggressive follow-up questioning.

By 1998, the labor movement's high-energy model had hit its stride. Working Partnerships' second research report, *Growing Together or Drifting Apart*, exposed the widening gap between the affluent and the poor in the new economy. Years before the media coined the phrase "digital divide," WPUSA shook the complacency of mainstream pundits who had been blithely claiming that the rise of information technology industries promised not merely greater wealth but also broadly shared prosperity. Through the debate over

Growing Together or Drifting Apart, the plight of the working poor in Silicon Valley had surfaced in a manner that made their presence on the local political agenda inevitable.

All of the elements of the labor-based coalition could now be joined together in two high-stakes campaigns, which made the fall of 1998 the time when labor in the South Bay would truly be put to the test.

First, as a result of term limits, the city council seat in district three, downtown San Jose, became open. Cindy Chavez, then political director of the CLC, announced her candidacy. The June primary narrowed the candidates to two: Chavez and Tony West, a Harvard-educated federal prosecutor who would carry the banner of the chamber of commerce and establishment interests.

Second, labor decided to press for adoption of a living wage policy while Mayor Susan Hammer remained in office. Hammer, a liberal Democrat, would also be termed out after 1998. Both of the leading candidates seeking to replace her opposed adoption of a living wage by the city. If this historic moment of opportunity was allowed to pass, the chance for a living wage might be lost for a decade. Despite the formidable challenge of undertaking two massive campaigns at the same time, the labor council pressed forward with the demand for a living wage.

Long years of precinct work, phone banking, and careful endorsements proved their worth. Labor had an excellent working relationship with Mayor Hammer. When WPUSA published an analysis calculating the level of income necessary for a decent standard of living in the valley, thereby demonstrating the need for a living wage policy, Hammer signed the report's introduction. Also, six of the ten city council members had received labor support in their election campaigns.

When the LCLI held its program in the spring of 1998, the participants chose the living wage as their class project. They and former LCLI graduates worked to form a broad coalition in favor of the proposal. The interfaith council offered opportunities to reach people of faith throughout the city. On Labor Day, living wage advocates spoke from the pulpit at eighty churches and synagogues, citing the moral validity of a "fair" wage. Thousands of support cards were collected in lobbies and parking lots after the services.

Opponents of the living wage fought determinedly to block its adoption. The *San Jose Mercury* lamented the "increasing influence" of labor on the mayor and urged the city council not to be "stampeded" into a "perilous" act that might damage the city's probusiness image. Chamber of commerce missives denounced the "job killer" policy that would "end our economic development program" and "drive businesses out of the city." Also, the conflict over the living wage spread out into the third district city council campaign. Cindy Chavez's opponent repudiated both the living wage and Chavez as a union-backed candidate. Chavez stuck to her guns and her identity, defending both the living wage and labor's agenda in the community.

On November 17, labor and allied groups initiated one of the strongest get-out-the-vote operations in the city's history. District three residents were reminded, urged, cajoled, and assisted to make it to the polls. Some enthusiastically, some grumbling, some getting dressed again after heading for an evening nap, they responded. Chavez won her seat by two hundred votes, fewer than three votes per precinct. Weary but elated volunteers at her victory party could identify by name more than two hundred persons they had managed to rally to the voting booths in the waning hours before the polls closed. In a desperate effort to stop Chavez, business interests had flooded the district with mailings paid through independent expenditures. Their late efforts proved fruitless. Labor prevailed in the trenches.

Two weeks after the elections, the city council held its dramatic hearing to decide on the living wage. Union members and living wage supporters jammed the chambers. Sensing defeat, only a handful of opponents appeared to testify. The margin of the victory astonished observers, as even one of the mayor's most persistent opponents voted "yes" on the living wage, explaining to the wildly applauding crowd that it was "the right thing to do."

The years between the establishment of WPUSA and victories of the fall of 1998 can be viewed as the formative period in the development of labor's new strength in the South Bay. From that time forward, each of the original pillars of capacity—policy analysis and research, organizing and coalition building, and political action—would at times play an advanced role in a strategy and receive support from the other two. Probably the best way to explain this mutually reinforcing process is to review a number of the situations in which it has actually functioned.

At times policy and research were the engines of action. In the spring of 1999, WPUSA released its most extensive report, *Walking the Lifelong Tightrope*, at a conference in the state capital, Sacramento. In this analysis, WPUSA expanded its analysis of the new economy to the entire state. Amid the drama of Initial Public Offerings (IPOs) and technological wizardry in California, the report discerned a work life characterized by extraordinary instability and insecurity. On a daily basis, working families confronted an economy in which median job tenure is three years, temporary employment is one of the fastest-growing industries, older workers are discarded as obsolete, and everything in major firms but the core occupations essential to product development is subject to outsourcing.

As a remedy, WPUSA discussed the design of a new social contract to modify the institutions that had once mediated harmful economic pressures on working families. Unemployment insurance, for example, was never designed to meet the needs of temporary workers. Similarly, new forms of portable health insurance will be required for workers who repeatedly change jobs.

This focus on the insecurity experienced by working families induced the labor movement to increase its efforts on behalf of contingent and temporary employees. To begin with, WPUSA secured funding for a large-scale temporary workers project with multiple components. This effort included a plan to organize a temporary-workers membership organization through which temps would secure access to health benefits, receive training opportunities, and develop forms of advocacy on their own behalf. By 2003, nearly 1,000 temps had become members and had become eligible to enroll in an affordable health insurance plan. Also, the project has established a model temporary employment agency that provides wages above industry standards and implements proworker administrative procedures.

Organizing led to advocacy. One of the early initiatives of the temporary workers project was to press for a code of conduct to be adopted by temporary employment agencies. The code, similar to standards proposed in South Carolina and New Jersey, calls for a living wage, access to affordable health benefits, training, and fair administrative procedures. In 2000, the subject for Labor Day sermons by activists was the plight of temporary workers. Once again thousands of worshippers signed cards, this time for the code of conduct.

However, it is one thing to gain letters and petitions in favor of a code of conduct and another to design a strategy that brings a code into practice. Labor planned to move the code forward by focusing on a "friendly" target—Santa Clara County government. A number of the members of the board of supervisors had been supported by labor in their election campaigns and were responsive to issues regarding low-income workers.

Since the county placed a substantial number of welfare-to-work clients in temporary agencies, the labor-community coalition asked the board of supervisors to perform a research project and determine whether those agencies lived up to the requirements of the code. The board agreed to send out a questionnaire on this subject. However, none of the temporary agencies responded. At this point, the coalition faced a political blind alley. It intended to ask the board to adopt a policy to give preferential treatment to agencies that met the standards of the code. However, without information, it was impossible to know how many, if any, agencies could reach such a standard. At the same time, the county social service agency entered the debate. Recognizing that federal legislation was requiring a speedy transfer from welfare to work, some of their managers with a long history of commitment to workers' rights expressed deep concern that they might be unable to locate alternative work options for those individuals losing eligibility for government entitlements. After some internal debate, the code of conduct strategy was deferred.

The setback regarding the code hardly even slowed down labor's momentum. It may be useful to consider why. Three factors appear relevant. First, the collapse of grassroots movements are often the result of self-inflicted wounds, and labor simply refused to wallow in disappointment over an unsuccessful tactic. It went back to the drawing boards to design new policy initiatives. In February 2003 it sponsored AB880, statewide legislation to impose a 5 percent payroll tax on temporary agencies, using the proceeds to enable local governments to provide services on which temp workers depend. Second, the deferral of the code in no way interfered with the other continuing programs of benefit to temps, such as the provision of affordable health insurance. Third, the labor movement was simultaneously involved in a number of other policy initiatives, some of which were spectacularly successful, as will be noted below.

Not all of WPUSA's policy proposals had their roots in a major research project. An alternative source of information and ideas was the accumulated experiences and institutional history of activists and local leaders in a wide variety of issue areas. WPUSA decided to systematically mine that wealth of knowledge through what became known as "the blueprint project."

The concept behind the blueprint was ambitious. WPUSA would hold roundtable discussions with the best local minds it could find on housing, environmental quality, health care, immigration, neighborhood concerns, and more. Participants would be asked to discuss the critical problems in their issue area and to suggest solutions. WPUSA staff would critically review this information from the perspective of economic and political feasibility. The best ideas would be published in a document, *The Blueprint*, which would guide the labor-community coalition for years to come.

In practice, the blueprint project revealed both the strengths and weaknesses of the stratagem of developing a formal "program" for the progressive movement in a region. Soliciting participation proved to be no problem. Most of the discussions were resounding successes, yielding enthusiastic and creative discussions. However, not every issue area could generate a "flagship" idea of sufficient scale and plausibility to warrant inclusion in a blueprint. Moreover, when the best ideas were gathered together, it was recognized that they constituted a list, not a strategy. In other words, they didn't build on one another or have links to one another or generate resources that would allow success in one area to lead to greater success in another. In consequence, *The Blueprint* was never published as a document in its own right.

What the blueprint process did accomplish was something quite different. In several cases, it revealed opportunities for individual policy initiatives that could produce major results. Such achievements would not serve to identify the labor-community coalition as a group with a brilliant coherent vision for the entire region. However, they could demonstrate that the coalition had the capacity to develop successful policies with extremely broad positive impacts that extended well beyond its own membership. In other words, they elevated the labor-community coalition to the stature of a group that could constructively exercise power on behalf of the community at large, a group that could govern.

The first of these initiatives came out of the blueprint's health care roundtable. Advocates and activists immediately agreed on the paramount problem: the large number of people lacking health insurance. The proposed solution, quite simply, was to provide that coverage. It didn't take WPUSA staff long to determine that this objective—universal health coverage in one region—could pass neither a political nor an economic feasibility test. But the analysis did not stop there. If universal coverage could not be achieved, what about covering a significant subset of the uninsured population? Would it be feasible to create a program that would provide health insurance for 100 percent of the low-income children in a city or county?

That question led to the launch of the Santa Clara County Children's Health Initiative (CHI), a project led by labor in coalition with People Acting in Community Together (PACT), a church-based activist organization. After six months of organizing, CHI had garnered commitments from local governments for allocations of $8 million from local tobacco settlement funds or tobacco taxes. Enrollment began half a year later. After thirty months, the program had processed applications from nearly 55,000 children and was widely recognized as the most successful effort of its type in the state. At least half a dozen other counties have generated their own programs based on the CHI model with many more imitators in the pipeline.

For the labor-community coalition, the CHI success had profound implications. It showed that the coalition could do more than follow the lead of other progressive coalitions; that is, add one more city to the list of those with living wage policies. In fact, it could *be* the leader. Moreover, CHI was widely popular throughout the valley. Even labor's harshest critics could not deny its value. Elected officials who had initially opposed it sought to rewrite history, arguing they were really among its strongest proponents.

A second blueprint proposal concerned affordable housing. Because of the meteoric rates of job growth in Silicon Valley, housing prices and rents have escalated wildly. Even relatively generous local government housing subsidies proved to be woefully ineffective in meeting the needs of low-income families. In addition, building affordable housing on infill sites in San Jose, the only Silicon Valley city with a substantial number of undeveloped sites still available, encountered serious obstacles. Expensive land costs necessitated massive government support for each project, and neighborhoods furiously resisted the high densities that could bring down per unit costs.

The blueprint discussion on housing had suggested inclusionary zoning. The idea had merit. But builders who confronted high infill costs could not possibly be required to also offer units affordable to extremely low-income households. The projects simply would not pencil out.

Further analysis suggested a variation of the inclusionary zoning proposal. Just south of San Jose lay the Coyote Valley, a 1,700-acre urban reserve designated in the city general plan for eventual residential development. Land in that area was less expensive. Neighborhood opposition would not be a problem; no neighborhoods existed yet. Why not apply inclusionary zoning to the 25,000 housing units planned for the urban reserve?

This time the proposal was included in a research document, WPUSA's report, "Everyone's Valley: Inclusion and Affordability in Silicon Valley." When the monograph was published, the far-reaching political effects of the CHI success became evident. City leaders immediately contacted the CLC and asked to make the proposal their own. At a press conference at city hall, the mayor endorsed the Coyote Valley recommendation. City council approval followed shortly. Literally without a fight, the labor-community coalition secured a commitment by the city to require 20 percent of the housing units in the Coyote Valley to be affordable

Other campaigns of the labor coalition had their genesis in organizing efforts either by coalition partners or by unions. Creating a network of activists that would help sustain coalition relationships had become an expanding part of labor's strategy. The LCLI model was replicated, allowing WPUSA to offer two new institutes—one for members of neighborhood associations and one for people of faith. Moreover, most of the 140 graduates of the initial LCLI formed a senior fellows program to maintain contact with one another, continue their education through speakers and workshops, and join together on common projects. When joint labor-community action was needed, the relationships essential for coordinated action had already been established.

A community-initiated issue soon surfaced when tenant advocates began pressing for stronger protection against arbitrary evictions. With a vacancy rate below 2 percent, landlords could issue a thirty-day "no-cause" notice and then raise the rents astronomically to a new tenant desperate to find a unit. Renters constitute less than 40 percent of San Jose's residents, and their level of organization cannot compare to that of the real estate industry. Unless they secured strong allies, their chances of convincing the city council to enter the hornet's nest of eviction policies would be slim.

By this time, labor had demonstrated convincingly both an interest in broader community issues and the capacity to produce results. When the renters asked for aid, numerous unions responded positively, noting their own members' problems with abusive eviction practices. Once WPUSA and the CLC entered the debate, the entire dynamic shifted. City leaders announced their intention to sponsor negotiations to forge a compromise reform. Landlord and real estate interests came to the table to face tenant advocates side by side with the labor-community coalition. A city ordinance providing renters with additional protections was drafted and adopted by the end of the year.

In other cases, union-organizing campaigns benefited from community assistance. When SEIU 250 struggled to secure first contracts with three hospitals owned by a nationwide health care corporation, the union could call upon a movement with experience in research, organizing, and politics. Policy briefs were generated indicating that the hospitals in question had violated state minimum staffing laws leading to complaints substantiated by state investigators. Religious and community leaders sent delegations and attended rallies. Elected officials requested meetings with hospital executives and explanations for the inadequacy of staffing ratios. When the contracts were signed, they provided improvements to the lives of thousands of health care workers in Silicon Valley and continued the momentum of successful organizing in the health care industry.

Politics—the third pillar of the strategy—offered continuing challenges and opportunities. Before the March 2000 primary a veteran assemblyman stepped down to seek a vacant congressional seat, setting the stage for a replay of the campaign in district three the previous year. In a solidly Democratic district where the primary winner is virtually assured of success in the general election, Manny Diaz, a city councilman who had strongly supported the living wage, found himself challenged by Tony West, the same candidate narrowly defeated by labor just thirteen months earlier. This time West had powerful allies—the state attorney general, the mayor of San Francisco, and a number of statewide business interests. Diaz campaigned as a labor Democrat, proudly announcing his intention to introduce a living wage bill in the state legislature. Diaz was outspent two to one, much of his opponent's funds going into a blizzard of negative mailings. Labor relied on its field operation. Some 10,000 hours of volunteer time produced a 53 percent victory for Diaz. The headline that followed, "Labor-Backed Candidates Stomp Big Business Boys in Legislative Races," left no doubt as to the basis for Diaz's triumph.

Following these victories, it was probably inevitable that conservative interests would seek to force the legitimacy of labor's political role in Silicon Valley to a public test at the ballot box. The battleground was an open city council seat in 2002. Business leaders argued that a labor victory would provide unions and their allies with seven votes, a working majority, on the city council. The chamber of commerce endorsed a local neighborhood leader; the CLC backed a school board member. The critical issues in the campaign centered on eviction protection, the living wage, and a more fundamental question—should the city council demonstrate balance between business and labor coalitions or have a pronounced slant toward the priorities of working families. Once again, the labor field campaign generated a maximum effort. Voters were visited and phoned repeatedly, with messages delivered in English, Spanish, or Vietnamese. The opposition relied on a costly mail campaign. When the votes were counted, labor's candidate had won with 62 percent of the vote. The debate regarding "balance" that business leaders had provoked had been decided—but not in the way they had envisioned.

Lessons from the Past, Visions for the Future

When reviewing the accomplishments of the combined efforts of the CLC and WPUSA in Silicon Valley, several conclusions potentially relevant to other regions can be advanced.

The first and most obvious is the extraordinary effectiveness of the three-pillar model. The expertise to define a meaningful policy agenda, the ability to engage in grassroots organizing to communicate the usefulness of these proposals, and the capacity to effectively engage in electoral politics are all essential and symbiotic elements of a strategy to increase labor's power.

An incredible public policy vacuum exists at the local and regional levels in many areas. This vacuum results partly from legislative gridlock, partly from term limits, and partly from politicians who have let pollsters do their thinking for them. Unquestionably, it is also a consequence of the failure of conservative philosophies to produce results in almost any of the critical areas of life for working families—from housing and health care to job security. However, labor must also recognize that the vacuum results from its own disappointing tendency to cede the terrain of policy development to "third way" Democrats.

This vacuum provides an unusual opportunity for labor and its allies— not just a chance to develop programs that meet its members' needs but also the chance to demonstrate that labor can be a powerful voice for community needs that are otherwise ignored.

High-quality research produces multiple payoffs. It creates the space for political action by raising issues into the public arena. In this manner, the WPUSA report on growing inequality set the stage for the living wage campaign. It also enables labor to enter policy debates and win. Finally, it provides insight into complex issues that can produce workable policy proposals that labor-backed candidates can embrace.

Without policy objectives that effectively improve the lives of working people, victories at the polls advance the careers of political leaders but not the role of labor in the community. It is the nature of the policy objectives that labor fights for that will motivate its volunteers and allow the expansion of its coalitions.

However, the bookshelves of America are crowded with policy proposals that—whatever their merits—have never reached beyond small circles of experts. Policy development has to be based on an interactive relationship with a community base. Policies have to meet real needs in an understandable fashion, and the fact that they meet this standard has to be communicated in the field through grassroots activity.

Networking, the organizational practice of executives and elites, can work for progressive activists too. The relationships established at community training institutes in Silicon Valley are the sinews of coalitions that have taken action successfully on specific issues. Increasingly, smart-growth proponents, tenant advocates, and health advocates are recognizing the usefulness of having a strong labor-community coalition in their region.

Expanding labor's policy agenda beyond its basic contract issues can produce both forms of organizational support and shifts in public opinion that pay off at the bargaining table. This spring, SEIU Local 1877 engaged in tough negotiations for a new master contract for janitors, seeking to protect their members from excessive increases in health insurance premiums. When the union made its demands, it did so in a political environment in which even industry spokespersons are acknowledging the unacceptable gap between rich and poor that was first identified and challenged by WPUSA. When Local 1877 sent delegations to meet corporate executives or held rallies and demonstrations, union members stood with clergymen and elected officials, neighborhood leaders and community activists. In Silicon Valley, labor does not have to fight alone, and that fact may help determine the scale of the ensuing conflict. Local 1877 won its contract in May 2002 without a strike.

Even if well communicated at the grassroots level, a policy agenda can not adopt and implement itself. Government decisions are necessary. Proposals to benefit working families usually require costs to be absorbed somewhere by some interest. Elected officials will not confront those forces unless they recognize there is real value in labor support—and a sobering price to pay if they take the other side. The connection between the outcomes of the district three and twenty-third assembly district races and candidates' positions on the San Jose living wage has been lost on no one involved in the local political arena.

The question that the future will answer is the extent to which the three-pillar strategy can be sustained and expanded. It is relevant to note that the labor-community coalition—despite its major successes—lacks both a formal structure and a concrete membership base. People and organizations make plans and take actions with the knowledge that the coalition exists. But it has no board of directors, much less an executive committee. Organizations participate when they choose to show up. Similarly, no one pays dues to the coalition, although they may be financial supporters of a coalition member.

Silicon Valley is the home of virtual organizations of numerous types. Many of them thrive on the flexibility such arrangements permit. Whether a labor-community coalition can prevail in the long term on this basis remains to be seen. At some point, the need to move toward a more formal structure may be unavoidable, and the outcome of confronting that challenge cannot be predicted today.

Finally, one of the intangible strengths of the coalition that deserves emphasis is its explicit commitment to values. Values are as important as interests when labor engages in political contests. The apostles of the new economy tend to be infatuated with the efficiency of markets. But in neighborhoods and communities, even in Silicon Valley, people seek an economic order that is both productive and fair. By their unwillingness to acknowledge the validity of fairness as an economic criterion, the opponents of the living wage left themselves no strategies other than distortion or the unimpressive assertion that fairness should be left only to higher levels of government. When labor states that it believes the economy should reflect community values, it strikes an instinctive chord with constituencies that range from civil rights advocates to proponents of homeless shelters to opponents of urban sprawl. Belatedly, opponents of labor are getting the message. As "born again" proponents of fairness, however, they will have to confront labor on its own ground.

12

Economic Development for Whom?

Labor Gets Involved in Massachusetts's Economic Development

Mary Jo Connelly, Peter Knowlton, Pete Capano, and Harneen Chernow

To many union activists, intervening in the economic restructuring that has stripped our communities of decent jobs has become a critical challenge. We do not see economic development work as an alternative to the labor movement's other imperatives—namely, organizing more and different kinds of workers as union members and mobilizing to gain a stronger political voice. We see it as a necessary complement to these struggles and to our efforts to influence global trade policy. Like union activists nationwide, the Massachusetts trade unionists whose works are described in this chapter launched their local economic development efforts *because of* their experience as workers in industries and regions decimated by industrial flight to countries such as Mexico and China.

Building Labor Capacity for Intervening in Local and Statewide Economic Development
Mary Jo Connelly

Why Economic Development?

Beginning with industrial plant closings in the late 1970s and intensifying in the late 1990s, growing numbers of union activists across the country have worked to influence the development of their local and regional economies. As corporate interests have led economic restructuring at all levels from global to local, unions have been involved in a variety of efforts to gain more say over job creation, job retention, job training, and community standards for public expenditures in these areas. Unions and their community partners have begun to pose and organize around alternatives to "corporate" models of economic development. These corporate models usually create low-wage jobs without benefits or opportunities, and promote contingent, disposable, transferable, or dangerous jobs and jobs that make it very hard for workers to organize. In addition, they often draw on public funds to perpetrate these evils.

State and local union activists who take on economic development quickly figure out that we need to do a lot of upfront learning. Few unions have the same level of knowledge about economic development systems as they have about politics or bargaining. This is not surprising, since the emerging interest in economic development represents a significant new direction for organized labor. In the thirty years following World War II, organized labor in this country played little more than a token role in shaping job creation or the structure of the economy at the national, regional, or local level. Instead, in the postwar years U.S. unions relied on two broad strategies for influencing the economy: a labor market strategy aimed at raising wages in key sectors, and a political strategy to create a wage floor and elements of a social safety net.

While labor's involvement in economic development began with campaigns to stop plant closings, it has evolved into a growing menu of policy and programmatic tools. Unions and their community partners are working to influence the quality of jobs created in their communities, the access to training that leads to high-wage jobs, and the climate and opportunities for workers to organize unions. For union activists, this direction means taking on a new and broader conception of "community unionism" and new roles with respect to community partners. These union-community economic development efforts include:

- Grassroots campaigns for living wages, community standards, disclosure of corporate subsidies, and linkage to provide job access to low-income residents
- Union-sponsored or -affiliated education and training programs to improve job access, career opportunities, and even industry competitiveness
- Campaigns by unions and community partners to influence the allocation of publicly funded workforce development and economic development resources toward jobs that can sustain families and communities.

Many of these efforts have been documented elsewhere by the AFL-CIO's Working for America Institute and by labor movement scholars.[1]

The Massachusetts Context: Why Labor Is Looking for New Strategies

Over the past three decades, working families in Massachusetts have been subjected to an intensified version of the negative economic trends familiar to low- and middle-income workers in other parts of the United States: the decline of real income and the rapid growth of income inequality; the disappearance of high-wage manufacturing jobs and the rise of a high-tech new economy demanding skills that few low-income workers have the opportunity to acquire; the growth of low-end service industries that rely disproportionately on contingent labor and easily exploited undocumented immigrant workers; the privatization of public and human services; and a badly sagging social safety net, exemplified by the nation's most punitive welfare reform policy. Not coincidentally, for the past generation Massachusetts has been governed by a fiscally conservative Republican administration.

Rapidly Growing Inequality

Restructuring to a "new economy" has meant creating jobs and generating greater wealth for Massachusetts's affluent residents, but at the expense of middle- and lower-income working families. Massachusetts is not only one of the most unequal states, it is the one where inequality is growing fastest.[2] The wealth gap between the top 5 percent and the middle 20 percent of Massachusetts's residents is growing at the same rapid rate as the gap between the richest and poorest. While family incomes declined, the Massachusetts cost of living remained 10 percent to 25 percent higher than the national average, and housing prices increased faster than anyplace else in the country, an average of 49 percent.

Decline of Regional Manufacturing Economies

Mirroring the restructuring of the U.S. economy, over the past three decades Massachusetts's economy has shifted from manufacturing to services. The manufacturing base has been declining during that time, but, unlike the rest of the country, Massachusetts manufacturing shrinkage intensified in the 1990s. The Commonwealth's manufacturing dropped from more than 30 percent of all jobs in 1969 to 13 percent in 1999.[3] Between 1992 and 1997, while total U.S. manufacturing employment rose 4 percent, Massachusetts lost 131,359 more manufacturing jobs.[4] Further, the North American Free Trade Agreement (NAFTA) has had a disproportionately negative impact on Massachusetts. Losing over 17,000 jobs in the first seven years of NAFTA, Massachusetts was harder hit than only California and six other heavily industrialized states.[5] (This reduction does not include additional losses to countries outside the NAFTA region.)

Manufacturing and manufacturing losses have been clustered in the northeast, southeast, and western regions of Massachusetts. The two cases described below are both from regions that historically have been among the most heavily industrialized and now have been heavily hit by deindustrialization. Between 1985 and 1999, the city of New Bedford in southeastern Massachusetts and the city of Lynn in northeastern Massachusetts both lost over *half* of their manufacturing base, a loss of more than 11,300 manufacturing jobs in New Bedford and more than 8,300 in Lynn.

For both cities, there may be even farther to fall, since both still rely on manufacturing far more than most other Massachusetts cities. Manufacturing still accounts for 25 percent of all jobs in New Bedford and 28 percent in Lynn, twice the 13 percent state average. No other industry has replaced the lost manufacturing jobs in either city. In 2001, New Bedford and Lynn each had 10,000 fewer jobs of all kinds than in 1985. Unemployment in New Bedford has run at twice or two-and-a-half times the state average and Lynn has consistently stayed about 25 percent above the state average, even in "boom" years. In 2002, with statewide unemployment up to 5.3 percent, the unemployment rate in New Bedford rose to 11.2 percent and to 6.65 percent in Lynn. Child poverty rates in both communities are about twice the state average.[6]

Economic Restructuring for a Knowledge-Based Service Economy

As the Massachusetts economy restructured, services grew to be the largest sector of the state economy, but this is a service sector sharply divided between low-skill, low-wage jobs and high-skill jobs in the new "knowledge-based service economy."[7] "We are an early-stage economy," says Rosabeth Moss Kantor, a professor at Harvard Business School. "We create the knowledge. When a product moves further along and becomes a commodity, it gets made someplace else."[8] Whether you call it an "early-stage" or a "knowledge-based" economy, it still includes low-level workers who lack advanced degrees. By the late 1990s, the "knowledge-based service economy"—industries such as software, research and development, biotechnology, consulting, and money management—grew to 79 percent of the Massachusetts economy, as compared with 42 percent of the U.S. economy.

Education and Training Gaps

Even as Massachusetts has been moving to a knowledge-based economy, it has failed to provide the education and training that would allow its workforce to follow. It is estimated that one in three workers is not adequately prepared for the new economy because of gaps in their basic or English language skills. The state's adult education and training system is woefully inadequate. Due to lack of funding, it has the capacity to serve less than 6 percent of the workers who need skills.[9] This segment includes limited-English–speaking workers, who account for a rapidly growing proportion of the state's workers. In fact, immigrants accounted for *all* of the net growth in the state's labor force in the 1990s.[10]

Organized Labor's Fight to Reclaim Ground for Working Families

Like its national counterpart, organized labor in Massachusetts has responded to economic restructuring with a mix of old and new strategies to influence economic opportunities for working families. An intensified commitment to organizing new members has generated innovative alliances and strategies. Labor and friends have won right-to-organize resolutions in more than twenty-two Massachusetts cities. Most central labor councils (CLCs) across the state have actively worked union city agendas. Industry organizing in health care, building services, telecommunications, manufacturing, building trades, and hospitality has reflected labor's aim to exert pressure on those key segments of the labor market. Massachusetts unions have also crafted campaigns to follow outsourced or privatized work in electronics, human services, and construction. Knowledge workers in a few private colleges and high-tech firms have joined unions, and more are organizing. Individual unions, labor councils, and the state federation have made a special commitment to building long-term relationships with immigrant communities and workers they seek to organize.

In defense of working families, Massachusetts labor has also mobilized for many political battles around the minimum wage and the social safety net. With a conservative Republican governor, far too many of these battles have been defensive ones. Most have involved alliances with community partners at both the state and local levels. Labor's recent key state policy battles have included efforts to roll back punitive welfare reform, fund paid family leave, establish publicly funded training for low-wage workers, and index the minimum wage to increases in the consumer price index. At the local level, labor-community alliances have succeeded in passing living wage ordinances in three Massachusetts cities and one county, as well as focusing media attention on the issue on one well-known college campus.

The Challenges in Moving an Economic Development Agenda

By the late 1990s, a number of Massachusetts labor activists recognized that even with strong organizing and a focused policy agenda, labor needed some new weapons in our arsenal if we were to regain ground for working families in a rapidly restructuring economy. The workforce and economic development systems have proved to be logical arenas for strategic intervention by organized labor at state and regional levels. Massachusetts labor activists and labor educators who sought new ways to intervene in state and local economic development confronted a number of challenges, which will be addressed in more detail throughout the following narratives. The challenges include:

1. *Building support within labor*: We needed to find ways to build understanding of and support for this work within our own unions, labor councils, and statewide labor movement. It has been a particular challenge to frame this work as a necessary complement to organizing and political action, at a time when our labor movement has been stretched thin meeting our existing commitments and surviving in a very tough political and economic environment. In addition, it has been challenging to try to build this support in unions representing different sectors, populations, and interests. Finally, it was important to carefully delineate the complementary roles to be played by state labor leaders, local leaders, and labor educators in advancing economic development agendas within labor institutions.

2. *Coalition building*: At the same time that we are working out certain issues "inside the family" of labor, to be effective on economic development issues we also needed to build and deepen relationships with community-based organizations and progressive policy advocates both within our regions and at a statewide level. In many cases, we faced the challenging of expanding or refocusing collaboration: moving from a labor-community partnership built around a training program to one focused on policy advocacy; or adding new partners to the core of a living wage collaboration to create a corporate accountability coalition. Of course, community organizations faced the same tough political and economic climate as unions did, with a scarcity of staff and activists struggling to fight many battles.

3. *Pulling together needed research and other information resources*: As mentioned, labor activists found that our organizations knew relatively little about state and local economic development systems, and that we had a lot to learn before we could identify effective ways to intervene to have our voices heard in setting job creation and workforce development agendas. We had to start with the most basic questions: What public and private institutions are involved? Who makes what kinds of decisions concerning public incentives and subsidies? How much money is involved? Where are

there openings through which labor and community allies might raise issues of wages, job standards, access to jobs and training, and access to union membership?

4. *Grounding economic development work in concrete organizing and political work:* An ongoing challenge is how to translate activists' vision of people-centered economic development into actionable campaigns. While it is important to articulate principles and criticisms of existing economic development priorities, it is equally important to find ways to challenge these more directly: for example, organizing for city council ordinances or state legislation to disclose corporate tax breaks and redirect these funds to labor priorities such as training, or translating "good jobs" principles into COPE principles that are used to screen candidates seeking labor support.

5. *Linking regional and state-level work:* Because in our state labor's economic development efforts have been a lively mix of region-specific and statewide initiatives, it has required active coordination on the part of activists, state leaders, and labor educators to keep each other current and to share information and research resources. For example, this work is being done in different venues in different CLCs: a few CLCs have established economic development committees while others locate their work within in a coalition effort. And while a general trajectory for corporate disclosure legislation and policy work is taking shape at the state level, its links to local tax disclosure work have been slower to emerge.

People First! Trade Union Activists Get Involved in Workforce and Economic Development in Southeastern Massachusetts
Peter Knowlton

Southeastern Massachusetts is historically a manufacturing and fishing industry region with a long history of labor activism. From the early days of Frederick Douglass and the *Liberator*, to the strike of 1928 involving more than 28,000 textile workers, to the innovative and radical approaches to fighting plant closings and the threat of taking a factory by eminent domain in the 1990s, southeastern Massachusetts has a rich tradition of workers struggling to improve their living and their place in society. As in other industrial regions across the country, however, the 1980s and 1990s gave rise to massive plant closings in southeastern Massachusetts, resulting in the loss of thousands of good paying jobs.

During this time the state allocated resources for dislocated workers through the creation of workers assistance centers (WAC). WACs employed union leaders and activists from closing workplaces to coordinate dislocation services for their laid-off coworkers. WAC staff assisted workers in finding new employment and education and training opportunities, and in getting access to financial assistance. The servicing work that stewards and officers had done in their workplace they now did for laid-off members. During this time the United Electrical, Radio, and Machine Workers (UE), the Union of Needletrades, Industrial and Textile Employees (UNITE), the United Auto Workers (UAW), and the United Rubber Workers (URW) all experienced plant closings, with the union playing a lead role in setting up and staffing a WAC.

Union-run WACs were more successful than city- and state-run centers for a number of reasons: (1) the centers were staffed by coworkers of the laid-off workers, who were also being laid off and were therefore quite sensitive to the challenges facing their coworkers; (2) WAC staff were previously stewards, officers, or activists and brought the knowledge, skills, and tools of union leadership as well as the respect of their coworkers to their work; and (3) bureaucratic hurdles faced by laid-off workers were addressed by WAC staff in the same way that problems in the shop had been addressed, and therefore workers secured the necessary assistance, education, or training.

By the late 1990s, the public system to support dislocated workers had changed. Rather than setting up WACs, the system sent these workers to regional one-stop career centers staffed by employment and training professionals and offered a narrow menu of standard job search activities. In 1996, for example, the members of UE 284 employed by J.C. Rhodes saw their profitable plant sold—despite efforts to defend their jobs and have the company taken by eminent domain—and moved to Georgia, where the company paid $2 to $5 per hour less to nonunion workers. Upon being laid off, many of UE 284's dislocated workers experienced a bottomless pit of bureaucratic roadblocks and frustration in dealing with the city and state worker dislocation services.

In late 1998, another company, M.I. Phoenix, closed, and UNITE members experienced similar problems. No longer were union officers hired to operate a workers' assistance center tailored to the needs of a specific workforce. Public resources dedicated to worker retraining and education seemed woefully inadequate and counterproductive. Dislocated workers could not qualify for training to learn new skills if jobs were available in the field from which they were laid off. Stitchers from M.I. Phoenix who qualified for extended benefits because they were laid off by foreign trade, for example, were unable to receive training to learn a new skill because stitcher jobs were available in the area. The system that was supposed to prepare workers for the next century seemed to keep them from diversifying their skills and from moving into industries with more of a future than the declining apparel industry.

A "Summit" on Regional Economic Development

In early 1999, discussions began among representatives from some area manufacturing unions (primarily UE and UNITE), the University of Massachusetts–Dartmouth Labor Education Center, the Massachusetts AFL-CIO, and the area's two AFL-CIO Central Labor Union bodies. Initially the discussion centered on laid-off workers: what they needed and what must change to make it happen. From there the discussion took a radical, but not unlikely, turn to focus on the region's economic development picture and what role, if any, unions and workers played in it.

After a few weeks of informal discussions, participants decided to pull together a "summit" of local union leaders, public officials, and economic development "wonks" to discuss the region's workforce development system, the creation of a working people's economic agenda for southeastern Massachusetts, and labor's future policy initiatives to improve working people's lives. Despite the fact that Representative Jim McGovern, the University of Massachusetts–Dartmouth chancellor, and the Massachusetts AFL-CIO secretary-treasurer were keynote speakers and presenters, only a handful of the fifty-plus attendees were public officials or economic development leaders. Not surprisingly, most participants were local union leaders and activists representing all industries from the public sector to the building trades. The absence of public officials and economic development staff sent us a message: When it comes to issues of economic development, labor is viewed as a nonplayer. Those who matter are the chamber of commerce, the industrial park agencies, big business, and the public and quasi-public functionaries in public service and economic development agencies.

The summit experience left us motivated to discuss, understand, and influence economic development in the southeastern region. We wanted to challenge and eventually change the corporate-driven model of economic development where public resources are used as corporate welfare to improve the employer's bottom line and not necessarily the welfare of the workers or the community. What happens to jobs in the corporate-driven economic development model could not be plainer.

Manufacturing: The average manufacturing job paid $10 to $12 an hour in the 1980s with a full benefits package. The region had high union density. Twenty years later, the average manufacturing wage had been driven down to $8 to $10 an hour, a full benefits package was nothing more than a pipe dream, and unions were all but irrelevant in the region. The area lost more than 15,000 good-paying manufacturing jobs in an area where only 100,000 people were living.

Seafood processing: In the early 1980s, most of the 2,000 seafood processing workers were members of the independent Seafood Workers Union with an average wage of $10 to $12 an hour with full benefits. Today the union has been busted, and the industry has half the number of workers, with a substantial number working as temps or part-timers with no health insurance and little to no paid time off. Only one seafood processor has a union. There, like most places in the United States, the momentum for organizing manufacturing workers under the rules of the National Labor Relations Board has ground to a halt.

Organizing Around a Different Vision

As one working group member and presenter stated during the summit, "It is indicative of this area's legislative, economic, and political priorities that when advisory and planning councils are established to deal with economic or community development, the labor movement, if included at all, is tokenized at best. This intent, and its success, is simply the societal expression of what companies insist on in every negotiation for a union contract—management rights. We may have a voice but we have no power." What came out of the summit was the recognition that for labor to become a player in workforce and economic development, we had to join up with friends and allies and come up with a plan that expressed our vision of development.

Currently our southeastern working group consists of local trade union leaders, activists, a local community economic development center, a growing number of academics, and ongoing assistance from the Massachusetts AFL-CIO.[11] Initial work of the group included (1) developing a document (*People First! A Plan for Sustainable Economic Development in Southeastern Massachusetts*) that outlines the basic principles and policies of an "alternative" economic development vision, and (2) increasing our visibility at those forums where economic and workforce development policy is made. We have also spent a tremendous amount of time over these last two years just learning the economic development "game."

The *People First!* document, which outlines the group's basic approach to economic development in both policy and principle, has been adopted by our local central labor council and appears on its Web site. A cornerstone of the document is to "guarantee that workers can exercise their rights under the First Amendment and the National Labor Relations Act without fear of retaliation or employer interference" (*People First: A Plan for Sustainable Development in Southeastern Massachusetts*, at www.nbclclabor.org/economic. html). We are first and foremost trade unionists who believe the best way for workers to improve their power at work and in the community is to organize freely, without threats or coercion, and to build unions. In addition, the document states:

Workers, residents, and community organizations traditionally play a very limited role, if any, in shaping our economic future. This has kept us on the "outside looking in." Economic development responds to corporate interests whose primary goal is making money rather than providing for the welfare of workers and our community. This creates a growing wage gap between the owners, the producer, and the consumers. Corporate influence and profits grow while our incomes and communities decline.

We need an economic development policy that puts improving the standards of people and our environment first—not last. We need a policy that gives our community more power over its economic engine and improves the economic, social, political, and spiritual well being of its residents. We need a policy that encourages alternative forms of business; including worker owned and operated enterprises, consumer and producer co-ops. We need a policy which supports a progressive tax structure and the delivery and expansion of public services.

We are continually taking the document to local unions and community, civil rights, women's, economic development, educational, and church-based organizations. We use this opportunity to build our labor community alliance for *People First!* economic development in several ways. We spend time learnings about what the group is working on and how we might be able to work together. We introduce and discuss *People First!*, ask for suggested amendments, and request that the organization endorse the principles and join the effort. We began this effort by presenting to existing allies to gain experience discussing and debating the issues surrounding economic development.

We will continue to use *People First!* to insert labor's agenda into southeastern Massachusetts economic development forums and discussions. We are considering using the principles and programs outlined in *People First!* during the next round of local elections. Those candidates that do not endorse the document would not get labor's support. We may also undertake a campaign to hold city governments accountable for tax breaks awarded to businesses in exchange for promises to create jobs.

We continually work to analyze, clarify, and guide labor's role on local workforce and economic development boards and forums. Labor has mandated seats on the local workforce investment boards (WIBs) that disburse federal and state funds to companies for training, education, and development. The WIBs also oversee the "one-stop" career centers that coordinate training and education opportunities for dislocated workers. Companies that receive these monies have minimal requirements or accountability for providing a secure, safe, and economically sustainable livelihood for its workers, families, and the community. The major economic development centers in the region, like most locales, are virtual creatures of the business community and disburse large amounts of public dollars for tax increment financing, loans, grants, and so forth, with little or no accountability. Labor has yet to have a presence in these organizations—but we will!

At some point, conflicts within the labor movement or with our allies will occur over specific development projects, for example, building prisons, casinos, or power plants. We view economic development in terms much broader than structures and brick or mortar. For us, it would be a mistake to allow an individual project to distract us from pushing forward to build a movement that bases economic development on people rather than profits, on workers rather than the stockholder, on the community rather than the boardroom, and on the environment rather than pollution. We are trying to unlearn bad habits and to put ourselves into a seat we have not sat in for decades. We are ready for the challenge and the responsibility that goes with it.

Building a Labor/Community Partnership for Living Wages Jobs: The ECCO-IUE/CWA 201 Jobs Team
Pete Capano

In November 1996, International Union of Electrical Workers (IUE)/Communication Workers of America (CWA) 201, representing workers at General Electric (GE) in Lynn, forged a partnership with the Essex County Community Organization (ECCO), an organization of fourteen faith-based organizations also in Lynn, to address the need for better jobs in our community. In response to years of downsizing at General Electric, IUE/CWA 201 got involved in this partnership to provide better job opportunities for our members who faced job insecurity. The goal was to provide living wage jobs with benefits and a career path for IUE/CWA 201 members and their children and for members of the ECCO congregations.

The Union's Goals for This Partnership

In addition to providing good jobs, IUE/CWA 201's goal was to build power to better effect change. The largest union on Boston's North Shore, working with the largest community organization, had great potential to shape economic and social policy in the region. We hoped over time to create a powerful coalition among labor, community, and religious people that can provide mutual support during times of struggle and a strong voice for social justice.

Another goal for IUE/CWA 201 was to change public opinion of the union. The local paper has depicted the union negatively for years, saying it is "greedy union workers" who are chasing GE out of Lynn. Meanwhile, GE has contaminated and abandoned acres of land where manufacturing used to thrive and has permanently laid off thousands of workers. Yet a $1,000 check given to Santa Claus around Christmastime by a GE executive makes a front-page news story.

We did not have a model for coalition work, but we understood the need for labor to reach out to the community, to form alliances with other social and economic justice organizations as a way of building power and credibility. We had also met with members of the nearby Merrimack Valley Project, a labor-community organization working on providing benefits for workers who were victims of plant closings. It was helpful to know that they had been working together for a few years, so a coalition was possible and not unprecedented.

Initial Strategy: Learn about the Players and the Jobs

To meet our goal of creating good jobs, we discussed a number of strategy options, which included a living wage campaign, increased access to quality job training, and a campaign for language in public contracts that would require the hiring of local residents. Techniques that we discussed to achieve our goals included lobbying public officials, action research, and public action. A "Jobs Team" with representatives of ECCO and IUE/CWA Local 201 was formed to lead the effort.

We soon learned that our first job would be to identify the players working on economic development and job-training issues in the Lynn area. We were a group of committed activists, but we knew little about these issues and decided we needed to educate ourselves as best we could. The Jobs Team launched "research actions" facilitated by ECCO and union leaders. As part of our fact-finding mission, we interviewed representatives of public and private organizations involved in economic development and job training in the Lynn area, including community development agencies, the U.S. Department of Housing and Urban Development (HUD), and what is now the Workforce Investment Board (WIB). We also interviewed elected officials, area employers, the regulars at the local soup kitchen, and laid-off workers.

One of our goals was to see who, if anyone, was providing the kind of opportunities we were seeking for our laid-off members and for residents of the local community. Another goal was to find out more about where people were working, who they were working for, whether they were doing part-time or temp work, what they earned, and whether they had health benefits and a career path. We were also trying to identify what job and job-training opportunities were available, who was hiring, and the minimum qualifications that employers wanted from potential employees. Finally, we were interested in finding out how public money allocated to employment services, job training, and economic development was being spent. We wanted to discover how open the city was to providing such information.

The Machinist Training Program

One of the most successful achievements of the Jobs Team was the creation of a machinist training program for the community and for laid-off members of IUE/CWA 201, their children, and IUE/CWA members wishing to upgrade their job skills. Employers throughout the region had identified the need for skilled machinists to fill current vacancies. We also learned that no machinist training program to fill this need existed in the region. Once we identified the training, we met with area machine-shop employers and got commitments from them to hire graduates of the program. There were many other challenges we had to address, including funding (we sought public funds from local and state elected officials), minimum qualifications, where the training would take place, who would do the teaching, and who would coordinate the project.

After eight years, over a hundred people have graduated and been placed in jobs through the machinist training program, in union and nonunion jobs, including eighteen union jobs at GE. These are living wage jobs with benefits and a career path. IUE/CWA 201 negotiated with ECCO to guarantee that 33 percent of the training slots would go to IUE/CWA members who qualified for the program. The machinist program is considered by many to be a success and is held up as a model program by everyone from the AFL-CIO to Massachusetts's Republican governor. Recent attempts to expand the concept to other sectors such as health care have been unsuccessful so far. Despite well thought out plans for training and commitments by employers to hire graduates, elected officials and funding agencies have been reluctant to fund program expansion.

Adding ESOL Expanded Access to Training

Early in the process, we realized that the machinist training program was screening out many potential applicants due to inadequate language and literacy skills. Seventy-five percent of applicants to the machinist training program did not qualify because the academic standards were too high for them or because of language barriers. Initially a tenth-grade math and reading level was needed to enter the program. (Ironically, the employers involved were hiring people off the street with no experience but were insisting on the highest possible standards for entry into the machinist training program.) These standards excluded many of the people for whom we were intending to provide job training. Eventually we were able to negotiate the use of eighth-grade levels as an entry requirement, but this level still excluded many people.

To address this problem, we created our own remedial adult education classes and classes in English for speakers of other languages (ESOL). This program, called Pre-Vocational Resource for Improvement, Motivation, and Opportunity (PRIMO), gives people the skills they need to qualify for entry into the machinist training program. It also gives us the opportunity to include information about unions and worker rights in the curriculum. Applicants can now improve their English, reading, and math skills and continue in the machinist training component of the program.

Winning Membership Support for Labor-Community Coalition Work

While we had very strong support from our union leadership for the Jobs Team's work, our membership also had to approve the coalition if we were going to work with ECCO as an organization. It took a campaign to get member support. We wrote articles for our union newspaper, performed one-on-one interviews with members in the shop, and spoke at membership meetings to advocate for IUE CWA/201's involvement with ECCO on the jobs project. We also wrote language that allowed laid-off members, members who wanted to upgrade, and children of IUE/CWA 201 members to qualify for the program. That language was voted on and approved by our membership.

Our local also had a long-term goal of expanding the coalition to the North Shore Labor Council (NSLC). Expanding the coalition to the council would increase the number of people involved and broaden the scope of the work, allowing other North Shore unions to reach out into their communities. And in order for the relationships between labor and community on the North Shore to grow, the coalition would have to move beyond IUE 201 and Lynn into other sectors and communities. ECCO had also expanded beyond Lynn into the rest of the North Shore, growing to include about thirty churches and social service organizations. The Jobs Team today consists of union and community members from all over the North Shore, and includes members of other NSLC affiliates.

While some union members question whether the work with ECCO is draining resources and time away from other issues that may be more important, most union members who have had anything to do with the project consider the machinist training program a success. We believe that it is meeting the union's goals. The most important lesson our labor council is taking from this project is that unions, churches, and community groups can work effectively together, that we can support each other's struggles. More than just a jobs initiative, this project forged a relationship between the two groups that has had a positive effect on both organizations and a noticeable impact on economic development in our region. Some of the ECCO members who were initially most uncomfortable working with unions walked the picket line with IUE/CWA Local 201 members at our June contract rally. Clergy have spoken about labor from the pulpit. In turn, unions have supported ECCO in its fight for affordable housing and for a public library.

Ongoing Workforce and Economic Development Work

The Jobs Team is an ongoing project, and many of its goals are being met. IUE CWA/201 and the labor council, however, have made commitments to other kinds of workforce and economic development projects to meet their broader goals of building power to create living wage jobs for local residents. First, in collaboration with many community groups, churches, and social service agencies, NSLC has invested a great deal of time in working with the regional WIB and with job-training providers to promote the inclusion of workers' rights and the importance of unions. We have also worked to broaden training access for low-income residents by expanding eligibility requirements and advocating for those who we feel have been unfairly denied training. We have also acted for more transparency and accountability in the publicly funded employment training system that the WIB oversees.

Further, in an effort to coordinate the growing level of involvement in workforce development activity on the North Shore, in January 2000 the North Shore Labor Council (NSLC) formed an economic development committee (EDC). This committee is composed of activists from within the council and community activists who have worked with the council on workforce development issues, as well as representatives from the Massachusetts AFL-CIO and labor educators.[12] Initially, the committee provided a forum for discussion and served as a clearinghouse for information about members' individual activities.

Over the EDC's first year, there developed a consensus that people wanted to work in a more focused way—doing both external work to move a labor-community agenda in new arenas where decisions affecting North Shore workers are made, and internal base-building, reaching out to a broader base of labor council members. Despite the fact that the labor council had established an EDC and heard from us regularly, there were few avenues for members to learn about the relevance of the work or to become involved in it.

In September 2000, the EDC held a retreat that generated two broad goals: (1) continue the work presently done to help individual members with support and advice while co-coordinating ongoing activities; (2) work toward positioning the NSLC to be a player in decisions made about the regional economy. Once again, we discovered that we had more research and learning to do. One of the EDC members, a labor educator at the state university, developed a participatory research project for committee members and their allies, the Job Toolkit. The goal of this project was to help the EDC and its allies identify more focused options for intervening in regional economic development: where can we have the most influence, and how can our work benefit and involve the council and the broader community?

Job Toolkit discussions took place over the first six months of 2001. Discussion and training topics included a profile of the North Shore economy and population and how they have changed in recent years; the kind of questions about the economy and proposed economic development efforts that are useful; who makes local and regional economic development decisions, and what their agenda is; how to track public money invested in economic development; and what kind of strategies labor and community activists in other parts of the country have used to influence economic development. Participants included not only EDC members but also interested members of other North Shore affiliate unions, several ECCO Jobs Team members, a legal services attorney, a community health educator, and a city councilor from the region's largest city, Lynn.

Job Toolkit participants identified a number of potential avenues for action, including campaigns for living wage, community benefit agreement, and accountability for local tax breaks. The training also helped broaden the concern for economic development beyond IUE Local 201, bringing in a number of NSLC activists from other unions; however, the training failed in its broader goal of translating this into new activism around a focused campaign. While labor and community activists worked together effectively in the training setting, this was not the venue where the terms of the partnership could be renegotiated. Ultimately, at that point the community partner was not ready to broaden its coalition work beyond training. In addition, the labor council EDC was not able to agree on and launch a campaign to draw in the new activists. Much of the EDC's time and energy was absorbed in the annual fight to obtain state funding for the E-Team and PRIMO projects. These same activists also had a number of other labor council priorities fighting for their attention during this period: electoral campaigns, including critical races for governor, congress, and state legislature; mobilization for anti-globalization events in Quebec; and mobilization around contract issues for IUE/CWA and other key unions.

Over a year later, the EDC is once again trying to spark a new wave of activism around economic and workforce development on the North Shore. In the throes of a severe state budget crisis that is decimating municipal and state services in their region, the EDC is putting together a campaign that could put some local tax money on the table. The EDC is examining records of tax breaks granted to companies in North Shore cities and town, in exchange for promises of job creation. We believe that we can get local officials to call in taxes owed by companies that have not created the required number of new jobs.

We see promise in this effort for several reasons. First, it has already brought in new labor activists to work on economic development, since more people see the immediate usefulness of this activity for saving union jobs (police, fire, teachers, etc). Second, rather than introducing an entirely new language and set of systems, it builds from political relationships and political advocacy work at which our labor council activists already excel. Third, we can broaden our coalition because a wide range of local groups are already invested in saving municipal services. Fourth, it will give us visibility that can get us to more of the arenas where economic development decisions are made. Fifth, we can expand the immediate "clawback" work into a broader public policy debate over economic development. What kinds of standards should be attached to jobs that receive tax breaks or public subsidies? Possible benchmarks include higher wages, benefits, career opportunities, local access to the jobs, funding for training, and protections for workers' right to organize a union. Finally, our work on local corporate tax breaks links to work being done by labor activists in other regions, as well as the Massachusetts AFL-CIO's efforts to advance state-level corporate disclosure legislation and policy.

A State Federation Organizes to Promote Worker-Centered Development
Harneen Chernow

The previous two regional experiences are good examples of the type of economic development initiatives that the Massachusetts AFL-CIO has worked to nurture and grow. Our foray into the economic development arena, however, came after considerable effort establishing programs in workforce development and worker training. Through these initiatives we came to realize the need for labor's voice in economic development.

Worker-Centered Workforce Development

In 1998, the Massachusetts AFL-CIO consolidated all its existing workforce development programs under a newly constituted Education and Training Department with two goals: expanding labor's role in the public workforce development system and organizing unions and labor councils to build and support worker education and training programs. While the Massachusetts AFL-CIO had always been involved in various workforce development initiatives, the high visibility of the new department represented an expanded commitment to involving labor in this arena.

Initial efforts focused on outreach to local affiliates to expand labor's role in the education and training of its members. New worker initiatives were implemented and resource materials were gathered to assist unions involved in training. We also spent time recruiting "activist" labor representatives to serve on the sixteen Workforce Investment Boards (WIBs) in Massachusetts and training those representatives to understand the systems and to promote a worker-centered vision of workforce development.

The Massachusetts AFL-CIO Education and Training Department collaborated with affiliates, education providers, and community organizations to develop and sponsor a number of programs for union affiliates and labor councils, including:

- Strategic planning sessions for labor representatives serving on WIBs
- Coalition building with advocates around issues of workforce development important to union members and low-wage workers
- Assistance in designing and negotiating incumbent worker training and education programs with strong union involvement
- Grant writing for union-based and joint labor-management training programs
- Technical assistance on the "how tos" of the grant review process to ensure quality training and union involvement
- Rapid response services for laid-off union members.

These programs and services have helped change the climate for worker education and training in Massachusetts. Policy makers and public and private agencies know that labor's voice must be represented when workforce planning takes place. In addition, many labor unions and labor councils have become increasingly involved in efforts to provide worker training to members, to assess the skill needs of their members, and to work with the Massachusetts AFL-CIO to serve as a key force in their regional workforce development system.

The Education and Training Department has also played a critical brokering and technical support role in a number of successful union workforce development efforts.

- The Massachusetts AFL-CIO brought together two locals of the Communications Workers of America, their employers, community colleges, as abstract as those just offered. The Wisconsin experiments, however, offer some real experience by which our application of the strategy outlined above can be assessed, which is what we aim to do in this chapter.

For the sake of brevity, we concentrate on the experience of the WRTP and, within that, on the first of the industry-sector partnerships under its direction—the one in manufacturing. This is the oldest of the projects noted above and the most advanced in realizing the different parts of the strategy just suggested. But we note immediately that other partnerships within the WRTP itself, and other projects—some relying on parts of the WRTP's own capacity, others modeled on it in other industrial sectors or other regional labor markets—suggest the wider utility and replicability of the broad strategy.

Economic Context and the Problem of Supplying
High-Road Inputs

Like many other midwest cities, Milwaukee was devastated by the "rustbelt recession" of the early 1980s, and even more by the massive flight of manufacturing firms over the subsequent decade out of Milwaukee Metro[3] to lower-cost "greenfield" sites. Milwaukee lost fully a third of its traditional industrial base during the period, a loss that sharply accelerated union decline state-wide and growing poverty in Milwaukee itself. Metro deindustrialization is expressed in Figure 13.1. Note that manufacturing employment in Wisconsin did not in fact decline over the period. It simply moved from Milwaukee and surrounding counties to more rural ones. Figure 13.2 shows some of the effects on Milwaukee, whose heavily African American central-city population was devastated by the industrial flight.[4]

In the early 1990s, as Milwaukee manufacturing firms began emerging from their prolonged slump, those firms discovered two things: (1) to remain competitive in high-end markets, they needed to upgrade the skills of their existing workforce, and (2) they needed to do so on a scale and scope beyond existing apprenticeship programs, which most of them had abandoned any-way during the slump's heyday of skilled-labor surplus. This situation made employers at least open to a constructive discussion with the labor move-ment about training problems. In turn, the labor movement realized that, to preserve membership and get on the high road, it needed to be much more involved in driving the firm's restructuring, modernization, and human capi-tal formation.

What became clear in this discussion, eventually formally facilitated by COWS, was the need for a joint labor-management structure of coopera-tion—or "partnership"[5]—covering multiple firms and ideally extending to enough of them to influence behaviors throughout the manufacturing sector.

Figure 13.1 **Metro-Deindustrialization in Wisconsin, 1979–95**

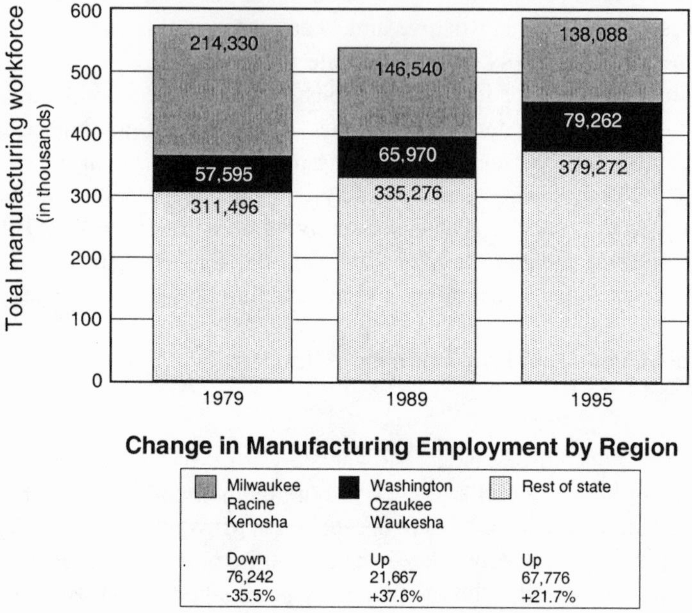
Total manufacturing workforce
(in thousands)
600
500
400
300
200
100
0
214,330
57,595
311,496
146,540
65,970
335,276
138,088
79,262
379,272
1979
1989
1995
Change in Manufacturing Employment by Region
Milwaukee
Racine
Kenosha
Washington
Ozaukee
Waukesha
Rest of state
Down
76,242
-35.5%
Up
21,667
+37.6%
Up
67,776
+21.7%

This need for a multifirm approach, rather than exclusive reliance on firm-specific collective bargaining or negotiation, followed from the fact that the sorts of supports needed for the high road were often a species of "public good" prone to "free-rider" problems.

Training itself is a classic instance of such a problem. Under otherwise unregulated and competitive market conditions, employers as a *group*—particularly high-roading employers—may benefit from the existence of a trained workforce, rich in generally applicable skills. But no *individual* employer has any incentive to provide the training needed to produce that workforce, since it lacks any assurance that its trainee may not one day become—through that individual's movement to a different employer—another firm's asset, without offsetting compensation. The result, widely achieved in fact in the United States, is that employers barely train frontline workers. But since a trained workforce, particularly in manufacturing, is essential to achieving reasonable wages, this situation is bad for individual workers and the society as a whole. Lacking an appropriately trained workforce, employers pursue low-road strategies that do not rely on one. But this result makes the high road less available even to those firms that wish to pursue it, since they now face conditions under which low-roading competitors are more or less settled in their ways, and the available workforce is insufficiently skilled to permit them to start on something better. (See Figure 13.3.)

The training of incoming workers fulfills a similar function. Wisconsin manufacturing was hit with tight labor markets and an aging workforce well before the rest of the country, and finding young workers who could operate the new machinery became increasingly difficult. By partnering with technical colleges and public agencies to provide customized training, the WRTP has ensured a sustained flow of skilled incoming workers. A major manufacturer in the region reports that this "managing of supply" allowed him to stay in Milwaukee and actually expand his plant. In health care, area hospitals have experienced an acute shortage of technicians and nursing staff. Here, the WRTP's role as intermediary has shortened the time prospective employees spend waiting for the clinical training they need.

Retaining incumbent workers is an equally important goal. Here again, the experience in health care is instructive. The WRTP helped one long-term care facility to solve its problem of high CNA turnover rates—and by extension, to rebuild its reputation for quality care—by introducing a mentoring program that greatly improved retention. The program, like other model WRTP programs in such areas as supervisor training and attendance improvement, was developed through the joint effort of industry partners.

It is also important to recognize that a low-wage business strategy brings its own set of costs—shirking, absenteeism, and lack of commitment and worker buy-in. These are incentive problems that the partnership model can also address. For example, worker-management teams charged with modernizing the workplace yield many of the benefits of employee involvement (Levine and Tyson 1990). The WRTP has successfully worked with several firms to convert temporary jobs back to permanent jobs by documenting in concrete terms the loss of revenue from the contingent strategy.

Thus the promise of the sectoral partnership model is that it can actually change the nature of jobs being created. But it is quite difficult to pull off. It requires a critical mass of employers and preferably unions in a given sector, as well as any number of public partners, such as community colleges, private industry councils, and community-based organizations. Coordinating among all the different players and identifying the interests and potential contributions of each is an enormous and constant challenge.

One major challenge is resistance from nonunion employers. In the Milwaukee metro area, many health care employers are reluctant to participate in joint activities with unions because they fear it will open the door to unionization at their facilities. However, unionized health care facilities that have good relationships with their unions are aware of the benefits that result from the partnership. This is also true in the construction industry, which has a long history of labor-management cooperation in workforce training, benefits administration, and so forth. The shared goal of expanding market share for union firms also strengthens the commitment of construction contractors to working with each other as well as with unions.

To Unions

The union and workforce perspective on the WRTP is a bit different, but no less important. Unions are involved because these projects provide real results for them. Unions that participate in these projects see old jobs improving and new jobs being generated. The very stability of their own firms rests on these initiatives to train, attract, and retain workers. Union members also see new pathways for skill development and career advancement as the projects extend within the firm. As they contribute positively to improving shop floor skills, unions also gain power to set the terms of compensation within the firm. These joint projects provide leverage in bargaining by allowing unions to be proactive partners on skill-upgrading issues that challenge the firms. It is critical, of course, that this leverage be exercised; a key balance throughout these projects is managing to keep engaged on issues of joint interest without selling out in negotiations. The WRTP not only helps union leaders and members work on issues of joint interest with management, it also provides linkages with other local leaders who have been through similar processes.

The union contribution to these projects increases union leverage, and the union contribution is substantial. Without labor union leadership at the partnership level *and* within participating firms, it is almost impossible to get inside firms and initiate broad, effective worker-training projects. Such projects require an economic incentive or source of pressure that makes firms willing to invest in upgrading the skills of workers. Some union firms have an incentive because high, contractually negotiated wages generate a need for equivalently high productivity. Other firms and unions find worker training an issue on which they can start discussions of interest to both parties. In these ways, unions can increase firms' commitment to worker training. Equally important, effective training also requires good information from shop floor workers. They have the most intimate knowledge of the content of work, wasted steps, and process problems. Unions provide independent workforce representation and so can contribute to making workforce training and modernization efforts more effective.

Unions are thus partners on development of these projects and recipients of the services that such projects create. They gain power through their increased knowledge, and they gain in strength as members themselves come to appreciate the union's role in remaking a worksite and improving their jobs.

Just as unions were at the forefront in forming the WRTP, they often take the lead in seeking out WRTP resources to help manage workplace change. In the case of the utility construction certification program described earlier, it was the union that initiated the training effort. In another instance, the union at a large telecommunications firm approached the WRTP about conducting "positive attendance workshops" for employees. The union was concerned that, because of high absenteeism rates, the company might transfer the work to its facility in another state. Shortly after the training, the absenteeism rate plummeted and the Milwaukee facility became competitive with its out-of-state counterpart.

It is not always easy for unions to participate in partnerships. In the health care industry in the Milwaukee metro area, for example, union representatives who service workers at many different facilities can find it difficult to play an active role. Again, construction may offer a useful model: it too has numerous sites scattered over a large area, and yet it still managed to build an impressive legacy of labor-management cooperation.

To Community Residents

Finally, there are evident payoffs to community residents—both to the general population in an area, and more specifically to populations of color, the poor, and others traditionally excluded from the full benefits of economic citizenship.

As a general matter, the WRTP increases investment, income, and employment in the community, all of which obviously increase its welfare and living standard. It also improves job quality for those fortunate enough to be employed at member firms, with spillover effects on nonmembers.

At least as important, however, the WRTP does all this in a way that specifically favors a fairer distribution of economic opportunity—for both incumbent and prospective workers—through its negotiated supports for worker training and advancement, career mentoring programs, and support for workplace diversity. And in so doing, it offers a bridge between labor and those portions of the community traditionally excluded from the benefits of good jobs.

The importance of this last point cannot be overstated. At the core of any labor-community alliance that matters is a clear exchange of benefits, as well as the shared solidarities that may come of fighting for social justice. The "community" wants jobs, ideally good ones, and opportunities for advancement currently denied to it. Labor wants political support for defending wage and other standards for which it has fought and which are now under unrelenting attack. Labor, having access to good jobs, can help the community concretely in meeting its need. The community, having votes, can help labor concretely in getting what it wants.

Replication

The Milwaukee experience suggests that strategies linking workforce and economic development can be successful at a local level, in ways that answer many of the questions posed at the outset. But is the Milwaukee experience somehow unique?

Decisively, we think not. All regions face a choice between encouraging low- and high-road competitive strategies. And in all of them there are clusters of firms that could be moving toward the high road if pushed, and assisted, by unions or public policy in solving the collective action problems that deny them public–goods-type high-road inputs. While circumstances vary, of course, that is our essential point on the replication question: "It can happen here"—meaning in any metro area.

Recently, national labor has come to be persuaded of this fact. And the Working for America Institute (WAI), the AFL-CIO's arm for workforce development, has taken significant steps toward providing the technical assistance needed to support labor and community leaders who wish to replicate WRTP-type "high-road regional partnerships" elsewhere.[10]

For activists, the basic opening moves in that replication are straightforward enough. From our experience, we would recommend that you:

- Do an industrial structure, demographic, and "power" map of your local labor market, identifying key sectors, workforce composition shifts, wage and income trends, and the available base, institutional or other, for advocacy.
- Target the sectors with the most immediate promise of success in taking the high road, or the most obvious demand for some of its ingredients, or the strongest union base—or, not infrequently, all three.
- Examine those sectors' problems in more detail, reviewing results with employers and worker representatives, as well as state officials, to get consensus on the description of existing problems. The range of strategies for solving shared sectoral problems will follow more or less straightforwardly from their description, but getting otherwise-divided actors to agree on that description is essential to acting on problems together.

From there, the harder work begins—hammering out specific agreements, finding the financing for specific program initiatives, training and then managing the staff for whom typically (and this is true on the labor and commu-

Index